"In this excellent collection the editors managed to assemble a star lineup to reflect on what is a crucial nexus in international politics. This is policy relevant research at its best, combining important policy hindsights with solid scholarship that will withstand the test of time. Recommended reading for both scholars and policy makers."

– *Matteo Legrenzi, Ca' Foscari University of Venice*

"Amid much that has been said and written on the topic, this volume presents fresh perspectives and insights into the critical and multi-dimensional relations of the states of the Persian Gulf with the rest of the world, ranging from the United States and Russia to India and Korea. This is an extremely timely and important volume, and I highly recommend it for anyone wishing to better understand a region that is once again at the epicenter of international competition and tensions."

– *Mehran Kamrava, Director, Center for International and Regional Studies and Professor, Georgetown University-Qatar*

External Powers and the Gulf Monarchies

The Gulf monarchies have been generally perceived as status quo actors reliant on the USA for their security, but in response to regional events, particularly the Arab Spring of 2011, they are pursuing more activist foreign policies, which has allowed other international powers to play a larger role in regional affairs.

This book analyses the changing dynamic in this region, with expert contributors providing original empirical case studies that examine the relations between the Gulf monarchies and extra-regional powers, including the USA, Russia, China, India, Brazil, Turkey, Japan, South Korea, France, and the United Kingdom. At the theoretical level, these case studies explore the extent to which different international relations and international political economy theories explain change in these relationships as the regional, political, and security environments shift. Focusing on how and why external powers approach their relationships with the Gulf monarchies, contributors ask what motivates external powers to pursue deeper involvement in an unstable region that has seen three major conflicts in the past 40 years.

Addressing an under-analysed, yet important topic, the volume will appeal to scholars in the fields of international relations and international political economy as well as area specialists on the Gulf and those working on the foreign policy issues of the extra-regional powers studied.

Jonathan Fulton is Assistant Professor of Political Science in the College of Humanities and Social Sciences at Zayed University, in Abu Dhabi, United Arab Emirates.

Li-Chen Sim is Assistant Professor and Chair of the Department of Social Sciences at Zayed University, in Abu Dhabi, United Arab Emirates.

Rethinking Asia and International Relations
Series Editor – Emilian Kavalski
Li Dak Sum Chair Professor in China–Eurasia Relations and International Studies, University of Nottingham, Ningbo, China

This series seeks to provide thoughtful consideration both of the growing prominence of Asian actors on the global stage and the changes in the study and practice of world affairs that they provoke. It intends to offer a comprehensive parallel assessment of the full spectrum of Asian states, organisations, and regions and their impact on the dynamics of global politics.

The series seeks to encourage conversation on:

- what rules, norms, and strategic cultures are likely to dominate international life in the 'Asian Century';
- how will global problems be reframed and addressed by a 'rising Asia';
- which institutions, actors, and states are likely to provide leadership during such 'shifts to the East';
- whether there is something distinctly 'Asian' about the emerging patterns of global politics.

Such comprehensive engagement not only aims to offer a critical assessment of the actual and prospective roles of Asian actors, but also seeks to rethink the concepts, practices, and frameworks of analysis of world politics.

This series invites proposals for interdisciplinary research monographs undertaking comparative studies of Asian actors and their impact on the current patterns and likely future trajectories of international relations. Furthermore, it offers a platform for pioneering explorations of the ongoing transformations in global politics as a result of Asia's increasing centrality to the patterns and practices of world affairs.

For more information about this series, please visit: https://www.routledge.com/Rethinking-Asia-and-International-Relations/book-series/ASHSER1384

Recent titles

External Powers and the Gulf Monarchies
Edited by Jonathan Fulton and Li-Chen Sim

China's Relations with the Gulf Monarchies
Jonathan Fulton

Advaita as a Global International Relations
Deepshikha Shahi

China's Great Power Responsibility for Climate Change
Sanna Kopra
Rethinking Asia and International Relations

External Powers and the Gulf Monarchies

Edited by Jonathan Fulton and
Li-Chen Sim

LONDON AND NEW YORK

First published 2019
by Routledge
2 Park Square, Milton Park, London, Oxon OX14 4RN

and by Routledge
52 Vanderbilt Avenue, New York, NY 10017

First issued in paperback 2020

Routledge is an imprint of the Taylor & Francis Group, an informa business

© 2019 selection and editorial matter, Jonathan Fulton and Li-Chen Sim; individual chapters, the contributors

The right of Jonathan Fulton and Li-Chen Sim to be identified as the authors of the editorial material, and of the authors for their individual chapters, has been asserted in accordance with sections 77 and 78 of the Copyright, Designs, and Patents Act 1988.

All rights reserved. No part of this book may be reprinted or reproduced or utilised in any form or by any electronic, mechanical, or other means, now known or hereafter invented, including photocopying and recording, or in any information storage or retrieval system, without permission in writing from the publishers.

Trademark notice: Product or corporate names may be trademarks or registered trademarks, and are used only for identification and explanation without intent to infringe.

British Library Cataloguing-in-Publication Data
A catalogue record for this book is available from the British Library

Library of Congress Cataloging-in-Publication Data
Names: Fulton, Jonathan, editor. | Sim, Li-Chen, 1972- editor.
Title: External powers and the Gulf monarchies / edited by Jonathan Fulton and Li-Chen Sim.
Description: Abingdon, Oxon; New York, NY: Routledge, 2018. | Series: Rethinking Asia and international relations | Includes bibliographical references and index.
Identifiers: LCCN 2018008459 | ISBN 9781138087590 (hardback) | ISBN 9781315110394 (e-book)
Subjects: LCSH: Persian Gulf Region–Foreign relations. | World politics–21st century.
Classification: LCC DS326 .E97 2018 | DDC 327.536–dc23
LC record available at https://lccn.loc.gov/2018008459

ISBN 13: 978-0-367-58736-9 (pbk)
ISBN 13: 978-1-138-08759-0 (hbk)

Typeset in Times New Roman
by Deanta Global Publishing Services, Chennai, India

Contents

	List of tables	ix
	List of contributors	x
1	Quo vadis? External powers in a changing Gulf region LI-CHEN SIM AND JONATHAN FULTON	1
2	The evolution of US–Gulf ties KRISTIAN COATES ULRICHSEN	17
3	Russia's return to the Gulf LI-CHEN SIM	36
4	Great Britain–Gulf relations: ties that bind? DAVID B. ROBERTS AND CINZIA BIANCO	56
5	French policy in the Gulf: the other Western ally JEAN-LOUP SAMAAN	74
6	A rising economic agenda: assessing current Brazil–GCC relations VÂNIA CARVALHO PINTO	90
7	Between geopolitics and economics: Turkey's relations with the Gulf BIROL BAŞKAN	106
8	India and the Gulf states DAVID BREWSTER AND KADIRA PETHIYAGODA	122

9 **Striking a balance between economics and security: China's relations with the Gulf monarchies** 140
JONATHAN FULTON

10 **South Korea–Gulf relations and the Iran factor** 159
JEONGMIN SEO

11 **Technology for oil: Japan's multifaceted relations with Saudi Arabia** 176
KOJI MUTO

Index 195

Tables

4.1	Significant outward and inward visits 2010–13	62
7.1	Turkey's trade statistics with the Gulf, 1950–79	108
7.2	Turkey's trade statistics with the Gulf, 1980–89	110
7.3	Turkey's trade statistics with the Gulf, 1990–99	111
7.4	The Gulf's share in Turkey's total exports and imports	112
7.5	Turkey's trade statistics with the Gulf, 2000–09	113
7.6	The Gulf's share in Turkey's total exports and imports	113
7.7	Turkey's trade statistics with the Gulf, 2010–16	117
7.8	The Gulf's share in Turkey's total exports and imports	118
7.9	Foreign direct investment (in million dollars)	118
9.1	China–GCC trade value (all figures in US dollars)	148
9.2	China's oil production and consumption	149
10.1	The establishment of formal relations between the two Koreas and the GCC	161
10.2	Amount of crude oil imports from the GCC states, Iraq, and Iran	169

Contributors

Birol Başkan is Assistant Professor at Georgetown University School of Foreign Service in Qatar. He has published in *Akademik Ortadogu, Arab Studies Quarterly, Comparative Political Studies, HAWWA: The Journal of Women in the Middle East and the Islamic World, Insight Turkey, International Sociology, Islam and Christian-Muslim Relations, The Muslim World, Politics and Religion, Turkish Studies*, and *Turkish Yearbook of International Politics*. He is the author of *From Religious Empires to Secular States* (Routledge, 2014), *Turkey and Qatar in the Tangled Geopolitics of the Middle East* (Palgrave, 2016), and the co-editor of *State-Society Relations in the Gulf States* (Gerlach, 2014).

Cinzia Bianco is a PhD candidate at the University of Exeter in the United Kingdom. Throughout her career, Bianco has served as a research fellow for the Institute for International Affairs (Italy) in the context of the European Commission's "Sharaka" project, researching European–GCC relations while based in Kuwait, Oman, Qatar, and the United Arab Emirates. Since 2015, she has been a non-resident research fellow at TRENDS Research and Advisory Abu Dhabi. Bianco received her MA in Middle East and Mediterranean studies from King's College London. Her PhD research focuses on the evolution of Gulf security after the 2011 Arab uprisings.

David Brewster is Senior Research Fellow with the National Security College, Australian National University where he works on Indian Ocean and Indo Pacific maritime security. His books include *India as an Asia Pacific Power* on India's role in the Asia Pacific, and *India's Ocean: The Story of India's Bid for Regional Leadership*, which examines India's strategic ambitions in the Indian Ocean. His most recent book is *India and China at Sea: Competition for Naval Dominance in the Indian Ocean*, published by Oxford University Press. Dr Brewster is also a Distinguished Research Fellow with the Australia India Institute, University of Melbourne and a Fellow with the Royal Australian Navy Sea Power Centre.

Vânia Carvalho Pinto is tenured Assistant Professor in the Institute of International Relations, at the University of Brasília, and Academic Productivity

Fellow (*Bolsista de Produtividade*) with the Brazilian National Council of Research. She is the author of several articles and book chapters focusing on gender issues, foreign policy on the Gulf, and Latin America and Gulf Arab relations. Her current research interests lay on comparative area studies, namely the Arabian Peninsula, Scandinavia, and Latin America, with a focus on the UAE, Norway, and Brazil, respectively.

Kristian Coates Ulrichsen is Fellow for the Middle East at Rice University's Baker Institute for Public Policy and the author of four books and three edited volumes on the political economy, international relations, and security of the Gulf States. Coates Ulrichsen is also an Associate Fellow with the Middle East and North Africa Program at Chatham House and an advisor at Gulf State Analytics in Washington, DC. His most recent book, *The United Arab Emirates: Power, Politics, and Policymaking*, was published by Routledge in 2016, and his most recent edited volume, *The Changing Security Dynamics of the Persian Gulf*, was released by Hurst & Co in 2017.

Jonathan Fulton is Assistant Professor of Political Science in the College of Humanities and Social Sciences at Zayed University, in Abu Dhabi, United Arab Emirates, where he researches China–Middle East relations, Chinese foreign policy, the global strategic implications of the Belt and Road Initiative, and international relations of the Gulf region. He has written several articles and chapters on China–Gulf relations, and is currently writing a book on China's relations with the Gulf monarchies.

Koji Muto is a director for the Planning and Project Division at the Japan Cooperation Centre for the Middle East (JCCME), Tokyo, Japan. Prior to this position, he worked for the Embassy of Japan in Saudi Arabia, the Saudi Electronics and Home Appliances Institute in Riyadh, and Japan Water Desk at Jeddah Chamber of Commerce and Industry. His main research interests focus on the political economy and business environment in Saudi Arabia and international relations between East Asia and the Gulf. He is a PhD candidate at Exeter University in the United Kingdom, where he researches the process of establishing multi-layered reciprocal relations between Saudi Arabia and Japan.

Kadira Pethiyagoda is non-resident Fellow at Brookings Doha Center, focusing on China and India's relations with the Middle East, and Research Director for Global Governance at the Lakshman Kadirgamar Institute of International Relations and Strategic Studies. Previously as a diplomat and Foreign Service officer, Pethiyagoda covered relations with Asia, trade, and public diplomacy. He was also Foreign Affairs advisor to a Shadow Foreign Minister. As a visiting scholar at Oxford University, Pethiyagoda researched South Asia's foreign relations. He is finalising two books on Indian foreign policy, one based on his doctorate. He has published in the *Independent*, *Guardian*, *Foreign Affairs*, and *HuffPost* among others and has been interviewed/appeared on BBC, Al-Jazeera, CNN, NY Times, and others.

David B. Roberts is Assistant Professor in the School of Security Studies at King's College London. He is the author of *Qatar: Securing the Global Ambitions of a City State* (2017) and dozens of articles on the international relations, security, and politics of the Gulf monarchies. Previously, David taught for King's College London at the Qatar Defence Academy and he was the Director of the RUSI Qatar think-tank.

Jean-Loup Samaan is Associate Professor of strategic studies at the United Arab Emirates National Defense College. Prior to that, he held various positions at the French Ministry of Defense, the NATO Defense College, and the RAND Corporation. He has published four books and several peer-reviewed articles in international journals such as *Survival, Orbis, Defence Studies,* and *Politique Étrangère*. His areas of research include the evolution of the regional security system in the Gulf and military doctrines against non-state actors.

Jeongmin Seo chairs the Department of Middle East and African Studies at Graduate School of International Area Studies, Hankuk University of Foreign Studies in Seoul, South Korea. Before he began the teaching position, Professor Seo worked as a Middle East correspondent in Cairo and dispatched from *Joongang Daily*, a major Korean newspaper. He holds a DPhil in politics from University of Oxford and two MAs from the American University in Cairo and Graduate School of Interpretation and Translation in Seoul. Seo also conducted one-year post-doctoral courses at Oxford Centre for Hebrew and Jewish Studies. His main fields of research are religion and politics of the contemporary Middle East and state–society relations of the region.

Li-Chen Sim is Assistant Professor and Chair of the Department of Social Sciences at Zayed University, in Abu Dhabi, United Arab Emirates. She is a specialist in contemporary Russian politics, and in particular the Russian oil industry and its impact on the country's politics, economic development, and foreign policy; and her concurrent area of research centres on the political economy of energy in the Middle East. She has also lectured extensively on renewable and nuclear energies at INSEAD Business School, New York University, Khalifa University, and the National Defence College in Abu Dhabi.

1 Quo vadis? External powers in a changing Gulf region

Li-Chen Sim and Jonathan Fulton

This volume analyzes the changing dynamics of the Gulf monarchies' (Bahrain, Kuwait, Oman, Qatar, Saudi Arabia, and the United Arab Emirates) international relations with extra-regional powers. Perceived as status quo actors reliant upon the USA as a security provider, the Gulf Cooperation Council (GCC) member states have pursued more activist foreign policies in response to regional events, especially in the wake of the 2011 Arab Spring. This in turn has created opportunities for other international powers to play a larger role in the Gulf region. In order to understand the extent to which these extra-regional powers have taken advantage of such opportunities, contributors to this book provide original empirical case studies examining the relations between the Gulf monarchies and ten interlocutors, namely, the USA, Russia, China, India, Brazil, Turkey, Japan, South Korea, France, and the United Kingdom. At the theoretical level, these case studies explore the extent to which different international relations and international political economy theories explain change in these relationships as the regional security environment shifts.

An important point that needs to be emphasized at the outset is that this book's focus is on how extra-regional powers approach their relationships with the Gulf monarchies. There is a vast literature from the other perspective, analyzing Gulf monarchies' use of great power partnerships to navigate a challenging neighborhood.[1] This volume asks instead, what motivates external powers to pursue deeper ties in a region that has seen three major wars in the past 40 years, within a larger unstable Middle East region? In addressing this, two broad themes provide an analytical framework. The first is shaped by political and security concerns, and the second by economic ones.

The first broad theme examines the deepening of ties between external powers and the Gulf monarchies from an international relations perspective. What political, diplomatic, and security issues drive these relationships? Are these relationships indicative of a change in the Gulf regional order? Or are they a function of a larger transition process at the international level? Contributors addressed a series of questions: Does the country in question perceive the regional balance of power to be shifting, and if so, does this power shift influence its foreign policy toward the Gulf monarchies? Does the country in question consider its relationships with the Gulf monarchies as a core strategic interest, or an economic opportunity? Are these external powers responding to a shift in global politics in pursuing ties to the Gulf monarchies, or are they being driven by their own domestic political concerns? What are the tools of influence – economic, cultural, military – wielded by these extra-regional powers, and how effective are they? In the case studies that follow, we see three common trends.

First, external powers have long taken advantage of the US security architecture and its military preponderance in the Gulf to develop stronger ties to the Gulf monarchies. Each of the case studies demonstrates that US security commitments have provided a low-cost entry into the Gulf, allowing other states to enhance their regional presence without the need to take on a corresponding security role relative to their expanding interests. Leaders in Washington have complained of free-riding,[2] a charge rejected by Gulf leaders who emphasize the economic relations and intelligence sharing that support US interests,[3] as well as leaders from other states who emphasize that they play important complementary or non-traditional roles in contributing to Gulf security. Hegemonic stability theory explains that these external powers, relatively satisfied with the norms of the existing international order, have thus far been willing to support the dominant power – the USA – in order to ensure that they continue to derive benefits from the continuity of this regional order. Instead of challenging US leadership directly, most have adopted a strategic hedging approach, in which they free-ride the benefits provided by the USA while steadily improving their economic and military capabilities within the Gulf. This is an effective strategic choice for second-tier states in a unipolar system that is demonstrating signs of possible power deconcentration.[4] The USA's relative disengagement from the region – whether in the form of 'pull back' or offshore balancing – and thus its ability to continue to deliver benefits to external powers in the Gulf, may alter the latter's level of support for the existing regional order underwritten by the USA.

This leads directly to the second trend: in the absence of major security commitments to the region, the structure of relations between extra-regional powers and the Gulf monarchies have thus far largely been dominated by economic interests, including trade, investment, finance, and labor contracting. The Gulf monarchies have combined their centrality in global energy markets with deft political economic strategies, becoming active participants in international organizations, important sources of foreign direct investment, generous aid donors, and significant customers in arms markets. A wide range of economic partners has contributed to a correspondingly wide range of states and firms that have a stake in the continued stability of the Gulf monarchies. Gulf development plans, such as New Kuwait 2035, Saudi Vision 2030, and Abu Dhabi 2030 all offer substantial opportunities for international firms to win lucrative construction and infrastructure contracts, which political and business leaders from the countries in this book have aggressively pursued. This too is consistent with a hedging strategy, where second-tier powers often focus on developing an economic presence while gradually increasing military or security capabilities.[5]

The third trend is that these relations are, in many cases, beginning to move beyond the economic to incorporate strategic concerns for both the Gulf monarchies and the external powers. This is a natural development, building upon the first two trends. Growing economic interdependence has led to an increase in state and commercial assets and expatriate populations for each of the states studied in this volume; it stands to reason that they will need to devise plans to protect these interests, rather than relying on the munificence of the USA. With the Belt and Road Initiative, China has already begun to articulate a vision of a greater Chinese presence across Eurasia, including the Gulf. India's Look West policy underscores the importance of the Middle East as a strategic consideration for Delhi. Russia's return to the Middle East requires a stronger presence in the capitals of GCC states. South Korea's considerable economic ties to the UAE have come with a limited but surprising military commitment. And the United Kingdom, France, and Turkey all have military installations on the Arabian side of the Gulf. It is important to emphasize that no other power offers a competing vision of Gulf order to challenge the USA, but as their strategic interests grow, it is likely that extra-regional powers will begin to pursue more assertive regional foreign policies. Hedging provides the space and time to increase a state's interests, but in a system where hegemonic relative power appears to be decreasing, regions become arenas for competition. Yetiv reminds us that regions are part of a broader international system, and external powers intervene in them for any number of reasons, impacting regional dynamics.[6]

Taken together, these three trends indicate that events in the Gulf regional order reflect changes in the international order. In recent years, a substantial body of literature has been published dealing with the theme of a transition from the US-led liberal order toward a less centered, multipolar one. Payne describes an inextricable link between the decline in US relative power and an end to unipolarity.[7] He believes that the rise of new powers, especially in the wake of the 2008 financial crisis, are evidence that the 'unipolar moment' has ended, and with it, Pax Americana. Taking a longer view, Buzan and Lawson describe an ongoing transition that has its roots in the nineteenth century, which is leading to a decentered globalism where the "core will become both bigger (absolutely and relatively) and less Western."[8] This is leading to a more diffuse distribution of power, and the end of superpower dominance: "with many states becoming wealthy and powerful, no single polity will be able to accumulate sufficient relative power to dominate international society."[9] The consequence will be a return to multipolarity in a more regionalized world order. Acharya sees a similar trend, in what he calls a multiplex world, using a multiplex cinema as a metaphor for international order: "in a multiplex world, the making and arrangement of order is more diversified and decentralized, with the involvement of established and emerging powers, states, global and regional bodies, and transnational non-state actors."[10] Central to his thesis is the assertion that the unipolar moment has ended. American power remains an important feature of the nascent order Acharya describes, but it is one of many elements, including the power and interests of emerging powers and regional economic and security cooperation mechanisms. This is consistent with Reich and Lebow's analysis, in which "we are witnessing a shift toward a world in which actors have differing forms of influence, contrasting balances between material and social resources that they use to effect in differing domains."[11] Kupchan also describes an order in flux, portending an end of Western dominance, replaced by a system that "will exhibit striking diversity; alternative conceptions of domestic and international order will compete and co-exist on the global stage."[12]

These visions of an international order in flux have serious implications for regional order in the Gulf, where regional ideological multipolarity has already resulted in fluid or 'liquid alliances.' Many have described the Middle East in general and the Gulf in particular as a 'penetrated region,' which Brown describes as one in which politics are not "adequately explained – even at the local level – without reference to the influence of the intrusive outside system."[13] At the same time, Gulf monarchies have long used relationships with these extra-regional powers to navigate a complex set of concerns at the domestic, regional, and international levels. David's concept of omnibalancing provides a useful theoretical approach to understanding the relationships between Gulf monarchies and external powers, explaining that foreign policy decisions in developing states reflect a need to ensure regime stability, and threats to this must be considered at both the systemic and domestic levels. Omnibalancing "assumes the decision maker asks, 'which outside power is most likely to protect me from the internal and external threats (as well as the combination of both) that I face'."[14] Alignment strategies are therefore chosen with the expectation that the external power (or powers) is willing to provide the security necessary to ensure regime continuity. A deeper pool of powers increases the likelihood of achieving this security.

For the Gulf monarchies, the primary external threats exist at the regional level, where they must navigate a dangerous neighborhood where Iran and Iraq have presented material and ideological threats to regional stability. As such, the Gulf can best be understood as a regional security complex, defined by Buzan as "a group of states whose primary security concerns link together sufficiently closely that their national securities cannot realistically be considered apart from one another."[15] Gause defines the Gulf as a security complex because the eight regional states (the six Gulf monarchies, Iran, and Iraq) "focus intensely on each other and devote the bulk of their security resources to relations with each other, and have done so for decades."[16] Consistent with the idea of the Gulf as a penetrated region, Buzan also emphasizes that "states outside the complex may play a major role within it, without the complex itself being central to their security concerns."[17] Alone among the external powers with interests in the Gulf, Gause includes the USA in this regional security complex, stating

> it is hard to argue with the fact that the United States determined the outcome of one Gulf war in 1991 and profoundly changed the distribution of regional power in 2003 by destroying what had been an important pole of regional power. The United States is directly involved in the region, but it does not completely control events in the Gulf.[18]

The inclusion of the USA is important in understanding order in the Gulf. As Coates Ulrichsen's chapter shows, the US role in the Gulf has undergone significant change over the years, but the imperative of a stable region, not dominated by another power, has been American policy since the Carter doctrine was announced in 1980.That the relationship was cemented during the Cold War underscores its structural nature. US–Gulf ties were not a reflection of shared values or norms, but rather a shared concern of a potential Soviet expansion into the region. As such, the relationship has always been somewhat of an elite bargain that papered over tensions at the public level.

There are concerns within the Gulf, however, that the US commitment to its security partnership with the Gulf monarchies is wavering. A series of strategic choices in Washington since the invasion of Iraq in 2003, including the pivot or rebalance to Asia and the Joint Comprehensive Plan of Action (JCPOA) with Iran, have contributed to a perception that Washington is less willing to continue its leadership position in the Gulf in service of the status quo. More worrisome was Washington's response to the Arab uprisings, especially its abandonment of longtime ally Hosni Mubarak in Egypt; for leaders in the Gulf, the implication was that they too could be dropped should the protests spread to their countries. Guzansky agrees that this has caused concern in the Gulf monarchies, leading "the elites in the Gulf to become skeptical of the certainty of American political backing should a domestic threat to their rule rise."[19] Gyrgiel and Mitchell also see a divergence in perceptions of regional politics, describing "a degree of strategic uncertainty that would not have been present at earlier stages of the post-Cold War era, when U.S. military commitments were more certain and aspirants for regional leadership more easily containable."[20] This plays into long-standing fears of abandonment among Gulf leaders, a common feature of asymmetrical alliances, a point emphasized by Kuwaiti political scientist Abdulla Al Shayji: "The GCC-U.S. partnership is a classic case study of the built-in dilemmas of an alliance between a stronger party and a weaker party."[21] A 2015 visit from then Secretary of Defense Chuck Hagel did little to comfort Gulf leaders, when he stated "Bilateral ties with the United States and American military presence are not enough to guarantee regional security. America's engagement with Gulf nations is intended to support and facilitate, not replace, stronger multilateral ties within the GCC."[22] Shortly after, an anonymous Gulf official expressed frustration, saying, "We need a dependable relationship with a major power. If the United States can't be counted on, then we will have to turn elsewhere."[23]

Among Gulf leaders, much of the rift between the US and the Gulf monarchies was attributed to President Obama, and the election of Donald Trump has been expected to bring the USA back to its 'natural' position as the primary security guarantor of the Gulf, reflected in a *Gulf News* headline when Trump made Riyadh the destination of his first overseas state visit: "US Policy Back on Track in the Region."[24] Trump has certainly aligned the USA closer to the Arab side of the Gulf and even further from Iran. In Riyadh, he promised closer cooperation with the GCC, and described the Iranian government as one that "speaks openly of mass murder, vowing the destruction of Israel, death to America, and ruin for many leaders and nations in this very room."[25] GCC leaders were clearly satisfied to have an American president who appears to share their view of regional events and US interests in the Gulf. The Trump administration's conflicted approach to the crisis between Qatar and the Anti-Terror Quartet of Saudi Arabia, the UAE, Bahrain, and Egypt, discussed in Coates Ulrichsen's chapter, indicates that Washington's vision for Gulf order remains unclear. Should this remain the case, it stands to reason that other powers will begin to take a more active role in shaping a new regional order to protect their assets and interests in the Gulf.

The second broad theme in this volume concerns the assessment by and behavior of extra-regional powers regarding the international political economy of the Gulf states since the start of the twenty-first century and, in particular, the Arab uprisings of 2010–2011. In other words, to what extent have the economic interests of the extra-regional powers in the Gulf region been affected by trends in international political economy; what has changed, what has stayed the same, and what will change in the next ten years to significantly impact on international relations? To address this question, the contributors were invited to approach it from different angles, including the following sub-questions: How likely are external powers to 'securitize' their economic relations with these states? Are the Gulf states – with their 'distribution' states, 'late rentier' systems, and state-directed economies – perceived as unique economic interlocutors for external powers and will the former continue to be treated as such? Do external powers simply react to changes in the political economy of the Gulf states, or do they attempt to shape the policy environment to their advantage?[26] To provide a context for case studies of selected external powers, an overview of trends in the global political economy that resonate with the Gulf states and their partners follows below.

Economic power and growth

It has become de rigueur to refer to the shift in global economic power away from the West and towards the East, with the latter including rapidly developing countries such as China, India, Brazil, Turkey, and South Korea. It is estimated, for instance, that while G7 economies will grow by 2.3% per annum between 2011 and 2025, emerging economies will outdo them at 4.7%.[27] As the share of global output by G7 economies declines – from 51% in 1990 to 31% in 2016 and 28% in 2022 – that by developing countries continues to rise and may reach 45% in 2025.[28] In terms of global investments, the top ten countries with net foreign assets comprised five developed European countries and five emerging economies in 2005; by 2014, two European countries and eight emerging economies shared the spoils.[29] South–North investment flows are not uncommon, with investors from the Gulf owning trophy properties and football clubs, and acquiring significant stakes in major companies in Europe and North America. The United Kingdom's Telegraph newspaper noted that Qatari investors "own three times more property in the UK than the Queen"[30] and the USA's largest oil refinery is owned by Saudi Aramco. South–South investment flows are also growing as noted in the chapter by Fulton: by one estimate, China has extended over US$65 billion worth of credit to energy companies in Africa, South America, and Russia since 2009.[31] Declarations of a 'pivot to Asia,' 'Look East policy,' and the 'Asian century' along with attention-grabbing projects like the 'Belt and Road Initiative,' the India-Africa Development Fund, and Saudi Aramco's IPO reinforce this impression.

Nevertheless, several caveats are in order. Despite their impressive growth rates and corresponding growth in national wealth, developing countries will continue to trail the purchasing power of consumers in developed countries. Even in China, one of the fastest growing economies in the world, citizens in Beijing will take 35 years to achieve a GDP per capita level comparable to that of New York in 2013; while citizens in Sao Paulo and Jakarta can expect to catch-up in 40 and 50 years' time, respectively.[32] In addition, while South–South trade has increased markedly and accounts for one-quarter of global trade today, North–South trade flows still predominate. In Africa, for example, trade with BRIC countries grew from US$23 billion to US$268 billion between 2001 and 2011; yet, this amounted to less than half of OECD–Africa trade in 2011.[33] Furthermore, Europe and North America continue to play host to the lion's share of investments from developing countries. In the case of Abu Dhabi, investors from the developed countries comprise the majority of those who purchased bonds issued by the emirate in 2017 and by one of its sovereign wealth funds (Mubadala) in 2009;[34] ADIA, its other sovereign wealth fund, is mandated to invest 55–85% of its portfolio in North America and Europe.[35]

The bottom line, therefore, is that centers of economic power will be distributed across both the developed and developing world. For countries external to the Gulf covered in this volume, this trend is an opportunity and a challenge. It is an opportunity because developed countries will continue to be courted by Gulf states keen to take advantage of the higher spending power, advanced technological prowess, and well-regulated financial markets there. However, the trend also poses a challenge since Gulf states can hedge their options through closer South–South commercial and financial exchanges at the expense of more conventional North–South flows. Consequently, East–West collaborative projects, such as the multibillion dollar investments earlier this year by Abu Dhabi's Mubadala and Saudi Arabia's Public Investment Fund into Japan's technology-based Softbank Vision Fund, may become more common.

Economic liberalization and diversification

The second trend that will have an impact on the external powers and their relationship with the Gulf is the latter's commitment to economic liberalization and diversification especially since, and in some cases prior to, the plunge in oil prices after mid-2014. These include the publication of forward-looking plans to diversify out of oil-led development, reductions in fuel and water subsidies to ease the burden on declining state budgets, regulatory changes to attract inward investment since foreign capital is spoiled for choice, partial privatization of state-owned companies, defense industrialization, and the introduction of consumption and other taxes to provide a more stable revenue stream for the government.[36]

Some of these reforms are not new, or were partially implemented, or were abandoned altogether. Saudi Arabia, for instance, has announced diversification plans since 1980 but much of it was limited to oil-related reforms – such as the creation of the energy-intensive petrochemicals industry – and ignored the development of non-oil sectors;[37] in Kuwait, a reduction in diesel and kerosene subsidies in January 2015 had to be partially reversed in the face of a huge public outcry. Moreover, only a few developing countries such as Malaysia, Indonesia, Chile, and Mexico, are widely acknowledged to have successfully diversified their economies away from primary commodities.

Nevertheless, there are good reasons to believe that the current commitment to economic reform by the Gulf states will be qualitatively different from previous attempts, and hence more sustainable. In the first place, proven oil reserves in these countries are declining precipitously: at the current rate of production, oil will last for 14 more years in Oman and 59 years in Saudi Arabia;[38] and no new supergiant oil fields have been discovered in the Gulf in recent years. Consequently, oil-rich Gulf states do not have a lot of time to use oil revenues to finance expensive diversification efforts. They also only have a limited window of opportunity to tap financial markets that are awash in liquidity and willing to lend to oil-rich countries. Saudi Arabia's indebtedness will rise from 8.4% of GDP in 2010 to 24.9% in 2022, while Oman's will balloon from 5.7% to 62.7% during the same period.[39] Second, the switch to non-oil electricity and modes of transportation will intensify, thereby reducing demand for oil, and resulting in a 'lower-for-longer' oil price during the next few decades. Gas is already the fuel of choice in power stations in Europe, energy-hungry economies like China and India are switching from coal or biomass to cleaner sources such as gas and nuclear, and even Gulf countries are embracing solar and nuclear power. Although electric cars make up just 0.2% of all passenger vehicles in the world today,[40] advances in supporting infrastructure including lithium batteries, prices of solar electricity, sales rebates, together with pledges from companies and governments to reduce the fleet of petrol-based cars may herald significant changes. Third, a new generation of younger leaders is in power in the more influential Gulf states: they are more aware about climate change, sustainable development, the perils of a mono-economy, and the role of human resources in a knowledge-based economy. Crucially, they also appear to have the drive, energy, and political will to implement such reforms. For instance, the Crown Prince of Abu Dhabi noted that "in 50 years when we might have the last barrel of oil, the question is: when it is shipped abroad will we be sad? If we are investing today in the right sectors, I can tell you we will celebrate at that moment."[41]

For external powers in the Gulf region, this trend of economic liberalization and diversification sustains existing commercial ventures and opens up new avenues – including food exports from Brazil, vocational training from Japan, armored vehicles and shipbuilding from the USA, polymer dispersants and sugar processing plants from the United Kingdom, military training from South Korea, nuclear-related imports from Russia – as the chapters in this book have noted. Saudi Arabia, Kuwait, and the UAE already mandate that successful arms exporters offset part of the value of major defense contracts through local joint ventures aimed at creating jobs in manufacturing goods or offering services in non-oil sectors. For example, Saudi Arabia reported that by 2006, 36 companies with a total capitalization of US$4.5 billion were created by the offsets program; while in the UAE, over 40 joint ventures were created by 2014.[42] Given that Saudi Arabia and the UAE are the Gulf's top two arms importers, more such diversification – aided by France, United Kingdom, and the USA as major arms exporters to the Gulf – can be expected.

Economic liberalization and diversification in the Gulf are also of interest to the scholarly community. The latter has been engaged in a long-running debate about the extent to which these states fit into political science literature on issues such as the democracy deficit, state autonomy, monarchial survival, alliance strategies, small states in international relations, and 'inside–outside' linkages. In this connection, the current wave of economic reforms appears to 'de-exceptionalize' the Gulf states. It is arguable that they are merely the latest participants of a trend that began in the 1980s with China and the Latin American countries, continued in the 1990s with the post-communist transitions away from central planning in Europe and the former Soviet republics, and which has now spread to the Gulf following pioneering efforts by the UAE in the first decade of the twenty-first century. While there are important differences between these periodic 'waves,' what is indisputable is the aim of reducing the direct role of the state in the economy, whether through public-private partnerships, corporatization of former government functions, partial privatization of the commanding heights of the Gulf economy, joint ventures, foreign direct investment, or a greater role for privately owned small-and-medium-sized enterprises.

It is also noteworthy that the commitment to liberalization and diversification among Gulf states reinforces scholarship regarding the 'varieties of capitalism' and how their different characteristics contribute to economic development. Khaleeji capitalism[43] is distinguishable from the liberal Anglo-Saxon model and the coordinated markets of Europe; it has more in common with the East Asian variant – given their relatively larger emphasis on state-led development – but is still differentiated from the East Asian model. Nevertheless, they are all stakeholders in the global capitalist economy. In this regard, one reason why incumbent elites in the Gulf support liberalization, diversification, entrepreneurship, and globalization – despite the consequences of demands for political change these may produce as seen in post-communist transitions – is that such economic reforms solidify and expand rentier networks among the population.[44] Consequently, the entrenched capitalist markets in the Gulf may "exist for state and family survival and wealth strategies."[45]

Energy security

The third trend in global political economy concerns the energy market. Energy is a key driver of international interactions between countries for at least two reasons. Its significant role in trade – the energy trade accounts for almost 20%

of global trade[46] – impacts on finance, revenues, and economic growth in energy consuming and producing countries. In addition, energy is closely correlated with geopolitics and power in international relations[47] as underlined by the decision by the British navy to switch from coal to oil, Adolf Hitler's invasion of the Soviet Union, Japan's bombing of Pearl Harbor, resource nationalism in oil-producing countries, and sanctions against imports of Iranian oil among others. Unsurprisingly, energy security or the "uninterrupted physical availability at a price which is affordable, while respecting environmental concerns"[48] has become a vital national interest for all countries.

In a recent report by the Institute for 21st Century Energy, the upward trend in China's energy security risk index since 2010 is a stark contrast to the sharp downward trend in industrialized countries. This shift in relative energy security away from the developing world and in favor of the USA/Europe is of tectonic proportions: it calls into question the sustainability of the energy rents, economic power, and political influence that accrued to the former in the 1970s and 2000s.[49] The fall in oil prices since 2014 explains some of this shift as wealth is redistributed from oil-producing countries, mostly in the South, to oil consumers in the North. Even more crucial, though, are long-term structural changes – including consumption, imports, efficiency, and technology – in the energy markets at the international and local levels.

Take energy consumption as an example: while it has plateaued in developed countries, it continues to grow rapidly in developing economies. Availability of and access to energy is therefore a bigger problem for the latter. Between 2005 and 2015, crude oil consumption in the USA and EU declined by 0.6% and 1.7% per annum, whereas in China, India, and the Gulf states, this grew by 5–6% per annum.[50] This decline in energy consumption in the West has also translated into a lower volume of energy imports. For example, US crude oil imports have declined from 10.1 million barrels per day in 2005 to 7.8 million in 2016,[51] thanks in part to rising shale oil production in the USA. Energy imports have also declined in the EU, partly offset by indigenous production of renewable energy which accounts for almost 30% of electricity generation in 2015 up from 15% ten years ago.[52] In contrast, crude oil imports by China have surged from 2.5 million to 6.7 million barrels per day between 2005 and 2015;[53] and 90% of oil from the Middle East is expected to go to Asia by 2035. Compounding the problem for developing countries is their relative energy inefficiency, which makes it even more difficult to temper consumption and import levels. It suffices to note the huge disparity in the energy intensity of the steel industry in the OECD countries and China;[54] and the fact that since 2000, energy efficiency levels have improved in many parts of the world but not in the Gulf,[55] partly because energy subsidies here are one of the highest in the world. Finally, technological advances have also changed the structure of energy markets. Companies specializing in horizontal drilling and hydraulic fracturing techniques have rendered unconventional shale oil and gas resources viable, hence increasing the supply of non-OPEC oil and keeping a lid on global oil price increases. Their technology-driven operating practices, including using advanced technology to identify the most prolific areas to target, to reduce well drilling times, and to improve oil rig productivity, have also forced conventional oil companies to be more cost efficient.[56] The end result is a reinforcement of the 'lower-for-longer' oil price scenario highlighted earlier, but this time from the supply side of the equation.

What do these aforementioned changes in the energy markets mean for external powers in the Gulf region? Two implications are highlighted here. First, foreign companies with the relevant know-how are well-placed to provide Gulf states with alternative energy for their electricity requirements. The UAE, which has been a net importer of gas since 2007, has chosen to ameliorate its vulnerability to gas imports through the construction of solar and nuclear power plants. Saudi Arabia has vowed to do likewise in order to free up domestically consumed oil for export revenues.[57] In this respect, a South Korean/USA consortium is close to completing the UAE's first nuclear power station while companies from Russia, China, and France have submitted expressions of interest to participate in Saudi Arabia's forthcoming tender for up to 16 nuclear reactors. In the solar industry, China's Shanghai Electric teamed up with Saudi Arabia's ACWA Power to submit a successful bid in 2017 for the fourth phase of Dubai's Mohamed Bin Rashid Solar Park, while Abu Dhabi's Masdar and Spain's FRV were 2016 winners for the third phase of the said Solar Park.

Second, Gulf states "may have to work harder to attract investors, previously taken as a given"[58] in the face of a less secure, low-carbon, and low-oil price future. Qatar, for example, lifted its 12-year moratorium on the development of its giant gas field in April 2017, partly to claim back its dominant position in the liquefied natural gas (LNG) industry from new players like Australia and the USA. As for Saudi Arabia, it may have to seek an alternative to the proposed sale of 5% of ARAMCO's stock value: the Chinese oil company that was in the running for a private placement seems to have declined the offer in favor of a US$9 billion stake in Russia's Rosneft. Rosneft's oil, largely delivered by overland pipeline to China, would enhance energy security for the latter since most of its current oil imports arrive via tankers. External powers interested in a stake in the Gulf's oil and gas industry may, therefore, have some room for maneuver.

Finally, the changing landscape of energy security implies that countries that have previously relied upon America's willingness to seek and maintain command of the global commons[59] – the air, sea, and land space that do not belong to any state but that provides the connections that sustain the international system from the flow of energy to communications – may have to step up. China's self-acknowledged 'Malacca dilemma' perfectly illustrates the dilemma: 85% of China's commodity imports transit the Malacca Straits, de facto control of which lies with the USA. Even though China now possesses two aircraft carriers (one locally made and the other bought second-hand from Ukraine), it cannot hope to compete with the 10 in the US navy, or with the latter's numerical superiority in destroyers and submarines, without diverting precious financial resources away from economic growth. As noted by all the contributors in this book, none of the external powers are able or willing to step into the USA's role in the Gulf, a role that is estimated to cost US$50–90 billion per annum, let alone globally.

However, they may have to 'show up' more often in anti-piracy and anti-terror operations led by the USA to entice the latter to retain its role in keeping trade routes open in the seas around the Gulf region. This applies particularly to Asian powers, since 90% of oil from the Gulf is expected to be shipped to Asia by 2035.

Bearing in mind the impact of these international political and economic issues, the chapters in this book discuss the changing nature of the roles of extra-regional powers in their relations with the Gulf monarchies within regional and international orders in transition.

In Chapter 2, Coates Ulrichsen provides an evolutionary account of the USA's relations with the Gulf monarchies, from the nineteenth century to the present. In it, he demonstrates that the expansion of US power in the Gulf was halting in depth and scope, and despite the strength of its regional presence by the end of the Cold War, the turbulent dynamics of the George W. Bush and Barak Obama presidencies led to troubled relationships with the Gulf states. He assesses how US–Gulf relations may evolve during the Donald Trump administration, as personalized networks appear to have a greater impact than institutional interests.

In Chapter 3, Sim sees Russia's Gulf policy as less of a grand strategy than as of defensive opportunism, driven by a combination of domestic pressures and economic incentives. She describes Russia's primary goal with Gulf states as an attempt to prevent blowback to the Putin regime caused by conflicts in the Middle East. As such, Russian interactions with the Gulf monarchies seem to be motivated by regime stability rather than commercial logic, resulting in a Russia that is unwilling, uninterested, and unable to take a larger role in providing regional stability.

In Chapter 4, Roberts and Bianco analyze the evolution of the United Kingdom's relations with the Gulf monarchies. Long the prominent power in the Gulf, the United Kingdom's role has inevitably diminished since leaving the region in 1971. With its depth of experience in the Gulf, there is a sense that the United Kingdom 'gets' the Gulf monarchies better than other external powers, an assertion that the authors consider in order to evaluate the modern basis of UK–Gulf relations and the prospects for their near-term development.

In Chapter 5, Samaan analyzes the deepening ties between France and the Gulf monarchies, noting that they have intensified in the face of negative French public opinion towards the Gulf. Trade and cultural interests have dominated, yet there are significant security issues, such as the Iranian nuclear program and the Syrian civil war, where French and the Gulf monarchies' interests converge. While 'Gulf-bashing' remains a constant in the French political discourse, Samaan anticipates a continuation of the enduring partnership.

In Chapter 6, Carvalho Pinto presents an overview of Brazil's relations with the Gulf monarchies, addressing both the opportunities and difficulties in deepening bilateral relations, and discussing areas that offer promise of stronger future ties. She focuses on the economic synergies that have been important drivers in the relationships, seeing an important role in private Brazilian economic actors.

In Chapter 7, Baskan provides an account of the evolution of Turkey's relations with the Gulf monarchies. He pinpoints the political and economic pivot points that have contributed to the changing nature of these bilateral relationships, noting that Turkey shifted from an indifferent actor in the Gulf to an increasingly important one, driven largely by economic opportunities in the 1980s. His analysis demonstrates that economic considerations were the primary drivers of Turkey's foreign policy in the Gulf, but geopolitics have always been in the background, especially in the wake of the Arab uprisings.

In Chapter 8, Brewster and Pethiyagoda analyze India's relations with the Gulf monarchies, demonstrating that Dehli's interests on the Arabian Peninsula are motivated both by economic concerns and the welfare of its massive diaspora in the region. While its influence in the Gulf has historically been limited because of ideological factors, domestic political concerns, and longstanding patterns of alignment and rivalry, they envision a new pattern of regional engagement for India as a result of a changing balance of power in the region, leading to an emerging political and security role for India in the Gulf.

In Chapter 9, Fulton traces the evolution of China's relations with the Gulf monarchies. China has transitioned from a marginal regional actor to a major partner of every state in the Gulf, with economic relations bringing the two sides closer together. The deepening of these economic relations coincide with China's rise to a power with global interests, and the Belt and Road Initiative's expansion of Chinese influence indicates a stronger potential role for China in Gulf security issues. He sees two competing approaches to a Chinese security role in the Gulf: a traditional power projection, using tools of military statecraft, and the one that Chinese officials describe as 'security through development.'

In Chapter 10, Seo considers the growth of South Korea's relations with the Gulf monarchies. He too finds that the focus of bilateral interests has shifted from commercial to more strategic areas, such as the nuclear energy sector and military cooperation. At the same time, Korean outreach to Iran is perceived as potentially problematic for its relationships on the Arabian side of the Gulf.

In Chapter 11, Muto provides a detailed analysis of Japan's relations with Saudi Arabia since 1955. His discussion of Japan's economic diplomacy with Saudi Arabia presents a model for understanding Japan's outreach toward other Gulf monarchies. He describes the foundation of this bilateral relationship as 'technological cooperation for energy,' a formula that has evolved into a multifaceted type of bilateral relationship in which both states pursue deeper economic relations in order to address national interests.

Notes

1 See F. Gregory Gause III, *The International Relations of the Persian Gulf.* (Cambridge: Cambridge University Press, 2010); Kristian Coates Ulrichsen, *Insecure Gulf: The End of Certainty and the Transition to the Post-Oil Era.* (New York: Columbia University Press, 2011); Mehran Kamrava ed. *International Politics of the Persian Gulf.* (Syracuse: Syracuse University Press, 2011).
2 See Jeffrey Goldberg, "The Obama Doctrine," *The Atlantic Monthly*, April 2016, https://www.theatlantic.com/magazine/archive/2016/04/the-obama-doctrine/471525/; "The Obama Interviews: China as a Free Rider," *New York Times*, August 9, 2014.

https://www.nytimes.com/video/opinion/100000003047788/china-as-a-free-rider.html
3 Turki al-Faisal Al Saud, "Mr. Obama, We are Not 'Free Riders'," *Arab News*, March 14, 2016, http://www.arabnews.com/columns/news/894826
4 Brock Tessman, "System Structure and State Strategy: Adding Hedging to the Menu," *Security Studies* 21, no. 2 (2012): 193.
5 Tessman, "System Structure and State Strategy,": 195–196.
6 Steve A. Yetiv, *The Absence of Grand Strategy: The United States in the Persian Gulf, 1972–2005*. (Baltimore: The John Hopkins University Press, 2008): 21.
7 Christopher Layne, "This Time It's Real: The End of Unipolarity and the *Pax Americana*," *International Studies Quarterly* 56 (2012), 204.
8 Barry Buzan and George Lawson, *The Global Transformation: History, Modernity and the Making of International Relations*. (Cambridge: Cambridge University Press, 2015): 275.
9 Buzan and Lawson, *The Global Transformation*: 276.
10 Amitav Acharya, *The End of American World Order*. (Cambridge: Polity Press, 2014): 8.
11 Simon Reich and Richard Ned Lebow, *Goodbye Hegemony! Power and Influence in the Global System*. (Princeton: Princeton University Press, 2014): 177.
12 Charles A. Kupchan, *No One's World: The West, the Rising Rest, and the Coming Global Turn*. (Oxford: Oxford University Press, 2012): 183.
13 L. Carl Brown, *International Politics and the Middle East: Old Rules, Dangerous Game*. (Princeton: Princeton University Press, 1984): 5.
14 Steven R. David, "Explaining Third World Alignment," *World Politics* 43, no. 2 (1991): 238.
15 Barry Buzan, *People, States & Fear: The National Security Problem in International Relations*. (Chapel Hill: The University of North Carolina Press, 1983): 106.
16 Gause, *The International Politics of the Persian Gulf*: 4.
17 Buzan, *People, States & Fear*: 106.
18 Gause, *The International Politics of the Persian Gulf*: 6.
19 Yoel Guzansky, *The Arab Gulf States and Reform in the Middle East*. (Houndmills, Basingstoke: Palgrave Macmillan, 2014): 14.
20 Jakub J. Grygiel and A. Wess Mitchell, *The Unquiet Frontier: Rising Rivals, Vulnerable Allis, and the Crisis of American Power*. (Princeton: Princeton University Press, 2016): 86.
21 Abdullah K. Al Shayji, "The GCC–U.S. Relationship: A GCC Perspective," *Middle East Policy* 21, no. 3 (2014): 61.
22 Andrew Critchlow, "US Says Can't 'Guarantee' Security in Oil-Rich Gulf States as Focus Turns to China," *The Telegraph*, May 15 2014. http://www.telegraph.co.uk/finance/newsbysector/industry/defence/10831872/US-says-cant-guarantee-security-in-oil-rich-Gulf-states-as-focus-turns-to-China.html
23 David Rothkopf, "The Middle East's Pivot to Asia," *Foreign Policy*, April 24, 2015, http://foreignpolicy.com/2015/04/24/the-middle-easts-pivot-to-asia-china/
24 "US Policy Back on Track in the Region," *Gulf News*, May 21, 2017, http://gulfnews.com/opinion/editorials/us-policy-back-on-track-in-the-region-1.2030740
25 Ben Hubbard and Thomas Erdbrink, "In Saudi Arabia, Trump Reaches Out to Sunni Nations, at Iran's Expense," *New York Times*, May 21, 2017, https://www.nytimes.com/2017/05/21/world/middleeast/saudi-arabia-iran-donald-trump.html?_r=0
26 Some of these questions are informed by recent works by Valbjorn Morten, "Strategies for Reviving the International Relations/Middle East Nexus after the Arab Uprisings." *PS: Political Science and Politics* 50 no. 3 (2017): 647–651 and Erin, A. Snider, "International Political Economy and the New Middle East." *PS: Political Science and Politics* 50 no. 3:664–667.

27 Hans Timmer, Dailami Mansoor, Jacqueline Irving, Robert Hauswald, and Paul Masson, *Global Development Horizons: Multipolarity – The New Global Economy*. (Washington, DC: World Bank, 2011).
28 GDP based on PPP, share of world. In *IMF Datamapper*. 2017; Timmer et al., *Global Development Horizons*.
29 "Global Financial Stability Report: Statistical Appendix." (Washington, DC: International Monetary Fund, 2015); Timothy Taylor, "US as a Capital Importer." *Conversable Economist*. 2013.
30 Lucy Burton, "Qatar looks to woo UK with 'Wall Street of the Middle East' Pitch," *The Telegraph*, May 21, 2017.
31 Michael Meidan, "China's loans for oil: asset or liability?" Oxford: Oxford Institute for Energy Studies, 2016.
32 "Global cities 2030: Future trends and market opportunities in the world's largest 750 cities." Oxford: Oxford Economics, 2014.
33 Daniel Poon, "South-South Trade, Investment, and Aid Flows." Ottawa, Canada: The North–South Institute.
34 See "The Report: Abu Dhabi." Oxford Business Group, 2016; Mahmoud Kassem, "Developed Markets Pique Interest in Oversubscribed $10bn Abu Dhabi Bond," *The National*, October 11, 2017.
35 "Mubadala Annual Report 2009." Mubadala, 2010.
36 For a discussion of some of these reforms see Martin Hvindt, "Economic Diversification in GCC Countries: Past Record and Future Trends." In *Kuwait Programme on Development, Governance, and Globalisation in the Gulf States #27*. (London: London School of Economics, 2013); Ulrichsen (2016), Saab (2014), and Young (2017).
37 The November 2017 announcement of a further US$20 billion investment in an oil-to-chemicals complex between two Saudi state giants ARAMCO (oil) and SABIC (chemicals) reinforces the dominance of this strand of diversification.
38 "BP Statistical Review of World Energy 2017." BP, 2017.
39 These levels of general government gross debt are, in fact, quite manageable and comparatively low. Saudi Arabia, for instance, had a gross debt level that was 100% of GDP at the start of the twenty-first century (see Chris Miller, "Russia Sets out to Bring the Middle East Under New Order." *YaleGlobal online*, 2016, https://yaleglobal.yale.edu/content/russia-sets-out-bring-middle-east-under-new-order) while the EU's indebtedness at 85.7% in 2016 is set to fall to 74.3% in 2022. See "General government gross debt as % of GDP." In *IMF Datamapper*, 2017a.
40 "The number of electric cars on the world's roads doubled last year." *Fortune*, June 7, 2017.
41 "Sheikh Mohamed's inspirational vision for a post-oil UAE." *The National*, February 10, 2015.
42 Bob Willen, Mauricio Zuazua, and Jim Hanna. "GCC Defense Offset Programs: The Trillion Dollar Opportunity," London: A T Kearny, 2014.
43 Adam Hanieh, *Capitalism and Class in the Gulf Arab States*. (London: Palgrave MacMillan, 2011)
44 Matthew Gray, "Political Economy Dynamics in the Arab Gulf States: Implications for Political Transition." In *The Arab World and Iran: A Turbulent Region in Transition*, ed. Amin Saikal. (Houndmills, Basingstoke: Palgrave Macmillan, 2016); Crystal A. Ennis, 2014. "Between Trend and Necessity: Top Down Entrepreneurship Promotion in Oman and Qatar." *The Muslim World* 105, no. 1:116–138.
45 Karen E. Young, "Markets Serving States: The Institutional bases of Financial Governance in the Gulf Cooperation Council States." London: LSE Kuwait Programme, 2015: 25.
46 "International Trade Statistics 2015." Geneva: World Trade Organization, 2016.
47 The classic work on this is Yergin.

48 Jessica Jewell, "The IEA Model of Short Term Energy Security." Paris: International Energy Agency, 2011: 9.
49 Roland Dannreuther, 2015. "Energy security and shifting modes of governance." *International Politics* 52, no. 4: 466–483.
50 "BP Statistical Review of World Energy 2017." London: BP, 2017.
51 Energy Information Agency report, "U.S. crude oil imports increased in 2016," April 11, 2017, https://www.eia.gov/todayinenergy/detail.php?id=30732
52 Hans-Wilhelm Schiffer, "Lecture on Successes and Challenges at Renewable Deployment in the EU Power Sector." (Washington, DC: US Energy Association, 2016).
53 Meidan, "China's loans for oil: asset or liability?"
54 Kira West, "Lecture on ETP 2015: Iron and Steel Findings." OECD Steel Committee Meeting, 2015.
55 Glada Lahn, Paul Stevens, and Felix Preston, "Saving Oil and Gas in the Gulf." London: Chatham House, 2013.
56 Diane Munro, "Navigating the New Oil Era." In *Issue Paper #10*. (Washington, DC: Arab Gulf States Institute in Washington, 2017).
57 A report in 2011 by the Saudi Electricity Company warned that nearly one-third of the country's oil production was being consumed locally and projected that by 2030, current production levels would be unable to meet the ever-increasing local demand for oil (Coates Ulrichsen 2016). A Chatham House report (Coates Ulrichsen 2016) went a step further by predicting that Saudi oil exports would cease after 2035 in the face of heavy domestic demand.
58 David Pike and Oliver Klaus, "The Mideast Gulf's New Oil Order." *Energy Intelligence*. 1 August 2017.
59 Barry R. Posen, "Command of the Commons: The Military Foundation of US Hegemony, *International Security*" 28, no. 1: 5–46; Collins, Gabriel, and Jim Krane. "Carter Doctrine 3.0: Evolving US Military Guarantees for Gulf Oil Security." Baker Institute for Public Policy, 2017.

2 The evolution of US–Gulf ties

Kristian Coates Ulrichsen

Introduction

More than 70 years have passed since the fabled meeting on February 14, 1945 between King Abdulaziz bin Abdulrahman Al Saud of Saudi Arabia and US President Franklin D. Roosevelt aboard a US Navy cruiser in the Great Bitter Lake adjacent to the Suez Canal. King Abdulaziz headed a 49-strong Saudi delegation that brought with them eight sheep, 100-lb bags of rice, and watermelons, as well as Persian rugs, ivory-handled swords, and Swiss watches as gifts. Their host on the *USS Quincy* was a fourth-term wheelchair-bound President who was, it turned out, less than two months from the end of his life. In much popular and political opinion, their one and only encounter has become a shorthand for the development of a relationship predicated on the exchange of oil for security. While oil and security remain important drivers of US interests in the Gulf, to focus on them exclusively and to imagine their subsequent evolution was predetermined would ignore the ebbs and flows of a relationship that goes back nearly 200 years.

This chapter provides an overview of the evolution of US–Gulf ties over the twentieth century and examines their multifaceted contemporary components. An opening section charts the historical development of US interests in the Gulf prior to the February 1945 meeting between King Abdulaziz and President Roosevelt. This period saw the growth of initial US diplomatic and commercial ties in Oman from the 1830s onward, the arrival of US oilmen in the Arabian Peninsula in the 1920s, and the securing of oil concessions for US companies in Bahrain and Saudi Arabia in the 1930s. Section two charts the emergence of a strategic component to US interests in the Gulf during World War II and analyzes the somewhat halting expansion of the scope of US–Gulf relations during the Cold War. The Cold War era witnessed also, for the first time, attempts by US presidents to articulate and define the nature and extent of US regional interests.

Section three analyzes how US policies toward the Gulf changed during the three major inter-state wars that shook the region between 1980 and 2003 when, again, policymaking was more reactive than proactive but resulted in a series of largely path-dependent decisions that influenced what came later. During this period, the US military footprint in the Arabian Peninsula expanded significantly and assumed its modern posture, with the reconstituted Fifth Fleet in Bahrain, the forward headquarters of Central Command (CENTCOM) in Saudi Arabia and, later, Qatar, and the patchwork of defense cooperation agreements signed with individual partners after the Gulf War in 1991. The US presence on Saudi soil after the end of the Gulf War also provided a powerful mobilizational tool for Al Qaeda and its leader, Osama bin Laden, with fateful consequences that became horrifyingly clear on September 11, 2001. More prosaically, the policy decisions made in the 1980s and 1990s meant that the US assumed the role of external security guarantor for the Gulf monarchies, after a 'lost decade' in the 1970s following Britain's military withdrawal from all positions east of Suez in 1971.

In section four, the analysis shifts to the turbulent dynamics that characterized the George W. Bush and Barack Obama presidency's troubled relationship with the Gulf States just as the shock of the Iraq War and the later Arab Spring upheaval reverberated across the region. Policymakers' perceptions of threat and national interest diverged on almost every major regional issue, from the uprisings of 2011 to the Syrian civil war, the nuclear negotiations with Iran, and the Gulf-led intervention into Yemen in 2015. This produced an atmosphere of mistrust and growing toxicity by the end of Obama's term in office, epitomized by the Justice Against Sponsors of Terrorism Act (JASTA) and President Obama's comment about 'freeloaders,' both of which infuriated Gulf leaders in 2016. Feeling they no longer had the US's 'back,' ruling elites in Gulf Cooperation Council (GCC) states became more assertive and interventionist as they developed a set of policies increasingly autonomous from US interests.

The diplomatic and economic standoff between three Gulf States plus Egypt and Qatar that erupted in June 2017 illustrates the 'post-American' landscape that confronts the most inexperienced and arguably unqualified US president in modern times. This chapter therefore ends with a look at how US–Gulf ties may evolve further in an 'alternative facts' environment and where the US president and his inner circle increasingly resemble a Royal Court where personalized networks appear to trump (pun intended) long-entrenched institutional interests.

Early relations

The first treaty relationship between the United States and a partner in the Gulf goes back nearly two centuries. In 1828, Edmund Roberts, a US merchant and diplomatic envoy, met with the Sultan of Muscat and Oman, Said bin Sultan, in Zanzibar. Although their meeting was designed only to discuss the removal of obstacles to trade in Zanzibar, which at the time was under the Sultan's control, it triggered negotiations between Roberts and the Sultan for a commercial treaty between Oman and the United States, which was signed in Muscat on September 21, 1833. The resulting expansion in commercial contact between the two countries led to the arrival of a US Consul, Richard Waters, in Zanzibar in 1837. Three years later, the Sultan dispatched a sailing ship, the Sultana, to New York laden with gifts for President Martin van Buren, which were passed to the Smithsonian Institution in Washington, DC, on its creation in 1848.[1] In response, President van Buren sent the Sultana back to Muscat with two of the largest mirrors ever made in the United States, along with a chandelier and a consignment of confectionary almonds.[2]

The early establishment of US treaty relations with Oman – only the second such tie with a state in the Middle East and North Africa after a treaty of peace and friendship with Morocco in 1786 – reflected the rise of Oman as a (short-lived) trading empire in the mid-nineteenth century. Consumers in the United States developed a liking for Omani dates and by 1875 US merchants were shipping nearly ten million pounds of dates from Oman to the United States annually.[3] However, the global economic slowdown of the 1870s and 1880s resulted in the separation of Zanzibar from Oman and a political and economic withdrawal from world markets that lasted until the present Sultan, Qaboos bin Said, took power in 1970. The slump in Oman left little US trade with the tribal leaders in the British-controlled coastal sheikhdoms along the Gulf shoreline or with the Al Saud leadership in the center of the Arabian Peninsula as it grappled with internal rivalries in the 1890s and later embarked on a process of territorial consolidation from 1902 until the early 1920s.

The contours of US involvement in oil in the Middle East originated in the mid-1920s before the actual discovery of oil on the Arabian Peninsula in Bahrain in June 1932. Charles Crane, a US philanthropist better known for co-leading the King-Crane Commission in 1919 that examined the future of the Ottoman Empire's non-Turkish territories after World War One, continued to take an interest in Arab affairs and visited Jeddah in 1923, when the Hijaz was still under the Hashemite control of Sharif Hussein of Mecca, and again in 1926, by which time the Hijaz had been conquered by the Al Saud. During Crane's second visit, he met with Prince Faisal bin Abdulaziz before he journeyed to Yemen, where he became acquainted with the mining engineer Karl Twitchell. In 1931, Crane returned to Jeddah where he met King Abdulaziz and subsequently engaged Twitchell to undertake a geological survey of the soon-to-be-formed Kingdom of Saudi Arabia's water and mineral resources. Twitchell found considerable quantities of both, as well as traces of oil deposits, and made a favorable impression upon the King and his influential financial advisor, Abdullah Sulayman.[4]

In January 1933, the Standard Oil Company of California (SOCAL, today Chevron) took Twitchell on as an advisor for their negotiations with King Abdulaziz over the oil concession they hoped to acquire in Saudi Arabia. SOCAL also held a similar concession in Bahrain which it had acquired from the Pittsburgh-based Gulf Oil Corporation in 1928. To get around the Red Line Agreement that effectively carved out zones of American and British influence in concessionary agreements in the Gulf, SOCAL established the Bahrain Petroleum Company (BAPCO) and registered it in the British Empire Dominion of Canada. The move paid off for SOCAL as Bahrain struck oil in June 1932, nearly a year before the company secured the Saudi oil concession in May 1933 against British competition. SOCAL formed a subsidiary, the California Arabian Standard Oil Company (CASOC), to operate the concession, and sold 50 percent of it in 1936 to the Texas Oil Company (Texaco, today a part of Chevron). Oil in commercial quantities was discovered in March 1938 and exports began after

World War II. In 1948, the Standard Oil Company of New York (today Exxon) and Socony-Vacuum (later Mobil) also bought into the concession, completing the four anchors of the company renamed the Arabian American Oil Company (Aramco) in 1944.

Expanding interests

World War II was the catalyst for the strategic partnership between the United States and Gulf States that augmented the pre-war US oil interests in Saudi Arabia and Bahrain. And yet, the growth of the strategic dimension to the partnership was neither preordained nor initially endorsed in policymaking circles in Washington, DC. In April 1941, the Chairman of BAPCO, James Moffet, requested that the Roosevelt administration provide financial assistance to the Saudi government after a drought and a spike in food prices caused significant hardship in the Kingdom. However, in August 1941, the White House rejected a State Department recommendation that Saudi Arabia be supported through the Lend-Lease program, and President Roosevelt himself signaled that he regarded political and financial assistance to the Kingdom a British – rather than American – responsibility. In rejecting the proposal to assist Saudi Arabia, Roosevelt requested that his officials 'tell the British I hope they can take care of the King of Saudi Arabia. This is a little far afield for us.'[5]

And yet, just 18 months later, Saudi Arabia was declared eligible for Lend-Lease assistance in February 1943 and described as 'vital to the defense of the United States.'[6] US calculations shifted after their entry into the war following the Japanese attack on Pearl Harbor in December 1941 while the strategic location of Saudi Arabia grew more acute as North Africa and Russia became major battlefronts in the war against Hitler and Mussolini (in October 1940, a long-distance Italian air raid on the oil refineries of Bahrain and Dhahran had illustrated their vulnerability but had not, at that early stage of the war, 14 months before Pearl Harbor, triggered a policy response to an attack on the US-owned installations). The search for Allied supply routes to the Soviet Union as well as growing US government appreciation for the strategic value of Gulf oil reserves lay behind the fundamental reassessment of US national interests in the region. Whereas pre-war diplomatic relations with Saudi Arabia had been managed by Alexander Kirk, a non-resident Ambassador from Cairo, in 1943 the US Legation in Jeddah was expanded, and a chargé d'affaires, James Moose, was appointed to represent formally the United States in the Kingdom.[7]

1945 was the year in which the rising US interest in Saudi Arabia supplanted and firmly eclipsed Britain's waning influence in the Kingdom, a quarter-century before it did so in the British-protected coastal sheikhdoms of Kuwait, Bahrain, Qatar, the Trucial States (today the United Arab Emirates), and Oman. President Truman maintained close contact with the Saudi ruling elite after he succeeded to the presidency following Roosevelt's death just two months after his meeting with the Saudi King. Abdullah Sulayman led a delegation of Saudi officials on a three-month tour of the United States in 1946 which met President Truman at the White House and negotiated for an array of loans as well as infrastructure and development projects. Major US initiatives in Saudi Arabia multiplied as a result, and included the opening of a US airfield at Dhahran in 1946 and the construction (by Bechtel) of the Trans-Arabia Pipeline (Tapline) to transport Saudi oil to the Mediterranean coast at Sidon in Lebanon between 1947 and 1950.[8]

American institutions and US-influenced organizations also played a pivotal role in the development of planning and governing functions in Saudi Arabia. A planning agency was established in 1958 on the advice of the International Monetary Fund (IMF) and was expanded into the Central Planning Organization in 1965, but its remit was limited by financial constraints. In the 1960s, both Aramco and the Ford Foundation in New York helped the Saudi government plan ministry activities and establish a civil service. By the end of the decade, the collection of statistics on non-oil related activities was becoming more urgent as the information was required by the growing number of international companies that sought to invest in Saudi Arabia. In 1970, the newly appointed head of the Central Planning Organization (which became the Planning Ministry in 1975 and still later the Ministry of Economy and Planning), Hisham Nazer, inaugurated the cycle of five-year development plans and contracted the Stanford Research Institute (today, SRI), a private US consulting firm, to draw up both the first (1970–75) and second (1975–80) five-year plans.[9]

Formal relations with the smaller Gulf States (other than Oman) had to await their declarations of independence in Kuwait in 1961 and in Bahrain, Qatar, and the UAE a decade later in 1971. British officials in Kuwait, for example, strongly resisted a State Department request in 1949 to open a consular office in Kuwait to represent US citizens living in the sheikhdom, who had to travel to the US Consulate in Basra for diplomatic services, and in 1951 expressed jaundiced (and stereotyped) unease at the prospect of Americans working on the Kuwaiti oilfields, arguing that 'We do not want to run the risk of American gunmen and others shooting up each other in the camp or Arabs outside the camp.'[10] The first US Consul to Kuwait was appointed in 1951 and developed close relations with Sheikh Fahad al-Salim Al Sabah, the influential brother of two successive Rulers of Kuwait in the 1950s and 1960s, and the first member of the Al Sabah to have visited the United States.[11] Kuwait became a sovereign state in June 1961 and in December 1968 Emir Sabah al-Salim Al Sabah of Kuwait became President Lyndon B. Johnson's last foreign visitor, during the period of transition to the incoming Richard Nixon presidency, when he led a Kuwaiti delegation to Washington, DC, in part to inquire about US plans for the Gulf in the wake of Britain's impending withdrawal from the region.[12]

Regional calculations – for both the United States and Gulf counterparts – shifted significantly when Prime Minister Harold Wilson declared, unexpectedly and without warning, in January 1968 that Britain would withdraw from all remaining positions East of Suez by the end of 1971. US officials expressed annoyance that their British counterparts had not informed them in advance of the sudden about-turn in British policy toward the Gulf. Secretary of State Dean Rusk reportedly admonished Foreign Secretary George Brown with the phrase,

'Be British, George, be British, how can you betray us?'[13] Whereas Gulf rulers lamented the loss of their external protector and, in some cases, offered to underwrite the costs of continuing Britain's military presence, US officials worried more about the power vacuum that might open in the region. This was a period, after all, when the Soviet- and Chinese-backed People's Democratic Republic of Yemen was becoming the first (and only) Marxist state in the Arab world, on the southern flank of the Arabian Peninsula, and actively assisting the Popular Front for the Liberation of the Occupied Gulf in its insurgency in neighboring Oman.[14]

And yet, the United States was not ready to fill the void in the Gulf left by the retreating British. US policies toward the Middle East during the 1970s were dominated by the Arab–Israel conflict and the geopolitical fallout from the 1973 war and Arab oil embargo, followed by the outreach to detach Egypt from the Soviet bloc and facilitate the negotiations with Israel that led to the Camp David Accords in 1978 and the Egyptian–Israeli peace treaty in 1979. To the extent that regional developments in the Middle East intersected with wider Cold War calculations in the eyes of US officials, they concerned Jordanian stability – after Black September in 1970 – and the cementing of the strategic relationship with Israel, rather than developments on the Arabian Peninsula.[15] In the Gulf, US policymaking coalesced gradually around the Nixon Doctrine, in which Saudi Arabia and Iran would work together in pursuit of regional stability and security. Despite their record of competing hegemonic designs, which had not yet acquired the sectarian tint of later decades, the Nixon administration hoped that it could 'keep reminding them [the Saudis and Iranians] that the best way to keep Nasser and the Russians out is to work together.'[16]

As such, the decade of the 1970s between Britain's pullout from the coastal sheikhdoms in November 1971 to the enunciation of the Carter Doctrine in January 1980 was one of great – and, in historical sweep, unparalleled – danger for the smaller Gulf States. For the first (and only) time in their history, the newly independent states lacked an external security guarantor, and were vulnerable to the expansionist designs of their larger neighbors. These emerging threats became manifest in different ways. The Shah revived Iran's longstanding territorial claim to Bahrain but this was settled peacefully through a UN mission that visited Bahrain and determined that its citizens wished to become an independent Arab state. Rather more worrying was Iran's seizure of the islands of Abu Musa and the Greater and Lesser Tunbs from the emirates of Sharjah and Ras al-Khaimah respectively, on the day before Britain's withdrawal in November 1971.[17] The young Gulf States' sense of weakness and vulnerability was further heightened by Iraqi involvement in the coup against the ruler of Sharjah in 1973, and in Baghdad's support for, and hosting of, revolutionary cells of the People's Front for the Liberation of the Occupied Gulf until 1975.[18]

The Twin Pillars policy, through which the Nixon Doctrine sought to use Iran and Saudi Arabia as conservative, anti-Communist, and pro-Western bulwarks in the Gulf, collapsed ignominiously with the Islamic Revolution in Iran in 1978–79 and the outbreak of the Iran–Iraq War in September 1980. Both developments forced US officials to reappraise their approach to the Gulf and to reevaluate the importance of regional security to US national interests.[19] However, it was a third event, the Soviet invasion of Afghanistan in December 1979 and resulting anxieties within the Jimmy Carter administration that it might be the prelude to a Soviet move toward acquiring a foothold in the Gulf or the Indian Ocean, which, for the first time, led to the proclamation for the United States of a position of predominance in the Gulf. President Carter used his annual State of the Union address to Congress in January 1980 to unveil what became known as the Carter Doctrine, when he declared that 'Any attempt by an outside force to gain control of the Persian Gulf region will be regarded as an assault on the vital interests of the United States of America, and such an assault will be repelled by any means necessary, including military force.'[20]

As the Cold War progressed, the attention of US policymakers gradually converged on the Gulf. Both the Truman and Eisenhower Doctrines in 1947 and 1957 – which pledged US economic assistance and military aid to countries that faced a Communist threat – were couched in broad regional terms, although their remit extended to include Saudi Arabia and Iran. By contrast, the Nixon Doctrine and the Carter Doctrine focused on the Gulf specifically, rather than the Middle East more generally, and linked regional and US security interests together. Beyond the network of defense and security agreements with Saudi Arabia, US military and strategic positions elsewhere in the Gulf remained small in scale well throughout the 1970s. Indeed, as the Iran–Iraq war began, the US security footprint in the smaller Gulf States was limited to the stationing of a small Middle East Force naval detachment based in Bahrain since 1949 and the acquisition of the former Royal Air Force base at Masirah in Oman in 1975, followed in 1980 by a ten-year access to facilities agreement signed with Sultan Qaboos bin Said.[21]

US preponderance

US force posture in the Gulf changed significantly and irrevocably from the 1980s onward, when the region became the site of three major inter-state conflicts: the Iran–Iraq war from September 1980 to August 1988, the Gulf War from January to February 1991 after Iraq occupied Kuwait in August 1990, and the US-led invasion of Iraq in March 2003. As in earlier decades, there was nothing predetermined about the gradual escalation of the US security footprint in the region, which proceeded instead in bursts of fits and starts, and was often reactive, rather than proactive, in nature. In the early 1980s, for example, Congress opposed a proposed sale of Stinger missiles to Kuwait, partly out of concern for Israeli security, prompting Kuwait to turn instead to the Soviet Union.[22] And yet, decisions made during the 1980s and 1990s, especially in the fevered aftermath of Saddam Hussein's move into Kuwait in August 1990, had significant consequences both for the United States and for their partners in the newly formed GCC.

The major trigger for the eventual uptick in US military posture in the Gulf was the succession of attacks on international merchant shipping and regional oil and gas facilities as the Iran–Iraq war progressed. The number of attacks on merchant shipping surged from 71 incidents in 1984 to 111 in 1986 and then jumped again to 181 the following year when they included vessels hit from Qatar, Saudi Arabia, the UAE, and neutral countries in addition to Kuwait. However, as Kuwaiti political scientist Abdul-Reda Assiri noted, the initial US response was 'lethargic and indeed ambiguous' as officials were anxious to avoid a potentially open-ended commitment in the Gulf, and only reversed course after Kuwait approached the Soviet Union for assistance instead.[23] The subsequent internationalization of Gulf waters occurred as the United States, the United Kingdom, France, Italy, and the Soviets all sent warships to conduct convoy operations that protected Kuwaiti re-flagged and chartered vessels during the 'Tanker War' phase of the conflict in 1987 and 1988. By the end of the Iran–Iraq War, there were 82 Western vessels, including 33 combat ships, in the Gulf and adjacent waters, along with 23 Soviet ships, minesweepers, and support vessels.[24]

Iraq's invasion and subsequent occupation of Kuwait in August 1990 was a cathartic reality check to ruling circles in all Gulf states. The Kuwaiti armed forces could hold back the Iraqi advance for only a few hours to enable the ruling family to escape into exile in Saudi Arabia. For a time, it appeared that Saddam Hussein might not stop at Kuwait's southern border but continue down the coast of the Arabian Peninsula to seize the oil reserves of the Eastern Province of Saudi Arabia. Despite years of multi-billion-dollar arms packages, the ease and speed of the Iraqi takeover of Kuwait showed Gulf States incapable of shouldering their own security, and reliant, once again, on an external power to do it for them – in this case the United States rather than Britain. It was decisions taken between August 1990 and February 1991 that subsequently exerted the decisive influence on the evolution of the Gulf security architecture and the US presence in the region.

King Fahd's decision on August 7, 1990 to host US-led military forces as part of *Operation Desert Shield* (which transitioned into *Operation Desert Storm*) was one of the few major decisions taken by a Saudi monarch without extensive prior consultation with major societal constituencies. The king took the decision to invite in foreign troops following a meeting with US Secretary of Defense Richard Cheney, on the promise that US forces would leave the Kingdom after the war.[25] The Council of Senior Scholars, led by Abd al-Aziz bin Baz, the senior religious authority in the Kingdom, declined initially to support the Saudi government's position, but later issued a fatwa on August 13, 1990 that endorsed the King's decision. Through its actions in 1990, the Saudi government alienated a significant element of the Salafi establishment, which divided into the *Sahwa* movement of religious–political activism and more extreme critics of Saudi policy such as Osama bin Laden, whose offer of the use of his Arab fighting force based in Afghanistan to repel Saddam Hussein had been summarily rejected by the Saudi government in August 1990. Whether through the *Sahwa* or Al Qaeda, the decision to rely on US-led military support unleased forces of domestic opposition that coursed through Saudi society for the remainder of the 1990s.[26]

Most US and coalition forces left Saudi Arabia after the successful conclusion of the Gulf War and the liberation of Kuwait in February 1991. US officials then concluded separate defense cooperation agreements with Kuwait and Bahrain

(1991), Qatar (1992), and the UAE (1994). These agreements added to the existing arrangements the United States had in place with Saudi Arabia and Oman and created defense and security partnerships with all six GCC states. Even these new agreements were unable fully to deter Saddam Hussein and they had to be reassessed in October 1994 after the Iraqi President massed two Republican Guard divisions near the Kuwaiti border. It was in response to this specific new act of aggression that the Clinton administration expanded its naval and military assets in the Gulf as part of a policy of 'Dual Containment' of Iraq and Iran.[27]

The increasingly visible presence of US troops and bases in the Arabian Peninsula – and particularly their air of permanence in Saudi Arabia – led to a growing divergence between political and public opinion as the US military footprint deepened throughout the 1990s. A part of the backlash that resulted was a reflection of greater popular skepticism of US motives and regional threat perceptions, especially after the election of the reformist Mohammad Khatami as President of Iran in 1997. Khatami's election was greeted with cautious optimism in GCC capitals and efforts to normalize relations between the Gulf States and Iran. A second source of disquiet among elements of Gulf societies was the growing influence of Islamism as a social and political force in all GCC states in the 1990s. The gap between the regime and public opinion over foreign and security policy opened a space for oppositional voices from across the political and religious spectrum to register their discontent at what Kuwaiti sociologist Ali al-Tarrah labeled the 'smothering embrace' of the US military presence in the region.[28]

In Saudi Arabia, an unpublished opinion poll in 2001 laid bare the scale of latent support for radical alternatives to governing elites as it revealed that 95 percent of young male respondents between the ages of 25 and 41 sympathized with Osama bin Laden.[29] In Qatar, too, the official rapport between Qatari and US military and defense interests was not universally acclaimed. Shortly after 9/11, Muhammad al-Musfir, a professor of political science at Qatar University, bluntly told Mary Ann Weaver of *National Geographic* that

> Your military is a very provocative element, and it's not just my students who are saying this. Go to the suq. Go downtown. Go to any café. The attitude is decidedly anti-American.[30]

Such ambivalence was most evident among Islamists in the Gulf although it also encompassed secular and nationalist strands of opinion as well. Most notably, it provided the background to Osama bin Laden's notorious declaration of 'Jihad against Jews and Crusaders' on February 23, 1998. In this proclamation, the dissident ex-Saudi founder of Al Qaeda stated menacingly that

> for over seven years the United States has been occupying the lands of Islam in the holiest of places, the Arabian Peninsula, plundering its riches, dictating to its rulers, humiliating its peoples, terrorizing its neighbors, and turning the bases in the Peninsula into a spearhead with which to fight the neighboring Muslim peoples.[31]

This statement represented an existential threat to the ideational and moral legitimacy of the Gulf monarchies and was especially potent in Saudi Arabia. Moreover, the advent of the Internet and Arab satellite television channels from the mid-1990s greatly facilitated the spread of oppositional messages and provided new forums for mobilization, a pattern that accelerated after public access to the Internet became widely available in Saudi Arabia in 1999.[32] The threat to US security from this radical backlash became dramatically clear when citizens of GCC states comprised 17 of the 19 airplane hijackers on 11 September 2001.[33]

9/11 illustrated the vulnerability of the United States and its regional partners to extremist rejection of the strategic relationship that had thickened so rapidly after 1991. The alleged mastermind of the Al Qaeda attacks on New York and Washington DC, Khalid Sheikh Mohammed, lived and worked in Qatar during the 1990s and was believed by US officials to have been tipped off by a member of the Qatari ruling family shortly before a failed FBI attempt to detain him in 1996.[34] Saudi Arabia and Dubai in the UAE played an active, if unwitting, role as hubs for the illicit networks that supported the terrorist networks and financial flows that made 9/11 possible. Although the final report of the 9/11 Commission found no evidence that the Saudi government as an institution, or senior Saudi officials individually, funded Al Qaeda, both it, and an independent task force set up by the Council of Foreign Relations in 2002, addressed the issues of terrorist financing and Saudi Arabia's alleged financial support for terrorism.[35] The Council of Foreign Relations report was particularly critical of Saudi-based support for international terrorist groups, and concluded bluntly that 'for years, individuals and charities based in Saudi Arabia have been the most important source of funds for Al Qaeda. And for years, Saudi officials have turned a blind eye to this problem.'[36]

By 2003, the present (as of 2017) US force structure in the GCC had emerged, as Qatar replaced Saudi Arabia as the site of the forward headquarters of CENTCOM while the US Fifth Fleet was headquartered in Bahrain and Kuwait and the UAE both hosted sizeable numbers of US forces. The transfer of the epicenter of US military power in the Gulf away from the Prince Sultan airbase south of Riyadh to the Al-Udeid airbase in Qatar, specially constructed and financed by the Qatari government, was in part a safety valve that released pressure on the US–Saudi relationship after the emergence of Al Qaeda in the Arabian Peninsula (AQAP) as a Saudi-based offshoot of Al Qaeda that was committed to ridding Saudi Arabia of Western influence.[37] Al-Udeid and a second military facility in Qatar – Camp as-Sayliyah – offer the United States an advanced command and control infrastructure and are the only facilities in the region that can host the B-52 bomber. As such, the two bases have become the central pivot that underpins US force projection in a wide array of regions, including against Islamist extremist groups in Africa and the so-called Islamic State in Iraq and Syria, as well as the ongoing stabilization operations in Afghanistan.[38]

And yet, it would be wrong to characterize US–GCC relations in the 1990s and early 2000s as solely or even primarily focused on (in)security and defense. This period saw the growth of significant reserves of US 'soft power' through the creation of educational offshoots of American universities, especially in Qatar but also in the UAE and Kuwait. Education City launched on the dusty outskirts of Doha in 1997 as an initiative of the Qatar Foundation for Education, Science, and Community Development, and has since partnered with six leading American universities: Virginial Commonwealth University in Qatar (opened in 1998), Weill Cornell Medical College in Qatar (2001), Texas A&M University at Qatar (2003), Carnegie Mellon University in Qatar (2004), Georgetown University School of Foreign Service in Qatar (2005), and Northwestern University in Qatar (2008).[39] Whereas the Education City campuses involved specific schools rather than entire universities, New York University went a step further and opened an entire portal campus in Abu Dhabi in 2010. The transplanting of an entire liberal arts research university was part of a broader push in the UAE to attract satellite university campuses, so that by 2009 the UAE was host to fully one-quarter of the 160 international branch campuses in existence worldwide.[40] In Kuwait, the American University of Kuwait was founded in 2003 as a collaborative venture with Dartmouth College in Hanover, New Hampshire, and sought to balance 'American expectations and Kuwaiti realities.'[41]

The invasion of Iraq and its aftermath

The US-led invasion of Iraq in March 2003 and the messy eight-year occupation that followed impacted US–Gulf ties in a myriad of ways. The plethora of defense and security links described in Part III meant that the GCC states served as the logistical and administrative hubs for the multinational coalition that mobilized to remove Saddam Hussein from power on a flimsy pretext that was perceived as less than legitimate by significant portions of the international community. In Kuwait, the government declared its northern border region with Iraq – amounting to one-quarter of the country – a no-go area reserved for coalition use in the immediate run-up to the invasion.[42] GCC leaders had to somewhat awkwardly balance their security ties with the United States with popular opposition to the invasion. This prompted many to publicly distance themselves from the United States while privately offering some degree of encouragement and support to the effort to oust Saddam Hussein's regime. Even so, levels of internal dissent took their most pronounced form in Saudi Arabia, where up to 97 percent of the population was reportedly opposed to cooperation with a US attack on Iraq.[43] Anti-war demonstrations occurred in other Gulf States, with those in Bahrain particularly well-attended, while in the UAE, the well-publicized opposition to the war of the Crown Prince of Ras al-Khaimah, Sheikh Khalid bin Mohammed Al Qassimi, may have played a role in his removal from his position in June 2003.[44]

While elevated levels of public disquiet at US actions in Iraq formed part of a larger chorus of anger at the Bush administration's Middle East policies more generally, the GCC states notably did not experience any significant blowback from their leadership's military and political alliance with Washington, aside from the campaign waged in Saudi Arabia by Al Qaeda in the Arabian Peninsula between 2003 and 2006. Officials in GCC states implemented hard security measures that ensured they remained relatively immune to the cross-border overspill of the multiple sources of insecurity, such as sectarian conflict, refugee flows, and terrorist attacks, and the destabilizing flows of men and money ran largely in the other direction, from the GCC into Iraq.[45] Militants from Saudi Arabia were estimated to constitute up to 60 percent of foreign fighters in Iraq as the Sunni insurgency against the US-led occupying forces escalated in the mid-2000s.[46] Moreover, in 2006, the Iraq Study Group appointed by Congress to assess the worsening violence in Iraq, observed that 'funding for the Sunni insurgency comes from private individuals within Saudi Arabia and the Gulf states.'[47]

In the absence of any direct overspill of instability from the Iraq War, leaders in Gulf States focused instead on the geopolitical and strategic implications of the war for the balance of regional power. This revolved around the perceived and actual expansion of Iranian influence following the removal of its main counterweight in the Gulf, and its consequences for the Shiite populations in the GCC. Officials and analysts in the GCC came to view the empowerment of Iraq's Shiite majority and the rise in Iranian influence in Iraq as the major, if unintended, consequences of the overthrow of the Ba'athist regime. The result was sustained suspicion of Iran's cultivation of extensive ties with both state and non-state actors in Iraq, which caused deep unease within the GCC and vocal frustration with US policies in Iraq.[48] As early as February 2003, the Saudi Arabian Foreign Minister, Prince Saud al-Faisal, warned President Bush that he would be 'solving one problem and creating five more' if Saddam Hussein was removed by force. Subsequently, in 2005, Saud al-Faisal claimed that the United States was 'handing the whole country over to Iran without reason.'[49] In March 2007, King Abdullah of Saudi Arabia even denounced what he labelled the 'illegitimate foreign occupation' of Iraq in an unprecedented public display of anger at US policy failures in the country.[50]

The sectarian lens constituted a powerful filter through which ruling elites throughout the GCC viewed developments in Iraq throughout the 2000s and early 2010s. Their deep distrust of Nuri al-Maliki after he became Prime Minister – with US backing – in 2006 contributed to a self-fulfilling cycle as the Gulf States' reluctance to increase their political and economic engagement with Iraq enabled Iran to take the lead in reconstruction and development projects.[51] GCC anger at Maliki's authoritarian tendencies escalated after the final withdrawal of US forces from Iraq in December 2011 and Maliki's subsequent marginalization and arrest of key Sunni Iraqi political figures. The ill-feeling ultimately magnified the threat to GCC interests posed by the self-proclaimed Islamic State of Iraq and Syria as it emerged as a destructive regional force in 2014.[52] Having spent much of the period after 2003 lamenting the plight of Iraq's Sunni communities and most of 2012 and 2013 channeling support to various Sunni rebel groups in Syria, officials in GCC states found themselves caught in a geopolitical straightjacket in 2014 as they struggled to limit their advance.

Relations between the United States and GCC states reached a nadir during Barack Obama's presidency as policy responses to the Arab Spring in 2011, the Joint Comprehensive Plan of Action with Iran in 2015, and the war in Yemen that began the same year strained ties of trust and confidence. And yet, the Obama administration differed notably from its predecessor in being willing to negotiate collectively with the GCC as a bloc rather than separately with individual states. Under President George W. Bush, US policy focused heavily on strengthening bilateral relations in the aftermath of 9/11 and refused to negotiate with the GCC as a trade bloc, borne in part out of a desire to dilute its collective bargaining power.[53] Instead, the Bush administration concluded bilateral free trade agreements (FTAs) with Bahrain in 2004 and with Oman in 2006, and began negotiations for separate FTAs with Qatar and Kuwait in 2006 that ultimately never came to fruition.[54] Saudi officials responded with fury to the bilateral US agreements with Oman and Bahrain, which Saud al-Faisal declared incompatible with the spirit of the GCC charter and designed to 'diminish the collective bargaining power and weaken not only the solidarity of the GCC as a whole but also each of its members.'[55]

In contrast, the Obama administration made concerted efforts not merely to engage but also to coordinate policy with the GCC as a bloc, particularly on defense and security policy during Hillary Rodham Clinton's tenure as Secretary of State in Obama's first term. A GCC–US Strategic Cooperation Forum was launched in March 2012 and in September 2013, a US–GCC Security Committee was formed to address common interests in counter-terrorism and border security. In December 2013, President Obama issued a presidential determination that made it possible – for the first time – for the United States to sell arms to the GCC as a bloc.[56] In Obama's second term, two US–GCC Summits were held at Camp David, in May 2015, and in Riyadh, in April 2016, although policymakers on both sides expressed frustration at the lack of tangible follow-up from each meet. By 2016, however, relations between President Obama and senior officials in GCC states had plummeted, with many in the Gulf reacting with fury and taking personal umbrage at a reference to 'free-riders' made in an extensive interview Obama gave to journalist Jeffrey Goldberg.[57]

Leaders in GCC states reacted viscerally to several key developments during the Obama presidency. The gradual recalibration of the focus of much US foreign policy toward the Pacific, encapsulated in the much-touted 'pivot to Asia,' was seized upon by officials in the Gulf to symbolize a supposed US disengagement from the region and abandonment of their interests just as US outreach to Iran reinforced such perceptions. For the first time since the United States became directly involved in Gulf security structures in the early 1990s, policymakers in GCC states no longer felt assured of US backing. This tapped into a general sense of incomprehension felt by ruling elites in GCC capitals at the administration's approach to regional affairs after the cathartic shock of the Arab uprisings in 2011. Beginning with the withdrawal of US support for Egyptian President Hosni Mubarak at the start of the Arab Spring and continuing with (muted) US criticism over the security response in Bahrain as the Al Khalifa ruling family restored order with GCC support, officials in Gulf capitals began openly to question US motives. As early as May 2011, influential Saudi foreign policy commentator Nawaf Obaid wrote of a 'tectonic' shift in the US–Saudi relationship and lamented that 'Washington has shown itself in recent months to be an unwilling and unreliable partner' against Iran. In a sign of the growing autonomy of Saudi policy calculations, Obaid warned – presciently, as it turned out – that 'in areas in which Saudi national security or strategic interests are at stake, the Kingdom will pursue its own agenda.'[58]

As frustrations with vacillating US policy toward the Arab Spring mounted in 2012 and 2013, declaratory and policy pronouncements from Gulf officials became shriller. The failure to take military action against the Bashir al-Assad regime in Syria following the August 2013 use of chemical weapons in Ghouta was greeted with dismay in GCC capitals, as were the signs of a rapprochement between the United States and Iran following the election of Hasan Rouhani as President in June 2013. Saudi Arabia's decision to turn down one of the ten rotating, non-permanent seats on the United Nations Security Council weeks after snubbing the annual meeting of the UN General Assembly revealed the depth of regional alarm at the direction of US policy in the Middle East. The extent of unease was illustrated in comments made shortly after the conclusion of an interim nuclear agreement between the United States and Iran (from whose negotiations GCC officials were excluded) by the former Saudi Ambassador to the United States, Prince Turki bin Faisal Al Saud, who stated that 'How we feel is that we weren't part of the discussions at all, in some cases we were – I would go so far as to say we were lied to, things were hidden from us.'[59]

Although the United States cooperated with GCC partners in the anti-ISIS air campaign that began in Iraq and Syria in late-2014 and provided logistical and intelligence cooperation to the Saudi-led coalition that launched military operations in Yemen in March 2015, the Yemen war brought into the open the different perceptions of Iran that divided officials in Riyadh and Abu Dhabi from their counterparts in Washington, DC. Whereas the former viewed Iran as a destabilizing 'meddler' in regional conflict zones, the latter under President Obama tended to view President Rouhani as a man they could do business with to defuse the longstanding standoff over Iran's nuclear program and international isolation. These tensions and the diverging views on how to view the unfolding disintegration of the Yemeni government peaked following the Houthi takeover of Sana'a in late-2014 and the ousting of embattled Yemeni President Hadi on the same day in January 2015 as the death of King Abdullah of Saudi Arabia. After Hadi escaped to the southern port city of Aden and re-established a base of control in the city, a further Houthi advance in March 2015 threatened to overrun the city and entrench Houthi – and, in GCC eyes, – Iranian power in Yemen. This led to Saudi Arabia and nine other Arab states, including every Gulf State bar Oman – to launch air strikes on Houthi strongholds in Yemen in Operation Decisive Storm, as the proxy struggle for influence between Iran and Saudi Arabia escalated into regional conflict.[60]

The conflict in Yemen highlighted the new assertiveness in GCC policies as the Gulf states acted collectively in a bid to secure regional interests, however narrowly defined. It constituted an important evolution in regional security structures as the locus of decision-making shifted to Gulf capitals rather than external partners in Washington, DC or, earlier, in London. Notably, the Yemen operation marked the first use of the joint military command that was created by the GCC in November 2014, alongside joint naval and police forces.[61] However, GCC officials continue to lack a viable alternative to the US-led security guarantee, and their failure to achieve any meaningful strategic or operational success in Yemen brought their defense and security reliance on US support into sharp relief. Furthermore, the longer the military campaign in Yemen has continued, the greater has been the private criticism of GCC actions from policymakers in Washington, DC, who question openly whether the Saudi-led coalition has realistic military and political objectives in Yemen, still less the tools of power and statecraft to achieve them.[62]

US–Gulf relations in the age of Trump

The opening year of the Donald Trump presidency has been as chaotic as many predicted, given the lack of prior political experience of the 45th president and most of his senior staff. The influence of several of the president's senior advisors, such as his son-in-law, Jared Kushner, and, in the early months, Steven Bannon, largely bypassed and undercut experienced colleagues such as Secretary of Defense James Mattis and Secretary of State Rex Tillerson. The significance of personalized ties among President Trump's inner circle provided an opportunity for figures such as Crown Prince Mohammed bin Salman in Saudi Arabia and Crown Prince Mohammed bin Zayed Al Nahyan in Abu Dhabi to reach out to shape the administration's thinking on regional issues. Their task was aided by the fact that key principals – such as Mattis and the incoming Director of the CIA, Mike Pompeo – had long espoused positions on Iran and the Muslim Brotherhood that aligned closely with those of Riyadh and Abu Dhabi. In the first week of the Trump presidency, a raid in Yemen conducted jointly by US and Emirati special forces, signaled the administration's intent to lean heavily on the UAE and Saudi Arabia in its approach to regional affairs.[63]

In June 2017, the decision by a quartet of US partners, Saudi Arabia, the UAE, Bahrain, and Egypt to withdraw their Ambassadors from Qatar, another US partner, and impose a range of economic and trade measures on Doha, placed the United States at the heart of a new regional fault line and illustrated the difficulty of conducting policy in the Trumpian era. Saudi and Emirati leaders evidently believed that their move to isolate Qatar after years of tolerating its maverick regional policies would enjoy the political support of the White House, and President Trump initially signaled his backing of their move when he Tweeted his support and linked it to (unpublicized) discussions he had had with Saudi and Emirati officials at the Arab–Islamic–American Summit in Riyadh in May. However, both the Secretaries of Defense and State mounted an institutional pushback to the president's sudden swing away from Qatar, cognizant of the commercial and defense value of the Qatari partnership to the United States, with the president seemingly unaware that Qatar hosted the fulcrum of US power projection in the broader Middle East at the Al-Udeid airbase.[64]

Several points emerge from the Qatar standoff, which remains unresolved at the time of writing in late-2017, and which all have implications for the future evolution of US–Gulf ties. One is that GCC states are diversifying their international relationships and adapting to a changing global order in which the sources of geo-economic power are more varied than ever before. An enduring irony of the visceral reaction of ruling elites in GCC states to the perceived US 'pivot to Asia' is that they themselves have already pivoted, at least in terms of economic and energy relationships. Such ties have yet to acquire an overt security dimension, as Asian energy importers continue to rely on the United States to guarantee regional security, but a US president aggressively committed to 'America First' nationalism may not continue to underwrite such guarantees indefinitely. Simultaneously, the internationalization of foreign relations of GCC states has created durable new linkages which, in many cases, do not always align with US interests, particularly in a context where GCC states more aggressively pursue their own national interests. The proliferation of investment ventures, energy and commercial agreements with Russian partners under US sanction since 2014 is one example; another is GCC states' participation in the Asian Infrastructure Investment Bank against US wishes after the Chinese-led initiative launched in 2015.[65]

As this chapter has made clear, the evolution of US–Gulf ties has rarely followed a clearly defined pathway in which US (or Gulf States') interests were clearly articulated ahead of time. Policies instead have largely been reactive in response to specific events, and established the United States as the dominant external power in the region more as an accumulation of disparate events than the product of a single grand design. The predominant US security posture in the Gulf is a product of the three inter-state wars that gripped the region between 1980 and 2003, and was neither preordained nor necessarily welcomed. The rise of the Gulf states as more proactive participants in regional and international affairs has provided regional policymakers with more political and economic options for their further enmeshment in networks of global power and politics. Officials in the United States have never set the agenda in determining policies and relationships in the Gulf, and they are likely to continue to lag changing patterns of international engagement going forward as well.

Notes

1 Jeremy Jones and Nicholas Ridout, *A History of Modern Oman* (Cambridge: Cambridge University Press, 2015), pp.61–62.
2 Jeremy Jones and Nicholas Ridout, *Oman, Culture and Diplomacy* (Edinburgh: Edinburgh University Press, 2012), p.138.
3 Fahad Ahmad Bishara, *A Sea of Debt: Law and Economic Life in the Western Indian Ocean, 1780–1950* (Cambridge: Cambridge University Press, 2017), p.203.
4 Fouad al-Farsy, *Modernity and Tradition: the Saudi Equation* (London: Routledge, 2009 edition), pp.96–97.
5 Eckart Woertz, *Oil for Food: The Global Food Crisis and the Middle East* (Oxford: Oxford University Press, 2013), pp.47–48.
6 Ibid. p.51.

7 Ibid.
8 Asher Kaufman, 'Between Permanent and Sealed Borders: The Trans-Arabian Pipeline and the Arab-Israeli Conflict,' *International Journal of Middle East Studies*, 46, 2014, pp.104–108.
9 Sarah Yizraeli, *Politics and Society in Saudi Arabia: The Crucial Years of Development, 1960–1982* (New York: Columbia University Press, 2012), p.62, p.124, and p.142.
10 Quoted in Miriam Joyce, *Kuwait 1945–1996: An Anglo-American Perspective* (London: Frank Cass, 1998), pp.7–8.
11 Ibid. pp.16–17.
12 Robert Jarman, *Sabah Al-Salim Al-Sabah: Amir of Kuwait, 1965–77: A Political Biography* (London: London Center of Arab Studies, 2002), pp.256–260.
13 Helene von Bismarck, *British Policy in the Persian Gulf, 1961–1968: Conceptions of Informal Empire* (Basingstoke: Palgrave Macmillan, 2013), p.211.
14 Ibid.
15 Joel Migdal, *Shifting Sands: The United States in the Middle East* (New York: Columbia University Press, 2014), pp.76–82.
16 Shohei Sato, *Britain and the Formation of the Gulf States: Embers of Empire* (Manchester: Manchester University Press, 2016), pp.70–71.
17 William Roger Louis, 'The British Withdrawal from the Gulf, 1967–71', *Journal of Imperial and Commonwealth History*, 31(1), 2003, p.102.
18 Christopher Davidson, *Dubai: The Vulnerability of Success* (London: Hurst and Co., 2008), p.251.
19 Henner Furtig, 'Conflict and Cooperation in the Persian Gulf: the Interregional Order and US Policy,' *Middle East Journal*, 61(4), 2007, p.628.
20 Gary Sick, 'The United States and the Persian Gulf in the Twentieth Century,' in Lawrence Potter (ed.), *The Persian Gulf in History* (New York: Palgrave Macmillan, 2009), p.298.
21 Jones and Ridout, *History of Modern Oman*, pp.191–92.
22 Abdul-Reda Assiri, *Kuwait's Foreign Policy: City-State in World Politics* (Boulder, CO: Westview Press, 1990), p.82.
23 Ibid. pp.103–105.
24 Ibid. pp.113–114.
25 Rachel Bronson, 'Understanding US-Saudi Relations,' in Paul Aarts and Gerd Nonneman (eds.), *Saudi Arabia in the Balance: Political Economy, Society, Foreign Affairs* (London: Hurst & Co, 2005), pp.385–386.
26 Andrew Hammond, *Islamic Utopia: The Illusion of Reform in Saudi Arabia* (London: Pluto Press, 2012), p.76.
27 Anthony Cordesman, *Kuwait:Recovery and Security after the Gulf War* (Boulder, CO: Westview Press, 1997), pp.127–128.
28 Abdullah al-Shayeji, 'Dangerous Perceptions: Gulf Views of the U.S. Role in the Region,' *Middle East Policy*, 5(2), 1997, pp.1–13.
29 Benjamin Schwarz, 'America's Struggle Against the Wahhabi/Neo-Salafi Movement,' *Orbis*, 51(1), 2007, p.124.
30 Mary Ann Weaver, 'Qatar: Revolution from the Top Down,' *National Geographic*, March 2003.
31 'Jihad against Jews and Crusaders,'*World Islamic Front Statement*, 23 February 1998. Available at www.fas.org/irp/world/para/docs/980223-fatwa.htm.
32 Khalid M. al-Tawil, 'The Internet in Saudi Arabia,' *King Fahd University of Petroleum and Minerals Working Paper* (undated). Available at www.faculty.kfupm.edu.sa/COE/sadiq/.../Internet%20in%20SA-update1.doc.
33 Fifteen of the 9/11 hijackers were from Saudi Arabia along with two from the United Arab Emirates. The remaining two hijackers were from Egypt and Lebanon.
34 John Hannah, 'Qatar Needs to Do Its Part,' *Foreign Policy*, May 22, 2017.

35 Christopher Blanchard and Alfred Prados, 'Saudi Arabia: Terrorist Financing Issues,' *Congressional Research Service Report for Congress*, Washington DC, September 14, 2007, p.2.
36 Maurice Greenberg, William Wechsler and Lee Wolowsky, 'Terrorist Financing. Report of an Independent Task Force Sponsored by the Council on Foreign Relations,' New York, October 2002, p.1.
37 Michael Gordon and Eric Schmitt, 'US Will Move Air Operations to Qatar Base,' *New York Times*, April 28, 2003.
38 David Des Roches, 'A Base is More than Buildings: the Military Implications of the Qatar Crisis,' *War on the Rocks*, June 8, 2017.
39 Kristian Coates Ulrichsen, *Qatar and the Arab Spring* (Oxford: Oxford University Press, 2014), p.43.
40 Jason Lane, 'International Branch Campuses, Free Zones, and Quality Assurance: Policy Issues for Dubai and the UAE,' Dubai: Dubai School of Government Policy Brief, No.20, 2010, p.2.
41 Marjorie Kelly, 'Balancing Cultures at the American University of Kuwait,' *Journal of Arabian Studies*, 1(2), 2011, p.201.
42 Peter Baker, 'Kuwait's Landscape of Tents and Tanks,' *Washington Post*, February 7, 2003.
43 Furtig, *Conflict and Cooperation*, p.638.
44 Simon Henderson, 'Succession Politics in the Conservative Gulf Arab States: the Weekend's Events in Ras al-Khaimah,' The Washington Institute, Policywatch No. 769, 17 June 2003.
45 David Pollock, 'Kuwait: Keystone of US Gulf Policy,' The Washington Institute for Near East Policy: Washington, DC, 2007, p.41.
46 Thomas Hegghammer, 'Saudi Militants in Iraq: Backgrounds and Recruitment Patterns,' Norwegian Defence Research Establishment (FFI) Report, 2007, p.11.
47 Christopher Blanchard, *Saudi Arabia: Terrorist Financing Issues* (Washington, DC: CRS Report for Congress, 2007), p.8.
48 Abdulaziz Sager, 'The GCC States and the Situation in Iraq,' Dubai: Gulf Research Centre, July 10, 2008.
49 Quoted in Nawaf Obaidi, 'Stepping into Iraq: Saudi Arabia will Protect Sunnis if the US Leaves,' *Washington Post*, November 29, 2006.
50 'Saudi King Calls US Presence in Iraq 'Illegitimate',' *New York Times*, March 28, 2007.
51 'US Wants Gulf States to Impose Curbs on Iran,' *Khaleej Times*, December 14, 2008.
52 Toby Dodge, *Iraq: From War to a New Authoritarianism* (London: Routledge, 2012), p.192; Patrick Cockburn, 'Isis Consolidates,' *London Review of Books*, Volume 36, Number 16, August 16–23, 2014, p.3.
53 John Fox, Nada Mourtada-Sabbah, and Mohammed Al-Mutawa, 'The Arab Gulf Region: Tradition Globalized or Globalization Traditionalized?' in John Fox, Nada Mourtada-Sabbah, and Mohammed Al-Mutawa (eds.), *Globalization and the Gulf* (London: Routledge, 2006), p.24.
54 Matteo Legrenzi, 'Gulf Cooperation Council Diplomatic Coordination: The Limited Role of Institutionalization,' in Jean-Francois Seznec and Mimi Kirk (eds.), *Industrialization in the Gulf: A Socioeconomic Revolution* (London: Routledge, 2011), p.117.
55 Cited in Abdulla Baabood and Geoffrey Edwards, 'Reinforcing Ambivalence: The Interaction of Gulf States and the European Union,' *European Foreign Affairs Review*, 12, 2007, p.548.
56 'US Approves Arms Sales to GCC As a Bloc, After Rulers Agree on Unified Military Command,' *Gulf States Newsletter*, Volume 38, Issue 961, January 9, 2014, p.1.
57 Turki al-Faisal Al Saud, 'Mr. Obama, We are Not 'Free Riders',' *Arab News*, March 14, 2016.

58 'Leading Saudi Researcher Warns West of a Newly Assertive Saudi Arabia,' *Gulf States Newsletter*, Volume 35, Issue 901, May 27, 2011, p.8.
59 'Iran and P5+1 Sign Breakthrough Nuclear Deal,' *Gulf States Newsletter*, Volume 37, Issue 959, November 28, 2013, p.3.
60 David Hearst, 'Has Iran Overreached Itself in Yemen?'*Middle East Eye*, March 26, 2015.
61 Frederic Wehrey, 'Into the Maelstrom: the Saudi-led Misadventure in Yemen,' *Carnegie Endowment for International Peace online analysis*, March 26, 2015.
62 Author interviews, Washington, DC, August 2015, March 2016, May 2016.
63 Kristian Coates Ulrichsen, 'US Policies in the Middle East Under the Trump Presidency,' *Orient XXI*, April 18, 2017.
64 'Mattis and Tillerson are Trying to Soothe a Crisis in the Persian Gulf, but Trump Keeps Picking On a US Ally,' *Business Insider*, July 1, 2017.
65 'US Urges Allies to Think Twice before Joining China-led Bank,' *Reuters*, March 16, 2015.

3 Russia's return to the Gulf

Li-Chen Sim

The headlines in the popular and scholarly presses leave little room for ambiguity about the level and significance of Russia's engagement in the Gulf and wider Middle East region. Examples include "Russia comes in from the cold – and towards the Gulf", "A Pax Russica in the Middle East", "Russia's new presence in the Middle East", "It's not Donald Trump who matters now in the Middle East – it's Putin", "How Russia became the Middle East's new power broker", and "Russia is expanding its great-power project in the Middle East".[1] According to conventional wisdom, not only is Russia back, it is also armed with an aggressive, expansive, and pro-active strategy to compete with, constrain, and perhaps even upend the role of the United States of America (USA) as the Gulf's hegemon for almost 40 years.[2] The visit by a ruling Saudi monarch to Russia in October 2017 during which an arms purchase agreement was concluded – both of which are firsts in their decades-old bilateral relations – has only fueled this perspective. As part of this 'new Cold War', Russia can draw upon some of the tactics used in Europe and in the former Soviet republics and apply them to its relations with the Gulf States.[3]

This chapter will review the above perspective of Russia's foreign policy in the Gulf.[4] It will argue that far from being a revisionist and pro-active external power, Russia is acting defensively to manage instability. Instead of seeking to replace the USA as a regional hegemon, Russia only desires recognition of its role in a multilateral and multipolar regional order. Rather than viewing Russia's behavior as coherent parts of an integrated grand strategy, it should be understood as ad-hoc, reactive, and opportunistic.

Russia's relations with the Gulf: a brief historical survey

The Gulf States did not play a significant role in the USSR's policy in the Middle East, the focus of which was on Egypt, Syria, Iran, and Iraq. These client states were provided with favorable terms for financing weaponry and economic development needs, with little expectation that these 'loans' would be repaid, except perhaps in the form of loyalty to the Soviet-led camp. With the exception of Kuwait and Saudi Arabia, diplomatic relations with the countries of the Gulf Co-operation Council (GCC) were only established after the mid-1980s with the winding down of the Cold War. However, bilateral cooperation continued to be insignificant until the 2000s, as a result of the turmoil of the post-communist transition in Russia and the country's Atlanticist orientation which prioritized relations with the West.

The first decade of the 21st century witnessed a marked increase in Russia's political and economic engagement with the Gulf monarchies. This was partly a result of Putin's growing disillusionment with the results of Russia's 'return to Europe' foreign policy, which had not stopped the North Atlantic Treaty Organization (NATO) from bombing its ally, Serbia, in 1998. It was also partly a reflection of Putin's belief that geo-economic competition was as vital as military supremacy; in his own words, "the modern world is a tough competition – for markets, investments, political, and economic competition … nobody is eager to help us. We have to fight for our place under the economic sun" (Tsygankov 2016). In 2005, Russia was granted observer status in the Organization of Islamic Countries, Putin visited Saudi Arabia and the UAE in 2007, bilateral business councils were established in several Gulf States, and trade turnover increased significantly albeit from an almost non-existent base. Saudi–Russian trade, for example, rose from US$60 million to US$1.3 billion between 2000 and 2012 (IMF 2017a,e), with the UAE emerging as Russia's largest trade partner among the Gulf monarchies. This period was also marked by challenges, the most significant of which was the assassination of Zelimkhan Yandarbiyev in 2004 by Russian agents in Doha, after requests for his extradition were repeatedly rebuffed by Qatar. Yandarbiyev had been regarded by Russia as a terrorist seeking funding and support for an independent Chechnya. Externally, the attempt to 'reset' Russian–American relations and to modernize the Russian economy through cooperation with the West under the tenure of President Medvedev (2008–2012), diluted any further momentum in Russian–Gulf relations.

The return of Putin to the presidency has since resulted in a much higher level of Russian engagement in issues relevant to the Gulf, sometimes to the chagrin of the latter. Russia continues to champion the Palestinian cause while improving relations with Israel, a country that is not officially recognized by the Gulf States; indeed, Russia's trade with Israel in 2016 was almost on par with the combined volume of trade with the Gulf monarchies (IMF 2017a,e). Russia has concluded civilian nuclear agreements with Saudi Arabia and is building reactors in Turkey and Jordan; at the same time, it has criticized Saudi Arabia for financing extremist Sunni groups and thereby extending its own influence in the Caucasus, Central Asia, and the Middle East (Katz 2012). Russia has secured lucrative arms deals with the Gulf States but has persisted in selling weapons to Syria and to Iran, as underlined by the US$8 billion deal with the latter for Sukhoi fighter jets and a S-300 missile defense system. Russia has been the recipient of Gulf largesse, including US$14 billion worth of contribution to the Russian Direct Investment Fund since 2011;[5] yet it has accused Saudi Arabia of unleashing an economic war at its expense by 'political manipulation' of global oil prices (Escobar 2014).

Consequently, Arab commentators have labeled Russia's foreign policy in the Gulf as "inconsistent" (Al-Hamli 2016) and have declared that "it is difficult to understand the motives behind Russian interests in enhancing its relations with countries in the Arabian Gulf region" (Bayoumi 2007). These seemingly contradictory actions arise because "Russians do not want to repeat the mistake of completely siding with one party ... Thus they maneuvre constantly, engaging in tradeoffs when necessary" (Trenin 2016, 4). This attempt to "dance simultaneously at everyone's wedding" (Blank 2006, 14) implies that Russia does not have permanent allies but, as noted by Richard Sakwa, a seasoned observer of Russia, "neither has it any deep seated adversaries" (Sakwa 2016, 14). This is arguably an advantage in a conflict-prone region with ever-shifting alignments.

Russia's interests in the Gulf region

Three specific and consistent goals inform these ad-hoc attempts to maximize freedom of maneuvre in the Gulf region.

Regional stability

The first is to stabilize the panoply of conflicts in the Middle East which have the potential to spill over into Russia's traditional 'soft underbelly', the Caucasus and Central Asia, and thereby undermine regime security in Russia itself. These traditionally 'foreign' conflicts have been increasingly securitized so that they are treated as threats to state security; and in Putin's Russia, state security has come to mean regime security (Snetkov 2015). In this regard, Russia's relations with the Gulf States are contingent upon their leverage over key actors – states and transnational groups – who can imperil domestic stability. Russia's fear of instability in its neighborhood is a product of historical and contemporary experiences. Citing "defensive aggressiveness" (Kotkin 2016) or "defensive imperialism" (Luxmoore 2014), the expansion of the Tsarist empire into contested lands in Eurasia was arguably predicated on attempts to pre-empt their use as beachheads by invading armies. The unleashing and revival of ethnic nationalism in the Soviet Union in the late 1980s – which often expressed itself violently in the Caucasus and Central Asia – contributed to the implosion of the USSR itself. Today, wariness about how instability in the Middle East has a knock-on effect on Russia is discernible in Putin's policy towards the Arab Spring and terrorism.

Russia has been unwavering in its support for the status quo during the 'color' revolutions that deposed pro-Russia leaders in the former USSR, the Euromaidan revolution in Ukraine in 2014, and the uprisings of the Arab Spring since 2011. From Moscow's perspective, these popular uprisings were illegal and usurped state sovereignty because they were facilitated by foreign agents. The latter are said to be intent on reducing Russia's influence in its own backyard or 'near abroad' and in the Middle East next door, having already wrenched its former Warsaw Pact allies out of its orbit via the expansion of NATO and the European Union; Putin would be next on their list (Hill 2015). Even if this scenario sounds implausible, the point is that Putin's interpretations of foreign policy matter enormously, and he "does believe that we [the Americans] are out to get him" (Remnick 2014).

Analyzing the huge anti-Kremlin demonstrations in Moscow in 2011 and 2012, for example, Putin blamed then-Secretary of State Hillary Clinton, saying that "she set the tone for some of our actors in the country and gave the signal. They heard this and, with the support of the US State Department, began active work" (Osnos, Remnick, and Yaffa 2017). It is this concern for regime survival, more than the pursuit of strategic competition with the USA, that drives Russia's engagement with the Gulf States (Trenin 2015, Mankoff 2012, Dannreuther 2012, Allison 2013).

A similar logic is at work in Syria, where rival foreign and local groups jostle for power. The fall of Bashir Al Assad as a result of a popular uprising would chip away at one of the pillars of Putin's instrumental legitimacy – his success at enhancing Russia's relevance in world affairs – at a time when his economic stewardship of the country is being undermined by low oil prices and financial sanctions. Putin faces reelection in 2018, and the fact that protest marches occurred in over 200 Russian cities in June 2017 cannot be comfortable for a leader who prides himself on his popularity. To make matters worse, the fall of the secular dictatorship in Syria is likely to usher in either a strongly sectarian and Sunni-based government or simply chaos. The former scenario would worsen the already fractious Sunni–Shiite cleavage and increase tensions with Iran with whom Russia cooperates, while the latter would make Syria a breeding ground for extremist Islamic groups who could further destabilize Central Asia and radicalize Russia's own Muslim population. In other words, instability in Syria – and by extension in Libya, Iraq, and much of the Middle East – is perceived to have an undesirable knock-on effect on regime stability in Russia. How the Gulf States can minimize this state of affairs is explained below.

Terrorism in the Middle East is the other source of instability that worries Russia. Up to 4,000 Russian citizens and 5,000 citizens from other post-Soviet states are estimated to be fighting in Syria and Iraq.[6] Most of them are affiliated to either the Islamic State (IS) or Al Qaeda and had previously belonged to local groups like the Caucasus Emirate or the Islamic Movement of Uzbekistan. Part of the fear is that the current decline of IS in Syria and Iraq may result in militants returning to their countries of origin to bolster existing and long-standing local insurgencies. In this regard, the April 2017 bombing of a St. Petersburg metro station, carried out by an ethnic Uzbek with Russian citizenship, presented the Russian authorities with the following quandary: was the attack blowback from Putin's military intervention in Syria, in which case more attacks would be forthcoming; or was it merely the resumption of attacks by local groups which had carried out several thousand attacks in Russia between 2007 and 2015 (Hahn 2017)? In any case, there are concerns that returning extremists will radicalize Russia's 15 million Muslims who account for 10% of the population and the 7 million migrant workers from North Caucasus and Central Asia working within Russia, all of whom face different degrees of persecution within Russian society (Tucker 2015). Consequently, the possible increase in violent conflicts and the reigniting of demands for representation by Islamic parties or the creation of separate Islamic statelets cannot be discounted.

For Putin, whose legitimacy and image as a strong leader was founded on his wars in and pacification of Chechnya, terrorism is a threat to his authority. On the premise that there are no moderate or good terrorists (RT 2015), Putin vowed in 1999 to "chase terrorists everywhere. If they are in an airport, then we will pursue them in the airport. And if we capture them in the toilet, then we will waste them in the outhouse" (RT 2011). It is a promise he has kept in Syria, where Russian airstrikes have targeted both IS and non-IS affiliated groups (Assil and Slim 2015). While the latter, including the Al-Nusra Front, are usually considered to be moderate Syrian opposition groups, Putin has branded them as terrorists just like IS and declared "now that those thugs have tasted blood, we can't allow them to return home and continue with their criminal activities" (Notte 2016).

Bearing in mind these two sources of instability in the Middle East, how has Russia tried to address them in relations with the Gulf States? Russia initially found common ground with the latter: it did not object to the Saudi/UAE-led military interventions in Bahrain in 2011 to quell popular protests and in Yemen in 2015 against rebellions in the south, both of which were consistent with Putin's distaste for chaotic revolutions from below. Sticking to this principle in Syria, however, has brought Russia into conflict with the Gulf monarchies who have privileged concerns over Iran's role in Syria over and above earlier expressions of solidarity with the status quo, and who thus seek Assad's removal. Russia is not pro-Assad as per the conventional narrative (Charap and Shapiro 2013); Russia has reiterated multiple times that its support of Assad is "not unconditional" (RT 2017). Instead, Russia is in favor of a pacted transition via the Geneva peace process, on the assumption that its implementation would result in more stability than an outcome imposed by any single party. Given that negotiations would take place only once all sides believe they have achieved parity in the form of a protracted stalemate in the conflict, Russia has tried to manufacture conditions for this to occur. For example, Russia's initiative to broker the deal over chemical weapons in Syria was aimed at pre-empting airstrikes by the West that would have severely weakened the Assad regime and advantaged the disunited opposition forces, while Russia's 2015 military strikes in Syria were aimed at bolstering Assad without giving him a decisive victory. In addition, Putin's overtures to Qatar, Kuwait, Oman, and also to regional powerhouse Egypt, may be attempts to pressure Saudi Arabia to reconsider its intransigence on a Syria without Assad (Ramani 2016, Todman 2016) and also to leverage on Qatar's relations with other Islamist groups in Syria to seek a back channel for a political solution (Ramani 2016, Korybko 2017).

With regard to terrorism, the other source of instability, Russia has had mixed success in engaging with the Gulf States. On the one hand, Russia has accused these states of supporting terrorism and its destabilizing effects. The arrival of foreign fighters, including prominent Saudi-born leaders such as Ibn Al Khattab and Abu Al Walid, into Chechnya in the mid-1990s, was partly responsible for transforming what was originally a local secessionist movement into a global jihadist cause as they provided access to tactics, material, and personnel (Hahn 2005). The Saudis certainly did themselves no favor when Saudi Arabia proposed to give Russia "a guarantee to protect the Winter Olympics in the city of Sochi on the Black Sea ... [since] the Chechen groups that threaten the security of the Games are controlled by us" (Ghoussoub 2013). Private donations originating from the Gulf States have been found to be responsible for financing the activities of Islamist groups fighting in Syria and Iraq (Keatinge 2014, Byman and McCants 2017), where Saudis comprise the second largest group of foreign fighters after Tunisians (Bremmer 2017). Money from the Gulf States to build mosques and schools have also been blamed for radicalizing local Muslim populations in the north Caucasus who were traditionally Sufi or who were relatively secular after almost 70 years of Soviet rule in the case of the Central Asians (Speckhard and Akhmedova 2007). Russia has been concerned enough to pass laws banning Wahhabism between 1999–2001 although there is no similar provision at the federal level. In October 2016, Ramzan Kadyrov, the leader of Chechnya and an ally of Putin, even went as far as to secure a controversial fatwa from Islamic scholars condemning Wahhabi Salafism as an extreme form of Islamic teaching.[7]

On the other hand, Russia is careful not to make itself an easy target for extremists by seeking good relations with the Muslim world, the leadership of which resides with Saudi Arabia as the custodian of Islam's two most holy cities. Putin, for example, has assiduously avoided using the term 'Islamic' to describe terrorists, remarking that he would "prefer Islam not be mentioned in vain alongside terrorism" (Kramer 2017). He has defended Islam as historically indigenous to Russian culture (it is one of the country's four traditional religions) and in 2015, he opened the Moscow Cathedral Mosque, the largest mosque in Europe. His policy of 'Chechnization', or appointing pro-Moscow Chechens to administer the republic, along with grants and subsidies from Moscow have ushered in a period of relative peace and development in the republic since 2000. Putin has also used Kadyrov to approach the Gulf monarchies about investing in Chechnya in the hope that economic prosperity would take the edge off some of the push factors for terrorism. Kadyrov, for instance, visited several Gulf capitals in 2013, 2015, and 2016 (Vatchagaev 2015, Araby 2016) where his youth, religion, and conservative values makes him a good ambassador for Russia among the new generation of leaders in the region.

The high stakes involved for Russia are sometimes given short shrift, with a Kuwaiti military commander opining that "few in the GCC believe that a handful of Islamist fighters are capable of wreaking havoc in such a big country" (Suchkov 2015). This is probably the result of an incomplete understanding of the global–local linkage between extremist fighters and of the conditions that have perpetuated grievances among migrant workers in Russia and among local communities in the north Caucasus and Central Asia. The Gulf States trace the root cause of the rise of extremist Islamic groups to the policies of Iranian-backed allies in the Middle East (Stephens 2016); Iran's subversion of the Middle East must hence be curtailed if Russia's fear of instability from terrorism is to be minimized – but this is a perspective that undermines Russia's own interests in Iran.

Recognition of Russia as a regional co-hegemon

Russia's second goal in the Middle East when dealing with the Gulf States is to "shake the region loose from American hegemony" (Miller 2016) and consequently, to be recognized and to play a role as an indispensable and influential extra-regional power. Russia seeks to reduce, not to replace or end, US hegemony, despite the hyperbole in the headlines cited at the start of this chapter.

This is because unlike the USA, Europe, or the former Soviet republics, the Middle East is simply not a core area of interest. Russia tends to look at the world as "a series of concentric circles spreading outward from its own borders and established priorities based on its appreciation of geographical proximity" (Caldwell 2007, 283). In this regard, the former Soviet republics occupy the first circle, the West the second circle, and all other states orbit the third and outer most circle; the Middle East is therefore too far to be a consistent foreign policy priority. This spatial orientation is reinforced by a tendency to self-identify as European or Western, which serves as Russia's frame of reference and comparison. Putin himself, for instance, remarked that "Russia is a very diverse country, but we are part of Western European culture. No matter where our people live, in the Far East or in the South, we are European" (Putin 2000, 169). Even while criticizing the West for having turned its back on its basic values, he has positioned Russia as the more conservative and more authentic part of Europe that will save European civilization from moral and religious decadence (Laruelle 2016). Throughout its history, Russia has sought to be recognized by the West, to modernize in the manner of the West, or in contested debates about identity, to seek to differentiate itself from the West (Leichtova 2014, Tsygankov 2016). The West has therefore always occupied a central place in Russian foreign policy, and it is shortsighted to assume that Russia's policies vis-à-vis the Middle East share the same primacy as its relations with the West. Likewise, the former Soviet republics represent Russia's 'near abroad' or sphere of 'privileged interests'. Russia's interests there cannot be conflated with those in the Middle East since Syria is not Ukraine – they are not both sides of the same coin.

The fact that the Middle East is a non-core region matters because this means that unlike the more zero-sum approach to the USA's involvement in Europe and the former Soviet republics, Russia in fact values the presence, albeit not the pre-eminence, of the USA in the Middle East (Katz 2008). For one thing, the USA's bases in and alliance with the Gulf States have brought relative stability, predictability, and unprecedented prosperity, which serves to protect Russia's growing trade and investments ties with these countries. For another, the USA's deep engagement in the Gulf and the Middle East acts as a lightning rod for extremist fighters; its departure would refocus their attention on Russia's transgressions in the north Caucasus and Central Asia. Characterizing Russia's policy in the Middle East as "an anti-American zero-sum geopolitical game" (Cohen 2012, 2) is, therefore, a gross oversimplification.

Toward this end, Moscow's interactions with the Gulf States demonstrate that it has the wherewithal to escalate or de-escalate an issue that is of primary interest to them, and that they now have to take into account Moscow's perspectives, something they have not done for almost 40 years. The comment by a senior UK parliamentarian that "there is no road to peace in Syria that does not pass through Russia" (Blunt 2017) seems to also apply to Libya, Iran, and elsewhere. In Libya, for example, the authority of the UN-recognized Government of National Accord (GNA) is being undermined most seriously by the Libyan National Army (LNA) in Tobruk led by General Khalifa Haftar. On the one hand, Russia has provided diplomatic, financial, and military support for General Haftar, whose patrons are the UAE and Egypt. Moscow has hosted General Haftar a few times, printed bank notes for use in the eastern oil-rich territories he controls, and supplied him with weapons delivered by Moldova and Egypt and financed by the UAE in contravention of a UN ban on weapons sales to Libya (Lewis 2017). On the other hand, Russia has good relations with the GNA, whose leader visited Moscow at the end of 2016 to request support to lift the arms embargo and asset freeze against Libya, while promising to look favorably upon weapons and oil deals with Russian companies. Russia also maintains contact with the Misratan brigades, another influential military force. The UAE, however, is discomfited by Russia's dealings with the GNA and Misratan partly because some of their members have radical Islamist orientations, and partly because Gulf rivals Qatar and Turkey are patrons of the GNA. The UAE is also wary that with Europe keen to stabilize Libya to stem the flow of refugees into Europe, Putin may seek a quid pro quo with the West, such as accommodating its preference for a post-war Syria (Korzhanov 2017). Which way Putin eventually leans is of crucial importance to the UAE and Qatar and their proxies. He can offer Russia's help as a mediator – the LNA and GNA were brought to Abu Dhabi in May 2017 for their first face-to-face meeting – or he can provoke further conflict by arming one or both sides; indeed, Russia is well-versed in playing dual roles as fireman and arsonist as the frozen conflicts in the former Soviet Union indicate.

There is certainly a case to be made that Russia's policy in Libya, like its policy in Syria, is part of the realization of a master plan for Russian access to and domination of the eastern Mediterranean, itself a centuries-old ambition (Valenta and Valenta 2016, Johnson 2015). Russia has recently expanded its network of overseas bases that can be used to project influence in the Gulf and the Middle East – two in Syria, two in Armenia, and one in Cyprus; it has been offered the use of bases in Yemen; it is in discussions with Egypt over the Soviet-era naval base in Alexandria and with Turkey over the shared use of NATO's air base in Incirlik. However, this chapter argues that Russia's behavior is more opportunistic than strategic. First, Russia's recent foray, starting in 2016, into the five-year-old Libyan civil war suggests that it is looking for a way out of Syria by supporting the Emiratis and Egyptians in Libya, who together with many north African countries, are less truculent about Assad's future. Second, its actions in Libya and Syria are low cost (Miller 2016, Charap 2015); in Libya for instance, the weapons were delivered and financed by others, and direct involvement has only required diplomatic facilitation of meetings thus far. Finally, Russia has no need for permanent naval bases overseas since the Russian navy has "no capacity for real power projection beyond home waters" for the foreseeable future (Mommsen 2016, 313). The navy has lagged behind the land and air forces in modernization; for example, it has only one aging aircraft carrier compared to ten in the USA, and the quality of its shipbuilding is abysmal as it loses more ships to fire than any other cause (Majumdar 2017). While Russia does not appear to have a grand strategy to be more involved in conflicts in the Middle East that concern the Gulf States, it is willing to consider taking advantage of relevant opportunities.

When Russia does take action, it is, paradoxically, aimed at maintaining, stimulating, and/or ensuring multilateral cooperation because Russia's leading role in these international fora reinforce its claims of being a great power (Stepanova 2016).[8] At the same time, this circumscribes unilateral action by the USA or another state at Russia's expense. A few examples should suffice. Russia voted in 2010 to approve sanctions against Iran for its covert nuclear program partly because the latter's non-cooperation with the International Atomic Energy Agency violated the non-proliferation regime dictated and upheld by the five nuclear powers including Russia. Likewise, in 2014, as Assad's position was weakening in Syria amidst a concerted push by the Saudi-led coalition, Putin refocused attention on the P5+1 negotiations over Iran's nuclear enrichment program by announcing that Russia would assist Iran in building additional nuclear reactors. In Syria, Putin's unilateral and brazen use of force in 2016 was aimed at getting Russia's co-stakeholders to resume the Geneva peace talks. As for Libya, to pre-empt calls to renegotiate the UN-brokered agreement, Russia hosted separate meetings with the LNA and GNA in 2017 and got them to agree to joint meetings in May in the UAE and in July in Paris. These resulted in agreements on a ceasefire and holding elections. In other words, as a permanent member of the UN Security Council and other international organizations, Russia wants to be seen as a state among equals enforcing what it deems to be legitimate, rules-based, and non-hegemonic arrangements (Pieper 2015); this is a more nuanced perspective than simply tarring Russia as 'revisionist' or 'anti-hegemony'.

Nevertheless, Russia's approach to multilateralism is more often instrumental and defensive (Ambrosio 2005) rather than principled; and selective and region-specific rather than consistent, despite claims of its commitment to a "polycentric world order ... based on the central coordinating role of the UN" (SputnikNews 2014). From Russia's perspective, multipolarity means that no one state, not even the USA, can act alone. Instead, the creation of "flexible international coalitions" of key states, including Russia, is the modus operandi that allows Russia to preserve its veneer of global influence (Tsygankov 2011). It will therefore reject the legitimacy of the outcome of negotiations in forums where it is not part of the decision-making (Lee 2010, Blank 2006). Russia is acutely aware that its resources are comparatively limited – Russia accounts for 3.6% of global GDP compared to the US share of 15.3%; Russia's GDP is less than 8% of the USA's; Russia's annual military expenditures are 11% of the USA (IMF 2017c, b, SIPRI 2017) – and it has little desire to squander them in a non-core region. At the same time, the Russian embrace of '*derzhavnost*' or 'great powerness' also shapes foreign policy. This is a deep-seated, persistent, and widespread belief in the existence of a manifest destiny, "a natural right to the role and influence of great power whether they have the wherewithal or not" (Levgold 2006), by virtue of its size, geography, resources, and history. This self-identity has had different incarnations over the centuries – Russia as the Third Rome or 'fuse of the world proletariat revolution' or vanguard against Western moral decadence – but the central idea is unchanged. One way of reconciling the contradictions between resource constraints and aspirational goals in a non-core region like the Middle East is, therefore, to champion the concept of multipolarity: it disguises Russia's diminishment, constrains US policy, and reinforces Russia's claim to be a great power.

Economic and commercial interests

Economic and commercial interests constitute Russia's third interest in relations with the Gulf States. The absolute volume of Russia's trade with the Gulf States has increased very significantly. Between 2000 and 2016, trade volume grew from US$0.27 billion to US$2.5 billion (IMF 2017a, e). 90% of the trade comprises Russian exports: the fertile soil in south Russia produce the cereals and barley that the non-arable deserts cannot, Russia's advanced refineries provide petrochemicals for use in the UAE and Saudi Arabia, and its precious stones find a market among end-users in these wealthy Gulf States or in the trading hub of Dubai for reexport to India and elsewhere. Russian oil exploration and oilfield services companies operate out of the Gulf, while around US$14 billion has been invested by Gulf countries into the Russian Direct Investment Fund. Russian-made weaponry is making inroads among states that have traditionally relied overwhelmingly on Western suppliers: Bahrain bought light arms and tanks from Russia, the UAE agreed in February 2017 to purchase anti-armor missiles worth US$700 million, Sukhoi fighters, and to jointly develop a light combat fighter jet in addition to previous purchases of Russian ground weapons, and Kuwait will take delivery of Russian tanks this year.

The push factor behind Russia's growing economic ties to the region is diversification. Russia has been obliged to seek out new markets because of the weakness of long-standing Soviet-era partners due to internal turmoil (Libya), international sanctions (Iraq and Iran), and because of sanctions imposed on it since July 2014 by the European Union and the USA for its incursions into Ukraine. Another aspect of diversification relates to the desire in Russia to build a modern, high-technology economy befitting a world power and to move away from serving as a raw materials appendage of the world economy much like a third-world country. At the moment, high-technology exports comprise just 14% of Russia's total manufactured exports, placing the country below the Philippines and Poland (IMF 2017d). To improve on this, Rosatom, the Russian state-owned company for nuclear technology, has been extraordinarily successful in winning contracts to construct and operate civilian nuclear reactors in Europe and also in Turkey and Jordan and has offered its help to build all 16 reactors in Saudi Arabia. It is Rosatom's comparative advantages in the nuclear industry, rather than any geo-strategic plot directed by the Kremlin to lock-in control of the nuclear energy market, that has accounted for its commercial success (Sim 2017).

The pull factor for Russia's interest in enhancing economic interactions concerns the receptivity of the Gulf States to Russia's outreach. Specifically, the perception among the Gulf States that the USA will be less engaged in the region has resulted in the former forging ties with non-traditional extra-regional powers such as China, South Korea, and Russia.[9] As noted by David Roberts (2017), "it is difficult to emphasize how betrayed the monarchies felt by this [the Joint Comprehensive Plan of Action]. The concept that the US would eventually do a deal with Iran at the expense of the Gulf monarchies had, for decades, been a fatalistic conspiracy theory permeating the Gulf. And then Obama made it so". The Joint Comprehensive Plan of Action (JCPOA) merely added fuel to earlier grievances, such as the USA's empowering of Iraq's Shiite majority and its 'pivot to Asia',[10] and made the Gulf States more open to Russia's overtures after the second decade of the 21st century. This is underlined by the growth in Russian–Gulf trade and investments during the latter period compared to the previous decade. In other words, the Gulf States are attractive and willing markets for Russia with their high per capita incomes, voracious appetite for arms – Saudi Arabia and the UAE were, respectively, the second and third largest arms importers globally in 2016 (Fleurant et al. 2017), interest in using nuclear energy to generate electricity and desalinate water, and development of non-oil sectors of the economies to create new commercial opportunities such as in space.

The growth in bilateral economic relations noted above, however, is tempered when viewed from a comparative perspective. The six states that comprise the GCC account for a mere 0.4% of Russia's overall trade in 2016, much less than its trade with Iran (0.6%), Egypt (0.7%), or Turkey (4%). The reverse also holds true: trade with Russia comprise of 0.2% of Saudi Arabia's and 0.3% of the UAE's total trade (IMF 2017a, e). The current trade structure offers limited room for expansion: grain exports from Russia will need to compete with the purchase or lease by Gulf States of overseas agriculture land on which crops are grown and then shipped back to Gulf consumers, and the petrochemicals industry in the Gulf States is increasingly sophisticated and has less need to import products from Russia. In the case of the arms trade, the Middle East is a very competitive market that has long been the purview of US (58.6%) and European (17.4%) suppliers (Cordesman 2016). Here, Russia accounts for a relatively modest 18.3% of all arms sales between 2000 and 2016, compared to its more dominant 43.1% share in Asia (Connolly and Sendstad 2017). Although much fanfare accompanied Russia's arms deals with the UAE and Saudi Arabia in 2017, they are the proverbial drops in the ocean compared to the hundreds of billions spent by the two Gulf States, who together account for one-fifth of all US arms exports in 2012–16 (Fleurant et al. 2017). There is also the issue of complementarity: in the same way that Russia's and Europe's differentiated economies make them good trade partners, the natural trade partners for the Gulf States are in energy-scarce Asia. With crude oil comprising the overwhelming majority of exports from the GCC, there is little scope for the latter to increase their exports to Russia; any improvement would depend on a successful effort to diversify Gulf exports away from oil.

Commercial relations aside, Russia also interacts with the Gulf States in energy markets. Russia and Saudi Arabia are the largest producers and exporters of oil globally, and their competition for customers and different break-even oil price positions have strained relations. Russian officials, for example, have implied that Saudi Arabia's overproduction to drive down the price of oil – to weaken Iran's geopolitical hand and squeeze out US shale oil producers – has done more damage to the Russian economy than sanctions imposed by the West (Koronowski 2014). On the part of the Saudis, there is little optimism that Russia will keep to the agreement to cut oil production in tandem with OPEC in the medium term, since Russia had reneged on promises to do likewise in 1998, 2001, and 2008 (Henderson and Fattouh 2016). Indeed, the fall in Russia's oil production during the first half of 2017 had little to do with compliance; it was due to routine well shut-ins and maintenance during winter. Also, no verification or enforcement mechanism is built into the deal; if OPEC has had little success in getting its members to keep to production quotas over the years – its core members cheat 96% of the time (Colgan 2014) – how could it enforce quotas with non-OPEC members like Russia? Looking ahead, competition between the Gulf States and Russia to supply the Chinese and Indian markets will only intensify. Nonetheless, such tensions are not new, reoccur periodically, and have not precluded cooperation in other areas of mutual interests.

Turning to the gas market, Russia and Qatar appear to be rivals. There is speculation, for instance, that Russia leaned on Assad to block Qatar's proposal to build a pipeline from Qatar to Turkey via Syria in order to pre-empt competition with Russia's own gas supply to the lucrative European market (Orenstein and Romer 2015, Escobar 2012).[11] Also, given that the USA – thanks to its shale gas bounty – now has little need for LNG gas from Qatar, there is some concern that Qatar will seek to redirect this surplus gas to Europe. After all, Russia and Qatar possess, respectively, the second and third largest gas reserves in the world and are also its two biggest exporters. However, a closer look at the structure of their gas exports suggests some complementary aspects. Russia dominates in pipeline exports, where 93% of its gas exports are via pipeline, while Qatar has a pre-eminent position in LNG exports with 84% of its gas exported in this form (BP 2017). In addition, LNG gas cannot completely substitute for pipeline gas in Europe since the latter currently has enough import and regasification capacity to cover only one third of its gas demand (Al-Tamimi 2015, Spalding 2016); any increase in capacity would be an expensive and time-consuming undertaking. Russia is likewise unable to refocus on and compete for consumers in Asia, the destination for two thirds of Qatar's LNG exports, for lack of pipelines to Asia and LNG export facilities from Russia.

It is, therefore, important not to exaggerate the degree of rivalry and tensions between Russia and the Gulf States in energy markets. While these are certainly present, they do not dictate the tenor of Russia's relations with these states, and neither do commercial interests highlighted earlier. In this connection, claims that Russia foments instability in and around the Gulf region in order to drive up the price of oil (Egan 2015) must be treated with caution. Price spikes due to short wars have historically been short-lived, as per Operation Desert Storm in 1990/1991; while a prolonged period of high oil prices is self-defeating since this incentivizes investments in alternatives to oil. Putin has, in fact, demonstrated repeatedly that while he is happy to grasp economic opportunities, he will not do so at the expense of Russia's other objectives, namely, stability and recognition of Russia's great power status. In 2008, Saudi Arabia offered economic incentives in exchange for an end to the latter's support towards Iran. In 2013, it allegedly proposed that Russia leave Assad's fate to the Saudis in exchange for US$15 billion in weapons contracts and Saudi cooperation with regard to the oil and gas markets (Ghoussoub 2013). More recently, in 2016, Saudi Arabia pushed Russia to "make a deal" by offering to facilitate a greater stake for Russia in the Middle East and access to "a pool of investment funds that exceeds that of China" if it disavowed Assad (Katz 2016b). Since Russia's involvement in Iran and Syria is closely tied to the twin prerogatives of stability and recognition, all such offers have predictably been declined. Consequently, even though the Gulf States are fully aware that Russia cannot be ignored in the region … there are clear limits to what the GCC can offer Russia to persuade it to modify its approach to the region, as economic incentives are clearly insufficient to alter Russian policy. (Sager 2016) This explains why the Saudis adopted a new, 'compartmentalization' approach during the king's recent visit to Russia, whereby discussions on economic and commercial relations were de-linked from demands regarding Assad.

Russia's bilateral relations with the Gulf States

The observant reader will have already surmised that for the most part, Russia does not approach the Gulf States as a homogenous unit. Russia–GCC strategic dialogues and Russia–GCC business forums exist alongside bilateral relations with each Gulf State, which in turn is a function of how each state responds or contributes to Russia's interests – stability, recognition, economic opportunities – in the region. Space constraints will allow only brief comments on the three most active sets of bilateral relations: with the UAE, Saudi Arabia, and Qatar.

Russia's best relations are with the UAE and are based primarily on the latter's equally uncompromising stand against "all forms of terrorism and religious extremism of any kind that destroy the social fabric of society, affect national harmony, and threaten global peace and security" (WAM 2016). It has been at the forefront of anti-terrorist operations against Al-Qaeda and IS in the Middle East and hosts the independent International Center of Excellence for Countering Violent Extremism. With the most diversified and business-friendly economy out of all the Gulf States, it is more receptive to commercial exchanges. For instance, non-oil exports account for 30% of total exports compared to 60–80% in the other Gulf countries, and the UAE's export diversity exceeds the levels in all Gulf States bar Bahrain (IMF 2016). The fact that Iran is a major economic partner for the UAE also makes it a relatively more pragmatic interlocutor on the Iranian issue than the Saudis. UAE–Iran trade, most of it in the form of reexports from Dubai to Iran, was worth US$12 billion in 2013 and accounted for 12% of all non-oil exports; the end of sanctions on Iran and resumption of trade is expected to add 1% of real GDP growth annually to the UAE (Bouyarmourn 2015).

At the other end of the spectrum is Russia's relations with Saudi Arabia. The decent working relationship masks long-standing tensions over the country's role in nurturing, supporting, and funding radical Islamist groups; it extends all the way back to Saudi Arabia's support for anti-Soviet mujahideen fighters in Afghanistan in the 1980s, and is underlined by the call by more than 50 Saudi clerics in 2015 for a jihad against Russia and Iran for their support of Assad. Saudi Arabia's obstinacy over the fate of Assad is the other sticking point. Tellingly, trade between Russia and Saudi Arabia has suffered since the conflict in Syria: the upward trend from US$56 million in 2000 reached a peak of US$1.36 billion in 2012, only to fall sharply over the next few years to US$485 million in 2016, which is even lower than the trade volume between Russia and Kuwait during the same year (IMF 2017a, e). Russia views Saudi Arabia's foreign policy in the Middle East as a threat to regional peace, and by extension to regime security and social stability in Russia. As noted by Katz, "while Russia wants increased economic ties to the GCC, Moscow is not going to sacrifice relations with a Tehran with which it shares security concerns in exchange for the promise of better relations with a Riyadh that it sees as implacably hostile toward Russia" (Katz 2016a, 4).

As for Russia–Qatar relations, they occupy the zone between the previous two sets of bilateral relations. Russia would relish a chance to supply arms to Qatar, but at the same time it appreciates that Qatar's economic outreach – such as its December 2016 purchase of a 19.5% stake in Russian oil company Rosneft worth US$11.3 billion[12] – comes with no political strings attached, unlike the pre-2017 modus operandi of the Saudis. While it is viewed, like the Saudis, as a protagonist in terms of its support for groups that Russia perceive as terrorists, Qatar's 'friends-with-everyone' approach and its interest in conflict mediation mean it is not as intransigent as the Saudis and that there is room for compromise. Turning to the 2017 row within the GCC over Qatar, it is arguable that Russia will not pick a side in the dispute. Actively backing Qatar risks blowback for Russia as it would be seen to be part of a Qatar-Iran axis; while openly siding with the UAE and Saudi Arabia would be a disservice to Qatar. This row also reinforces one of the claims advanced here that Russia is not in a stand-off with the USA in the Middle East: the USSR would have thrown its weight behind Qatar in response to the USA's backing of Saudi Arabia/UAE since geopolitical considerations, including the fact that NATO member Turkey has provided military, economic, and diplomatic support to Qatar, would have outweighed domestic consequences for Russia. Today's Russia has simply called for dialogue so that the efficiency of joint efforts on combatting terrorism – one of its prime concerns in the region – is not compromised (Reuters 2017).

Conclusion

This chapter has traced the evolution of Russia's extra-regional engagement with the Gulf States from a footprint that was barely perceptible in the 1990s to a diplomatic, political, military, and economic presence that is unmissable and unavoidable. In interacting with these states, Russia has no specially concocted strategy to expand its network of permanent military bases, it is not mired in a zero-sum competition for client states with the USA, and it has no desire to see the latter ejected from the region. Instead, Russia's interactions are largely opportunistic, low cost, and defensive tactics aimed at securing regime and social stability in Russia itself, and at ensuring a place for Russia at multilateral negotiating forums in the region. Putin has simply made the most of a weak hand in Russia's relations with the Gulf monarchies.

Russia's longer-term ambitions in the region are circumscribed by several factors. It has limited resources even in the medium-term to expend on a region that does not form the core of its vital national interests. Its remarkable progress in engaging the Gulf monarchies is partly due to the voluntary disengagement by the USA and their subsequent attempt to compensate by bringing in non-traditional stakeholders. This situation may still shift given the ongoing debates about America's role in the 21st century, which will reduce the window of opportunity for Russia's activism in the region. Moreover, there is no clear interlocutor for Russia among the Gulf States: the rivalry between Saudi Arabia/UAE and Qatar, the subtle tensions between Saudi Arabia and the UAE over Yemen and funding of Islamic groups, and the relative neutrality of Oman and Kuwait complicate the emergence of an undisputed leader that can represent a common position vis-à-vis Russia. There are, however, two possible platforms upon which to build more stable and constructive relations in a volatile part of the world. Moscow's assistance with civilian nuclear energy will result in long-term contracts for construction, fuel supply, maintenance, and operator training, and hence contribute positively to low-carbon, sustainable development goals. Its role as an extra-regional balancer and preference for multilateral negotiated settlements also augurs well in the current circumstances. To this extent, therefore, Russia is not always an "eternally negative force" (Blank 2015, 76).

Notes

1 See Alami (2016), Narbone (2017), Blank (2015), Frisk (2016), Matthews, Moore, and Sharkov (2017), and Ramani (2017) respectively.
2 For a discussion of alarmists versus skeptics on the existence of a Russian grand strategy, see Monaghan (2013) and Tsygankov (2011).
3 It is beyond the scope of this chapter to discuss in detail each of these tactics. For a useful overview see Starr and Cornell (2014).
4 Key proponents of this school of thought include John Mersheimer, Stephen Blank, S. Frederick Starr, Svante Cornell, Stephen Kotkin, and Ariel Cohen. Their works are cited in the references.
5 The breakdown of the US$14 billion contribution is as follows: US$250 million from Bahrain, US$1 billion each from Kuwait and the UAE, US$2 billion from Qatar, and US$10 billion from Saudi Arabia.

6 The figures vary depending on source and time period. The numbers cited here are from Putin (MT 2017). For other estimates see MacFarquhar (2015) and Khatib (2016).
7 Kadyrov was later compelled to apologize to the Saudis for this.
8 The argument here is limited to Russia's policy in the Middle East, where it has a relative deficit of resources and interests and excludes its approach to the post-Soviet region.
9 See the chapters by Fulton and Seo in this volume.
10 See the chapter by Ulrichsen in this volume.
11 For critical responses to this speculation see Mills (2016), Butter (2015), and Cochrane (2017).
12 Most of this stake (14.16%) was sold in September 2017 to CEFC China Energy for US$9.1 billion.

Bibliography

Al-Hamli, Ahmed. 2016. Introduction: Russia's foreign policy and the GCC. In Russian Foreign Policy and the GCC, TRENDS Working Paper 04/2016, edited by TRENDS. Abu Dhabi.

Al-Tamimi, Naser. 2015. Navigating uncertainty: Qatar's response to the global gas boom. In *Brookings Doha Center Analysis paper*. Doha: Brookings.

Alami, Mona. 2016. "Russia comes in from the cold – and towards the Gulf". *Middle East Eye*, 12 July 2016.

Allison, Roy. 2013. "Russia and Syria: explaining alignment with a regime in crisis". *International Affairs* 89 (4):795–823.

Ambrosio, Thomas. 2005. *Challenging America's Global Preeminence: Russia's Quest for Multipolarity*. Aldershot: Ashgate.

Araby, Al. 2016. "Leading UAE royal courts controversial Chechen leader". *Al Araby*, 27 November 2016.

Assil, Ibrahim Al, and Randa Slim. 2015. "Debating Russia's aims in Syria". *Middle East Institute*, 10 November 2015. http://www.mei.edu/content/at/debating-russias-aims-syria.

Bayoumi, Sami. 2007. *The New Russian Role in the Arabian Gulf Region*. Abu Dhabi: Emirates Center for Strategic Studies and Research.

Blank, Stephen. 2006. *Russia and the US in the Middle East: Policies and Contexts*. Swindon: Defence Academy of the UK.

Blank, Stephen. 2015. "Russia's new presence in the Middle East". *American Foreign Policy Interests* (37):69–79.

Blunt, Crispin. 2017. "Engage but beware: dealing with Russia in Syria". *Middle East Eye*, 12 March 2017. http://www.middleeasteye.net/columns/engage-beware-dealing-russia-syria-1636284810.

Bouyarmourn, Adam. 2015. "UAE economy to gain US$13 bilion from lifting of Iran sanctions, IMF predicts". *The National*, 6 August 2015.

BP. 2017. *BP Statistical Review of World Energy*. London: BP.

Bremmer, Ian. 2017. "The top 5 countries where ISIS gets its foreign recruits". *Time*, 27 April 2017.

Butter, David. 2015. "Russia's Syria intervention is not all about gas". Carnegie Endowment for International Peace, 19 November 2015. http://carnegieendowment.org/sada/62036.

Byman, Daniel L. and William McCants. 2017. "The danger of picking sides in the Qatar crisis". *The National Interest*, 17 June 2017.

Caldwell, Lawrence T. 2007. Russian concepts of national security. In *Russian Foreign Policy in the Twenty-First Century and the Shadow of the Past*, edited by Robert Levgold. New York: Colombia University Press.

Charap, Samuel. 2015. "Is Russia an outside power in the Gulf?" *Survival* 57 (1):153–170.

Charap, Samuel and Jeremy Shapiro. 2013. "How the US can move Russia on Syria". *Al Monitor*, 22 July 2013.

Cochrane, Paul. 2017. "The Pipelineistan conspiracy: the war in Syria has never been about gas". *Middle East Eye*, 10 May 2017. http://www.middleeasteye.net/essays/pipelineistan-conspiracy-why-war-syria-was-never-about-gas-144022537.

Cohen, Ariel. 2012. *How the US Should Respond to Russia's Unhelpful Role in the Middle East*. Washington DC: The Heritage Foundation.

Colgan, Jeff D. 2014. "The emperor has no clothes: the limits of OPEC in the global oil market". *International Organizations* 68 (3):599–632.

Connolly, Richard and Cecilie Sendstad. 2017. *Russia's Role as an Arms Exporter: The Strategic and Economic Importance of Arms Exports for Russia*. London: Chatham House.

Cordesman, Anthony H. 2016. *The Changing Patterns of Arms Imports in the Middle East and North Africa*. Washington, DC: Center for Strategic and International Studies.

Dannreuther, Roland. 2012. "Russia and the Middle East: A cold war paradigm?" *Europe-Asia Studies* 64 (3):543–560.

Egan, Matt. 2015. "Putin's air strikes in Syria stir up oil prices". *CNN*, 12 October 2015.

Escobar, Pepe. 2012. "Syria's pipeliniestan war". *Al Jazeera*, 6 August 2012. http://www.aljazeera.com/indepth/opinion/2012/08/201285133440424621.html.

Escobar, Pepe. 2014. "The Saudi oil war against Russia, Iran and the US". *RT*, 15 October 2014. https://www.rt.com/op-edge/196148-saudiarabia-oil-russia-economic-confrontation/.

Fleurant, Aude, Pieter D. Wezeman, Siemon T. Wezeman, and Nan Tian. 2017. Trends in international arms transfers, 2016. In SIPRI Fact Sheet. Stockholm: Stockholm International Peace Research Institute.

Frisk, Robert. 2016. "It's not Donald Trump who matters now in the Middle East – it's Putin". *The Independent*, 10 November 2016.

Ghoussoub, Sahar. 2013. "Russian president, Saudi spy chief discussed Syria, Egypt". *Al Monitor*, 22 August 2013.

Hahn, Gordon M. 2005. "The rise of Islamist extremism in Kabardino-Balkariya". *Demokratizatsiya* 13 (4):543–594.

Hahn, Gordon M. 2017. "The Petersburg jihadi attack in context: recent developments in Jihadism in Russia 2014–2017". https://gordonhahn.com/2017/04/07/the-petersburg-jihadi-attack-in-context-recent-developments-in-jihadism-in-russia-2014-2017/.

Henderson, James and Bassam Fattouh. 2016. *Russia and OPEC: Uneasy Partners*. Oxford: Oxford Institute for Energy Studies.

Hill, Fiona. 2015. How Vladimir Putin's world view shapes Russian foreign policy. In *Russia's Foreign Policy: Ideas, Domestic Politics and External Relations*, edited by David Cadier and Margot Light. Houndmills, Basingstoke: Palgrave Macmillan.

IMF. 2016. *Economic Diversification in Oil-Exporting Arab Countries*. Washington, DC: International Monetary Fund.

IMF. 2017a. "Exports". Washington, DC: International Monetary Fund.

IMF. 2017b. "GDP based on PPP, share of world". Washington, DC: International Monetary Fund.

IMF. 2017c. "GDP, current prices". Washington, DC: International Monetary Fund.

IMF. 2017d. "High technology exports". Washington, DC: International Monetary Fund.

IMF. 2017e. "Imports". Washington, DC: International Monetary Fund.
Johnson, Keith. 2015. "Putin's Mediterranean power play in Syria". *Foreign Policy*, 2 October 2015.
Katz, Mark N. 2008. "Comparing Putin's and Brezhnev's policies toward the Middle East". *Society* 45 (2):177–180.
Katz, Mark N. 2012. "The impact of the Arab Spring on Saudi-Russian Relations". *Orient* (IV), 6 October 2012.
Katz, Mark N. 2016a. *The GCC View of Russia: Diminishing Expectations*. Washington, DC: Arab Gulf States Institute in Washington.
Katz, Mark N. 2016b. "Is Saudi Arabia really inviting Russia to play a bigger role in the Middle East". *Lobelog*, 2 August 2016.
Keatinge, Tom. 2014. "The importance of financing in enabling and sustaining the conflict in Syria (and beyond)". *Perspectives on Terrorism*, 8 (4). http://www.terrorismanalysts.com/pt/index.php/pot/article/view/360/html.
Khatib, Hakim. 2016. "How many foreign fighters in Syria are there?" *International Policy Digest*, 15 October 2016. https://intpolicydigest.org/2016/10/15/how-many-foreign-fighters-in-syria-are-there/.
Koronowski, Ryan. 2014. "Dropping oil prics and sanctions are hurting Russia to the tune of $140 billion". *Think Progress*, 25 November 2014.
Korybko, Andrew. 2017. "Russia and Qatar: back channel diplomacy over Syria". *Global Research*, 25 April 2017.
Korzhanov, Nikolay. 2017. "Moscow's presence in Libya is a new challenge for the West". *The Maghreb Times*, 30 May 2017.
Kotkin, Stephen. 2016. "Russia's perpetual geopolitics". *Foreign Affairs* 95 (3):2–9.
Kramer, Andrew E. 2017. "The phrase Putin never uses about terrorism (and Trump does)". *The New York Times*, 1 February 2017.
Laruelle, Marlene. 2016. Russia as an anti-liberal European civilisation. In *The New Russian Natonalism: Imperialism, Ethnicity and Authoritarianism 2000–2015*, edited by Pal Kolsto and Helge Blakkisrud. Edinburgh: Edinburgh University Press.
Lee, Hongsub. 2010. "Multilateralism in Russian foreign policy: some tentative evaluations". *International Area Review* 13 (3):31–49.
Leichtova, Magda. 2014. *Misunderstanding Russia: Russian Foreign Policy and the West*. London, Oxon: Routledge.
Levgold, Robert. 2006. Russian foreign policy during state transformation. In *Russian Foreign Policy in the 21st Century & The Shadow of the Past*, edited by Robert Levgold. New York: Columbia University Press.
Lewis, Aidan. 2017. "Covert Emirati support gave east Libyan air power key boost: UN report". *Reuters*, 9 June 2017. https://www.reuters.com/article/us-libya-security-idUSKBN1902K0.
Luxmoore, Matthew. 2014. "Defensive imperialism: the evolution of Russia's regional foreign policy". *International Journal on World Peace* 31 (2):73–112.
MacFarquhar, Neil. 2015. "For Russia, links between Caucasus and ISIS provoke anxiety". *The New York Times*, 20 November 2015.
Majumdar, Dave. 2017. "The Russian navy is powerful (but suffers from two big flaws)". *The National Interest*, 3 March 2017.
Mankoff, Jeffrey. 2012. "Why Moscow fears Arab unrest". *Current History* 111 (747): 258–263.
Matthews, Owen, Jack Moore, and Damien Sharkov. 2017. "How Russia became the Middle East's new power broker". *Newsweek*, 9 February 2017.

Miller, Chris. 2016. "Russia sets out to bring the Middle East under new order". *Yale Global online*, 8 November 2016.

Mills, Robin. 2016. "Syria's gas pipeline theory is a low-budget drama". *The National*, 1 October 2016. http://www.thenational.ae/business/energy/robin-mills-syrias-gas-pipeline-theory-is-a-low-budget-drama.

Mommsen, Klaus. 2016. The Russian Navy. In *Handbook of Naval Strategy and Security*, edited by Sebastian Bruns and Joachim Krause. London, Oxon: Routledge.

Monaghan, Andrew. 2013. "Putin's Russia: shaping a 'grand strategy'?" *International Affairs* 89 (5):1221–1236.

MT. 2017. "4,000 Russian now fighting in Syrian insurgency, says Putin". *The Moscow Times*, 23 February 2017. https://themoscowtimes.com/news/4000-russians-now-fighting-in-syrian-insurgency-says-putin-57259.

Narbone, Luigi. 2017. "A Pax Russica in the Middle East? Putin will have to do more to make it stick". *Huffington Post*, 25 February 2017. http://www.huffingtonpost.com/entry/a-pax-russica-in-the-middle-east-putin-will-have-to_us_58b1de8fe4b0658fc20f9606.

Notte, Hanna. 2016. "Russia in Chechnya and Syria: pursuit of strategic goals". *Middle East Policy Council* 13 (1):59–74.

Orenstein, Mitchell A. and George Romer. 2015. "Putin's gas attack". *Foreign Affairs*, 14 October 2015.

Osnos, Evan, David Remnick, and Joshua Yaffa. 2017. "Trump, Putin, and the new Cold War". *The New Yorker*, 6 March 2017. http://www.newyorker.com/magazine/2017/03/06/trump-putin-and-the-new-cold-war.

Pieper, Moritz. 2015. "Between the democratisation of international relations and status quo politics: Russia's foreign policy towards the Iranian nuclear programme". *International Politics* 52 (5):567–588.

Putin, Vladimir. 2000. *First Person (translated by Catherine A Fitzpatrick)*. New York: Public Affairs.

Ramani, Samuel. 2016. "How Russia is courting the Gulf". *The National Interest*. http://nationalinterest.org/feature/how-russia-courting-the-gulf-17207.

Ramani, Samuel. 2017. "Russia is expanding its great-power project in the Middle East". *The National Interest*, 12 October 2017.

Remnick, David. 2014. "Watching the eclipse". *The New Yorker*. http://www.newyorker.com/magazine/2014/08/11/watching-eclipse.

Reuters. 2017. "Kremlin wants stability and peace in the Gulf despite Qatar diplomatic row". *Arab News*, 5 June 2017. http://www.arabnews.com/node/1110431/world.

Roberts, David B. 2017. "The US, Saudi Arabia, and the Gulf". *Global Policy Journal*, 1 March 2017.

RT. 2011. "Putin on 'wasting terrorists in the outhouse': wrong rhetoric, right idea". *RT*, 15 July 2011.

RT. 2015. "Putin: no need to distinguish between 'moderate' and other terrorists". *RT*, 22 October 2015.

RT. 2017. "Moscow's support for Damascus 'not unconditional' – Assad doesn't follow Russia's orders – Perkov". *RT*, 6 April 2017.

Sager, Abdulaziz. 2016. "GCC–Russia relations: a lot of rhetoric but little substance". *Saudi Gazette*, 21 June 2016. http://saudigazette.com.sa/opinion/gcc-russia-relations-lot-rhetoric-little-substance/.

Sakwa, Richard. 2016. Shifting plates and perceptions. In Russian Foreign Policy and the GCC, Trends Working Paper 04/2016, edited by TRENDS. Abu Dhabi.

Sim, Li-Chen. 2017. Economic diversification in Russia: nuclear to the rescue? In *Economic Diversification Policies in Natural Resource Rich Economies*, edited by Sami Mahroum and Yasser AlSaleh. London, Oxon: Routledge.
SIPRI. 2017. "World military spending". https://www.sipri.org/media/press-release/2017/world-military-spending-increases-usa-and-europe.
Snetkov, Aglaya. 2015. "From crisis to crisis: Russia's security policy under Putin". *Russian Analytical Digest* (173):2–5.
Spalding, King. 2016. LNG in Europe: An Overview of European Import Terminals in 2015. Atlanta, GA: King & Spalding.
Speckhard, Anna, and Khapta Akhmedova. 2007. "The new Chechen jihad: militant Wahhabism as a radical movement and as a source of suicide terrorism in post-war Chechen society" *Democracy and Security* (2):103–155.
SputnikNews. 2014. "Russia, China to seek polycentric world – Lavrov". *Sputnik News*, 15 April 2014. https://sputniknews.com/voiceofrussia/news/2014_04_15/Russia-China-to-seek-polycentric-world-Lavrov-7696/.
Starr, S. Frederick, and Svante Cornell, eds. 2014. *Putin's Grand Strategy: The Eurasian Union and its Discontents*. Washington, DC: Central Asia-Caucasus Institute & Silk Road Studies Program.
Stepanova, Ekaterina. 2016. "Russia in the Middle East: Back to a 'grand strategy' or enforcing multilateralism?" *Politique etrangere* (2):23–35.
Stephens, Michael. 2016. "GCC security priority sets it at odds with West". *Gulf Affairs* (Spring 2016):26–27.
Suchkov, Maxim A. 2015. "Why Russia's Mideast agenda doesn't appeal to GCC". Foreign Policy Advisory Group. http://www.foreignpolicy.ru/en/analyses/why-russia-mideast-agenda-doesn-t-appeal-to-gcc/.
Todman, Will. 2016. *Gulf States' Policies on Syria*. Washington, DC: Center for Strategic and International Studies.
Trenin, Dmitri. 2015. Russian foreign policy as exercise in nation building. In *Russia's Foreign Policy: Ideas, Domestic Politics and External Relations*, edited by David Cadier and Margot Light. Houndmills, Basingstoke: Palgrave Macmillan.
Trenin, Dmitri. 2016. *Russia in the Middle East: Moscow's Objectives, Priorities, and Policy Drivers*. Moscow: Carnegie Moscow Center.
Tsygankov, Andrei P. 2011. "Preserving influence in a changing world: Russia's grand strategy". *Problems of Post-Communism* 58 (1):28–44.
Tsygankov, Andrei P. 2016. *Russia's Foreign Policy: Change and Continuity in National Identity*. 4th ed. Lanham: Rowman & Littlefield.
Tucker, Noah. 2015. *Central Asian Involvement in the Conflict in Syria and Iraq: Drivers and Responses*. Washington, DC: USAID.
Valenta, Jiri, and Leni FriedmanValenta. 2016. "Why Putin wants Syria". *Middle East Quarterly* 1–16.
Vatchagaev, Mairbeck. 2015. "Moscow uses Kadyrov in Kremlin push for rapprochement with Saudi Arabia". *Eurasia Daily Monitor*, 24 July 2015.
WAM. 2016. "UAE reiterates stance against terrorism, extremism, sectarianism". *Emirates 24/7*, 20 September 2016. http://www.emirates247.com/news/emirates/uae-reiterates-stance-against-terrorism-extremism-sectarianism-2016-09-20-1.640666.

4 Great Britain–Gulf relations
Ties that bind?

David B. Roberts and Cinzia Bianco

Introduction

The British Embassy in Kuwait City takes up much of a city block prominently close to the Kuwait Towers along the corniche. It is a lush green space, with a bar, housing a hodgepodge of buildings where old meets new. Verandas reminiscent of colonial times looking out to sea mingle with submarine-like security doors stuck onto old buildings with rickety windows struggling to keep in the refrigerated air. The United Kingdom (UK) Embassy in Abu Dhabi is similarly located in Abu Dhabi's prime real estate, stubbornly refusing to move as a forest of skyscrapers emerge around it. The ambassador's residence in Muscat is a palace by the sea. In Riyadh, the embassy is as grand as you might expect, though similar to many others. In Doha, the old embassy has been swapped for a new building that looks like an electricity substation that is now dwarfed by the Turkish Embassy next door. And in Manama, the embassy is a dull modernist construction in an ode to form over function.

Doubtless someone could write an interesting thesis on the architecture of embassies and how they reflect the nature of bilateral relations. British embassies in the Gulf monarchies are typically found in conspicuously prominent areas, taking up prime real estate, often in the heart of the cities, or at least in highly desirable locations. This is reflective of the important nature of historic bilateral relations. The fact that the UK Embassy in Doha is so utilitarian-looking and comprehensively dwarfed by the ornate and imposing Turkish Embassy next door also seems to fit a certain pattern of wider international relations.

For much of the nineteenth century, the UK was the decisive power in the Gulf region. Barely a handful of regional representatives – 'residents' as they were known – managed regional affairs; strove to quieten truculent naval spats; fretted about powers emerging from inside the Arabian Peninsula; and acted as judge, jury, and on occasion, punisher-in-chief courtesy of a quick, retributive, and 'pacifying' bombardment from the sea. During this era, the only power to vie with the UK in the region was the Porte: the Ottoman Empire based in Constantinople. And vie they did with, for example, fifty years of boots-on-the-ground in Qatar that lasted until 1915. Nevertheless, Britain sailed imperiously around its Gulf lake, and that was, as far as London was concerned, what it was all about.

But the question remains: what impact does this history have on modern-day Gulf–British relations? Has Britain retained some kind of a 'special place' in the foreign policies or the hearts of Gulf rulers? The history is certainly dense, and the UK's colonial role does not loom as gloomily as it does elsewhere. And there are clearly interesting legacies and linkages. The UK Army's officer training college at Sandhurst educates most senior Gulf royals. British citizens typically comprise the largest grouping of Western expatriates across the monarchies. And the British Royal family is often seen as some kind of a diplomatic secret weapon as if speaking royal-to-royal is axiomatically special and important. However, evidence of the tangible translation of these unique British selling points into actionable advantage for the British government or British companies is painfully thin on the ground. Though the pageantry of a state visit to Buckingham Palace is perhaps an asset of sorts, the reality is that Britain is not special any more. Only in defence and security does the UK play an outsized role compared to its wider geopolitical and economic ranking, and even then, Britain is a distant second to the United States (US) in terms of importance.

When it comes to investments, Gulf royals and regional Sovereign Wealth Funds (SWFs) often display a particular affinity for investing in London; the opportunity cost for them to invest instead in Berlin, Hong Kong, or Washington DC is not that great. But for the UK it is somewhat akin to a zero-sum game. The UK strapped for investment increasingly turned to the monarchies after the financial crash. During the Arab Spring, the monarchies flexed their muscles to persuade (or coerce) the UK to more assiduously follow their policy prescriptions. And now with the UK staring into the Brexit abyss or at least facing deeply uncertain times, plans to court the monarchies have been codified and the security of the monarchies has been translated into British national security strategy. This chapter follows the journey of British engagement with this strategic region: starting from the roots of British hegemony, it examines how the power balance has evolved throughout the twenty-first century. Overall, the aim of the chapter is to determine to what extent, for what reasons and with which implications the tables have been turned in the context of UK–Gulf Cooperation Council (GCC) relations.

A mutually beneficial beginning

Trade was the key motivator for the British entrance to the Gulf in the early seventeenth century, both to secure trading markets for the Crown and to deny them to others. Factories were established in Iran in the 1610s under the auspices of the British East India Company along with a political residency, which moved to Bahrain in 1723. Initially, the Portuguese largely controlled Gulf waters for a century and were Britain's principal rivals. The French and the Dutch were also intimating that they wanted a slice of the Gulf pie. Nevertheless, though the Gulf was an area of proxy conflicts for influence, they were relatively tepid as trade and commerce in, to, from, and through the Gulf was not all that great.[1]

But for the UK, this was to change markedly with Clive's victory at Plassey in 1757, the end of Mughal dynasty, and Britain assuming direct rule of India in 1758. All told, this transformed the importance of the Gulf to the UK.[2] As far as London was concerned, India ascended to another plane of importance and a rising tide lifts all boats. The Gulf thus became critical to the Crown as the historical Bombay to Basra shipping route was refreshed in importance for communication, trade, and post.[3]

Britain exerted its authority and ultimately its rule in the Gulf not through deploying garrisons of troops throughout the region, nor did British soldiers retreat to key strategic fortifications. Rather, Britain relied on asserting control via co-opting existing mechanisms of rule.[4] Indeed, without the troops to enforce unwanted political control (though the UK did retain punishment power from its navy in the Gulf, which was unmatched), the UK relied on local proxies. A series of 'never more than four or five' British political residents controlled the overarching structure of alliance politics in the Gulf for a century or more forging alliances and treaties with local leaders.[5] As such, Britain slotted into the existing hierarchies of rule on the Arabian Peninsula.

Britain's treaties were full of conditions and demands as stipulated by the Crown, but they also promised varying measures of protection too. As such, they were, particularly for the smaller entities, critical ways to secure a relatively large amount of independence and security. In other words, they benefitted both the British and the elites that the agreements froze in power as the key interlocutors.[6] There were several major treaties including the General Treaty in 1820, the Maritime Truce in 1853, and formal treaties of protection and exclusivity from the 1880s onwards, alongside approximately 200 smaller treaties and agreements.[7] The British were not concerned with state-building or otherwise improving the lives or even the economy of the proto-states in the Gulf as much as simply pacifying piratical waters, facilitating safe passage for the Bombay to Basra route, and rendering the region as uniquely a British sphere of influence as possible.

It was only with the end of World War One and the dissolution of the Ottoman Empire that Britain became the unrivalled external power in the region for the smaller monarchies. But by this time Britain was a declining empire and America was increasingly building relations around the Gulf, particularly in Saudi Arabia.[8] The trickle of post-World War One decline became a flood with the end of World War Two as Britain struggled to right itself after the most sapping of conflicts. The desire to secure favourable economic terms with the proto-states in the Gulf for oil concessions to fuel a recovery was crucial to London's calculations. Lingering colonial mindsets also prevailed, as did a fervent desire to hive off as much of the region from escalating American interests as possible.[9] Nevertheless, cooperation was possible between London and Washington, such as with the joint 1953 decision to overthrow Iran's populist Prime Minister Mohammed Mossadegh, who was stoking up public support for the nationalisation of the Iranian oil industry.[10]

Indeed, though the Gulf monarchies developed a solid income stream from their oil revenues, typically exponentially larger than any previous one derived from trading, pearling, or agriculture, the British (and American) exploitation of control over their oil resources was, understandably, an emerging bone of contention.[11] In the 1950s and 1960s, the rising pan-Arabist narrative emerging from Cairo and Baghdad stoked a nationalist, anti-colonial rhetoric around the Middle East and North Africa region. This put pressure on governments to appease a growing populism within their states. A frequent demand from protestors was to nationalise the oil industries controlled by Western firms.[12]

Despite riots of varying scales throughout the Gulf monarchies, the leaderships stood fast against such protests. This is perhaps explained by the nature of the UK–monarchy relationship – in that it was truly a relationship with the monarchies themselves. In the smaller states in the Gulf, the UK played arguably the central role in anointing and securing in place the monarchies (and the subsection of each family) from the mid-nineteenth century onwards.[13] The parts of the ruling families in charge were, in essence, grateful to London for securing their rule, and they were getting enough oil funds for themselves and their immediate families.[14] Wider development did not matter as much.

The British era in the Gulf came to an end on its own terms. Partly driven by decolonisation-related ideological concerns and partly by a desperate economic state, in 1968 the UK announced it was leaving its possessions 'East of Suez' by 1971. This meant that Qatar, Bahrain, and the Trucial States (Oman and modern-day UAE) would become independent states and in charge of their foreign policy for the first time.[15] The monarchies were initially not happy to be cast adrift so abruptly. This was, after all, a region that had just seen the shocking 1967 war with Israel. Closer to home, Saudi Arabia and Iran still loomed ominously over the smaller proto-states, often with a range of unresolved irredentist issues. Also, it must not be forgotten that Britain had proved its utility only in 1961. In that year, Kuwait had received its independence from the UK and immediately Iraqi troops amassed on their border. Britain swiftly dispatched Operation Vantage, which saw the deployment of British forces to successfully deter Iraqi aggression. This vividly demonstrated the depredations that lurked in the region, the inability of the monarchies on their own to counter any would-be threats, and the importance of extra-regional allies coming to the aid.

Nevertheless, Britain proved to be unmovable and independence arrived in 1971. The post-independence relationship with the UK shows a mixed set of relations. Unencumbered by the exigencies of being British protectorates, the monarchies, quite naturally, strove to diversify their relations to an even greater degree and to see what better deals they could strike elsewhere. Journals and magazines that covered trade in the Gulf at this time like *Middle East Economic Survey* and *Middle East Economic Digest* are replete, as the 1970s progressed, with articles focusing on states like Japan and France quickly developing their relations with the monarchies. Though British relations were not jettisoned and Britain as a military training partner in particular was retained, there is little evidence of some residual preference for maintaining particular UK trade relations by the monarchies through the 1970s or 1980s.[16]

When significant deals were struck between the Gulf monarchies and the UK, they are noteworthy precisely because of their relative rarity. The set of al-Yamama weapons deals that the UK and Saudi Arabia signed in the early 1980s provide an emblematic case in point.[17] In their day, these deals were the largest weapons sales agreements ever made, which certainly shows a willingness to invest heavily in UK exports. But the overriding reason that this deal came about was not because of Saudi Arabia's primary desire to buy British kit or to augment its British relations, but because their first choice – an equally large weapons deal with the US – was scuppered.[18] The US Congressional representatives complained bitterly about such a prospective weapons deal with Saudi Arabia based on their unwavering desire for Israel to maintain a 'qualitative edge' over all other weapons sales to the Middle East.[19] Saudi Arabia's rulers – not unsurprisingly – saw this as a significant and somewhat humiliating slight. Assiduous courting from Prime Minister Margaret Thatcher then secured the deal for the UK.

This point here is not that the UK vanished from the region; far from it. The UK remained a significant trading partner for the Gulf monarchies, and it was particularly involved in military sectors. But any notion of special treatment for the UK because of its unique history in the Gulf is difficult to match with the reality. Operation Granby, the significant British contribution to the liberation of Kuwait in 1991, was motivated by a variety of factors. That the UK had a unique historical role in the region might have played a role in the decision-making process of prime ministers Margaret Thatcher and John Major. Similarly, the principle that 'an aggressor must never be allowed to get his way', as Thatcher argued, may also have been a factor.[20] But it was impossible for the UK to stand by while Saddam Hussein controlled 65 percent of the world's oil supplies and other leading members of the international community saddled up.[21] Again, pragmatism as opposed to sentimentality likely pervaded decision-making in London.

A rising Gulf

After a period of slow, steady relations, the UK was thrust back into the thick of Gulf politics with the 2003 invasion of Iraq and the aftermath. The war was wrenching and destructive for Iraq and it placed the Gulf monarchies in a political bind, not least for their hosting of so many military facilities used during the campaign. But it also made them far wealthier with the skyrocketing oil price, which, by the end of 2004, was at its highest level in two decades.[22] The next year, annual oil revenues jumped sevenfold compared to 1999 levels and in the first decade of the 2000s the economies in the GCC, the regional political body comprising the six monarchies, tripled in size.[23] Vast surpluses were partly accumulated in SWFs, state-owned investment funds mandated to invest in a diverse set of assets as a way to increase diversification of the GCC economies away from dependence on oil and gas revenues. Though some SWFs date their origin back to the 1970s, by the mid-2000s there were an estimated forty SWFs throughout the GCC.[24]

As international observers began to notice the SWF phenomenon, countries around the world battled to attract inward investments. European countries, a long-time destination for GCC investments, were particularly proactive in this quest and the UK was by far the most successful of the European states at attracting Gulf SWFs. During the first decade of the 2000s, the UK was the world's number-two recipient of inward investments, the bulk of which came from the Gulf: Saudi Arabia, the UAE and Qatar in particular.[25]

Some GCC funds invested in British infrastructure. The Abu Dhabi Investment Authority (ADIA) acquired a stake in London's Gatwick airport as well as a 9.9 percent stake in Thames Water, and Kuwait Investment Authority (KIA) bought a stake in London City Airport. Other SWFs were instrumental in providing liquidity to the British financial system, distressed by the Eurozone and the global financial crisis. In 2007, the Borse Dubai and Qatar Investment Authority (QIA) acquired, respectively, a 28 and 15 percent stake in the London Stock Exchange Group. In 2008, Barclays successfully turned to the UAE and Qatar for an investment of up to £7.6 billion, rather than accepting British government bailout funds.

Most Gulf cash was ploughed into safe long-term investments, such as high-profile real estate and commercial property. In the period 2005–10, Gulf SWFs tripled their share in the UK's market of commercial property: in 2009 alone they provided 16 percent of all foreign investment in the sector.[26] These types of deals also often involved trophy assets and flagship properties in London, such as Harrods, Canary Wharf, the Shard, Madame Tussauds, and the London Eye. These acquisitions were particularly symbolic, as they represented tangible signs of the rising posture of the monarchies and embodied the influence that the GCC countries were able to purchase in the UK. Indeed, from the early 2000 onwards, the GCC governments would seek to leverage their investments as an additional tool of influence in dealing with the UK – a case in point being the controversy between the UAE and the UK on the issue of political Islam during the Arab Spring, detailed in the next section.

Beyond investments, bilateral trade increased 39 percent between 2010 and 2012, peaking at around £30 billion.[27] To put this in context, this meant that the UK 'exported more to the Gulf in 2011 than to all of Latin America and the Caribbean, or to India, Russia and Mexico combined'.[28] Understandably, the British government was eager to encourage these investments and expanding business and political ties with the Gulf states increasingly became a priority. The partnership with the GCC states was viewed through the lens of mitigating the hardships experienced by Western countries precipitated by the 2007 financial crisis. As such, it was ever more becoming a partnership of equals with both sides benefitting.

Aside from areas of finance, the GCC states became increasingly important to the UK as energy suppliers. Gas as a source of fuel had long become more significant for the UK, from 5 percent of the energy mix in 1970 to 35 percent in 2012.[29] The UK became a net gas importer for the first time in 2004 and, as Qatar's liquefied natural gas (LNG) arrived from 2006, this source became particularly important. While Norway remains the main supplier in the UK's gas mix, in 2011 Qatar's LNG represented nearly 40 percent of all imported gas, and in 2016, it was approximately 33 percent.[30]

The unprecedented role played by the GCC countries in the UK's economic security via its investments and energy supply arguably represented a tipping of the scales between the former empire and its former protectorates. Certainly, on many occasions in the nineteenth or early twentieth centuries, the protectorates bargained hard and achieved significant concessions from the Crown. For example, when the Royal Air Force needed to establish an emergency landing strip in Qatar in 1932, the Qatari emir realised that this provided him with a strong negotiating position. Duly, he extracted a variety of concessions from the UK that it was initially unwilling to give.[31] Since the millennium, though the monarchies were keen to invest in the UK not least because it was simply perceived as a safe long-term bet, an awareness was building that the UK needed investment perhaps more than the monarchies needed to invest in the UK.[32]

This was promptly recognised by Downing Street. In 2010, the government launched the so-called 'Gulf Initiative', aimed at increasing the strength, breadth and depth of its relationship with the Gulf.[33] Rather than a formal strategy, the Initiative was a statement of intent aimed at providing a formal framework to support increased contacts with the creation of a commercial diplomacy project to promote UK interests in the region and the position of defence special adviser to the Middle East. The Gulf Initiative sought to harness the willingness of the GCC states to invest in and increase their involvement with the UK and to tie them yet further into the UK economy. The Gulf Initiative inaugurated a phase of intense exchange of official visits by ministerial delegations and formally acknowledged the centrality of the Gulf in the network of the UK's alliances in the MENA region, to the satisfaction of the monarchies. These strengthened bonds would soon be called into question, as UK–GCC relations came under the test of the 2011 Arab uprisings (Table 4.1).

Table 4.1 Significant outward and inward visits 2010–13[a]

Outward (to Gulf)	Inward (from Gulf)
Over 230 outward visits by ministers from all government departments since 2010, including: • Four visits to the Gulf by the current UK prime minister since 2010 • State visit by the queen in November 2010 to Oman and the UAE • Visit by the prince of Wales and the duchess of Cornwall in March 2013 to Saudi Arabia, Jordan, Qatar, and Oman.	Over 100 inward visits from senior Gulf interlocutors including: • Inward visit by the emir of Qatar in October 2010 • Inward visit by the emir of Kuwait in November 2012 • Inward visit by the president of the United Arab Emirates in April–May 2013 • Inward visit by the king of Bahrain in November 2012 and August 2013.

[a]Table taken from: House of Commons Foreign Affairs Committee, 'The UK's relations with Saudi Arabia and Bahrain'. Fifth Report of Session 2013–14, Vol.1, 22 November 2013, www.parliament. ul/business/committees-a-z/commons-select/foreign-affairs

Arab Spring

Amid flourishing UK–GCC relations, in December 2010 the Arab Spring erupted. While Qatar saw this as a once-in-a-generation opportunity to increase its influence in the region and support the revolutions, all other Gulf monarchies greeted the upheavals with deep and abiding trepidation. The UK government position mirrored that of most GCC states, initially greeting the Arab Spring with consternation.[34] However, Her Majesty's Government was caught on the horns of a traditional foreign policy dilemma, stuck between wanting to support existing elites with whom the government had working relations in the name of wider British foreign policy goals and a desire to be 'on the right side of history'.[35] This dilemma was exposed right from the beginning of the uprisings.

In February 2011, British Prime Minister David Cameron addressed the Kuwait National Parliament declaring that people in the MENA region were as entitled to civil rights and freedoms as British citizens were and that it was misleading to consider autocratic regimes a prerequisite for stability in the region.[36] Cameron was, of course, soon pilloried for giving this speech with a retinue of arms salesman in tow during this visit, symbolising support for precisely the kind of autocracy in Kuwait that he was verbally critiquing. Moreover, it should not be forgotten that the six GCC countries combined represented over 50 percent of the market for UK arms at that time.[37] Nor is there any sign of this trend stopping. Saudi Arabia has long been a critically significant client. In 2007, the UK and Saudi Arabia signed two defence agreements – the Saudi-British Defence Cooperation Programme and the Salem Project – and in the following five years the UK granted export licenses for over £4 billion worth of defence equipment.[38]

Such sales struck at the core of the UK's Arab Spring foreign policy dilemma when it was alleged that equipment sold by the UK was used by Saudi Arabia in suppressing protests in Bahrain in 2011.[39] This prompted an enquiry into the UK's relationship with Saudi Arabia and Bahrain by the House of Commons Foreign Affairs Committee (FAC), a decision met with considerable agitation in Manama and Riyadh. The Saudi ambassador in London, Prince Mohammed bin Nawaf Al Saud, informed the BBC that his government was 'insulted'.[40] The context for such reaction was a previous report compiled by the FAC looking into 'British Foreign Policy and the Arab Spring', released in July 2012, that advised the government to learn the lessons from the 'revolutions' and apply them to 'its relations with other Arab and Gulf states, … that are actively resisting reform, by encouraging democratic and liberalising reforms'.[41] Despite the worries expressed by the UK's Gulf allies, the FAC did go forward in compiling the inquiry on the UK's relations with Saudi Arabia and Bahrain, but its conclusions were markedly different from those reached the year before. In fact, the new report, released in November 2013, emphasised the importance of the UK's relations with the two Gulf powers, and approved the government's approach of 'gradual [political] reform based on participation and consent'.[42] This change of tone is the result of assiduous damage-limitation exercises by the government that sought to water-down criticism to benefit continued Gulf engagement.[43]

Nevertheless, despite the best efforts of British diplomats and ministers (including two visits by David Cameron in 2012), the Saudis decided not to revive the annual 'Two Kingdoms Dialogue', which lapsed in 2011. In addition, as indicated in the FAC report, Bahrain threatened to withdraw from defence cooperation with the UK in 2011.[44]

Ultimately, the assiduous courting of the monarchies paid off for the government. By October 2012, the UK had signed a new defence cooperation accord (DCA) with Bahrain, that included British training of Bahraini police in riot control, and won public praise from the Bahraini Crown Prince. But Cameron's courting of, for example, the Bahraini government allowed for Britain to not only boost its relations with counterparts in Manama but to offer 'friendly' critiques. The 2013 FAC report acknowledged both the allegations of widespread human rights abuses and the version of the Bahraini government: that opposition groups were not pro-democracy but violent and inspired by Iran and its sectarian agenda.[45]

But there were limits. Regarding the protests that swept the oil-rich, Shia-majority Eastern Province of Saudi Arabia, the UK refrained from addressing them *tout-court*. These markedly anti-regime protests, centred on the Shia cities of Awwamiyya and Qatif and inspired by the same grievances protested by Bahraini Shias, were likewise blamed by Riyadh on Iranian interferences in stirring up the discontented Shia population, allegedly with the intent of destabilising the Gulf monarchies and extending its influence in the region.[46]

Although not directly threatened by popular uprisings, the UAE was also irritated with the UK's handling of turmoil in the Middle East and North Africa (MENA) region. The Emiratis were particularly concerned that Islamists groups like the Muslim Brotherhood would take advantage of the political chaos to entrench themselves across the region.[47] Long-regarded as a destabilising and hostile force by elites in Abu Dhabi, when the Brotherhood won the Egyptian and Tunisian elections in 2012, the UAE, together with Saudi Arabia, led efforts supporting opposition movements including heavily backing the Egyptian military coup against the government in 2013.[48]

In this context, UAE leaders were concerned that several Brotherhood-affiliated dissidents sought and received refuge in the UK, benefiting from the freedom of expression guaranteed by the UK's democratic system.[49] Already in the 1990s, London had become a destination for Arab Islamist dissidents – mainly from Algeria, Egypt and, Yemen – bent on removing their own governments, earning the contemptuous nickname of 'Londonistan'.[50] Decades later, members of the Egyptian Brotherhood fled to the UK after the July 2013 coup and subsequent crackdown against the organisation. Even the former foreign affairs secretary for the Brotherhood's Freedom and Justice Party Muhammad Soudan was sentenced, in absentia, to 12 years in prison by an Egyptian court and fled to Windsor just before military officials raided his home in Alexandria.[51] It seems that the UK was a destination of choice not only for its past record of tolerating Islamist dissidents but also because it had given an impression of embracing the protest movements.

Emirati leaders raised these issues with British counterparts in June 2012. In a meeting with David Cameron, the Crown Prince of Abu Dhabi and *de facto* leader of the country, Sheikh Mohammed bin Zayed Al Nahyan, complained about the complacent tone with which the British public media, the BBC, was covering the Brotherhood.[52] Some reports of the meeting indicate that the UAE leader leveraged, in return for a tougher approach on Islamists, the possibility of lucrative deals including expanding Emirati investment in Britain, allowing British Petroleum (BP) to bid for a share in Abu Dhabi's oil, a potential £6 billion Typhoon fighter jet deal, and further deepening of the intelligence and military relationship.[53] What is clear is that a few months later BP was temporarily excluded from bidding for an extension to onshore oil concessions in the Gulf, in what was widely interpreted as a sign of dissatisfaction with the UK and EU's continuing dialogue with the Egyptian Brotherhood.[54] Also, at the end of 2013, the UAE declined to buy the Typhoon fighter jets.[55] In January 2014, it was confirmed that several leaders of the Emirati Brotherhood (Al Islah) had received political asylum in London and four months later dozens of British military advisers to the UAE armed forces were sent back when their contracts were not renewed.[56] Finally, the pressure mounted to the point that the Cameron government commissioned a review of the Muslim Brotherhood's activity in Britain with the possibility of eventually changing the policy towards the group. The review was led by John Jenkins, then Britain's ambassador to Saudi Arabia. In November of the same year, the UAE designated dozens of organisations, allegedly tied to the Muslim Brotherhood, as terrorist groups. The list included several UK-based organisations such as the Federation of Islamic Organisations, Muslim Association of Britain, and the charity Islamic Relief UK, which was occasionally involved in projects with the British government. However, despite such clear signals coming from Abu Dhabi, the Jenkins report, published after long hesitation out of concern that it could further irritate the Emiratis, did not designate the Brotherhood as a terrorist organisation.[57]

Making matters worse, the UK played a major role in the negotiations and ultimate signing of the Joint Comprehensive Plan of Action (JCPOA – aka the Iranian nuclear deal) with the government in Tehran in July 2015. After the nuclear deal, the UK and Iran took initiatives to improve their bilateral relations: the UK reopened its embassy in Tehran and Iran re-established its representation in London in August 2015.[58] The British government subsequently encouraged British banks and companies to do business with Iran – especially in the energy sector – including by confronting setbacks caused by primary and other sanctions being still in place in the US.[59] These moves did not sit well with Britain's Arab allies in the Gulf, in particular those most hostile to Iran: Saudi Arabia, Bahrain and the UAE. Reports indicate that 'the UAE was disturbed by Britain's uncritical acceptance of the Geneva agreement on Iran's nuclear ambitions',[60] while Saudi Arabia's ambassador to Britain branded the rapprochement with Iran as a 'dangerous gamble'.[61] From its side, the UK government insisted that the negotiations and the deal were exclusively related to neutralising Iran's nuclear weapons potential and did not deal with regional geopolitics.[62] Additionally, the government leveraged the fact that it had a staunch reputation as a hawk when it came to sanctions on Iran.[63]

Feeling marginalised by the international agreement with Iran, and alarmed by the reticence of President Obama in keeping the US in its traditional role as a security guarantor of the Gulf, the GCC countries were seeking a new level of commitment on the part of the UK to deter what they perceived as Iran's hegemonic ambitions following the nuclear deal. It was hard security and defence cooperation they were after, and from there the UK–GCC relations started to overcome the many post-revolutionary controversies.

Back to the future

Even before signing the *ad interim* nuclear agreement with Iran in 2013, the UK had gradually scaled up its already substantial defence cooperation with the GCC countries. The moves were intended to reassure the monarchies worried about an emboldened Iran and its attempts to exert influence in Iraq, Syria, Lebanon, Yemen, and the GCC itself. The centrepiece of such UK efforts was the announcement of the establishment of a 'permanent' naval base in Bahrain, which heralded a range of headlines about the UK's return to 'East of Suez'.[64] Though this sounds grandiose, the UK's Maritime Component Command (UKMCC) had long been based at Al Jufair, and the UK policy amounted to erecting a few concrete walls on existing facilities such as at the Mina-Salman Naval Support Facility (NSF). Nevertheless, these symbolic efforts as well as the remarks of then-Foreign Secretary Philip Hammond in 2014 that 'Your security is our security' reinforced the perception of a growing British role in the region.[65]

At the end of 2012, David Cameron signed a long-term defence partnership with the UAE involving increasing the number of joint military exercises, and a commitment to invest in the British military presence in the UAE, including the intention to upgrade the UK presence the Al Minhad air base in Dubai, where a Royal Air Force squadron was stationed.[66] British military officials also became increasingly involved in training efforts in Saudi Arabia, Kuwait, Qatar, and Oman, where army personnel are near-permanently based. The creation of the defence advisor for the Middle East (essentially, a Gulf-focused region-spanning defence attaché) was important in seeing through these changes, providing a single senior point of contact for Gulf leadership. Otherwise, these measures undertaken to strengthen defence cooperation were accompanied by multiple reassurances about the UK's commitment to Gulf security. This commitment made it to the official government documents through the 2015 'National Security Strategy and Strategic Defence and Security Review', where Gulf security was treated as central to British national security interests.[67] Similarly, in 2015 London's Whitehall started working on a 'Gulf Strategy', a roadmap for broadening the already strong defence and security relations into a wider set of engagements, prioritising the UK's prosperity agenda in the region. Analysing these developments both in light of the contingency of UK–GCC relations and of the international context, it could be argued that the resolve to underpin Gulf security was embraced both out of necessity and of desire, including as a way to counter-balance the UK's support for the Iran deal and to demonstrate the UK's commitment to the preservation of monarchical regimes against the revolutionary forces sweeping across the region.

When a small majority of UK citizens voted to leave the European Union in the June 2016 'Brexit' referendum, it represented a watershed moment for the UK's international relations. Soon after the UK government accelerated its efforts in reaching out to Gulf partners. In fact, the referendum result immediately raised concerns among the British business community about the future of the UK's economy outside of the European single market, given that the EU has been the first among the UK's trading partners and among the major sources of investments.[68] A way to meet such concerns for the government was to promote the policy of a 'global Britain' by easing barriers to economic exchanges with other partners around the world.[69] The GCC countries, due to the longstanding relations, their unique financial capabilities, and the coincidental political opportunities for partnership, were natural interlocutors. Indeed, by some estimates, in 2015 UK exports to the GCC stood at roughly £22 billion, a figure that exceeded British exports to China and India, and UK businesses won £11.2 billion worth of contracts across the Gulf.[70] In December of the following year, the Foreign Secretary Boris Johnson delivered a speech in Manama titled 'Britain is back East of Suez' regretting the decision of a few decades before to leave the protectorates.[71] A few weeks later, Theresa May was the first ever British prime minister to attend a GCC summit in Bahrain, an occasion that definitively marked the UK government's intention of scaling up Britain's role in the Gulf. The post-summit joint statement addressed the Syrian and Yemeni issue, with the UK firmly standing behind positions long held in the GCC, and announced a UK–GCC shared intent to deter Iran's predatory behaviour in the region.[72] Moreover, the parties pledged to start establishing joint economic and trade committees to conclude a free trade agreement (FTA) between Britain and the GCC.

The reactions to the prospect of a UK–GCC FTA in the region were positive: commentators highlighted the positive coincidence that put the UK in the frame of mind to reach out to the region at a time when all the regional countries were pursuing wide-ranging plans for economic diversification.[73] In fact, since a historic peak in June 2014, when Brent crude was sold at $115.19 per barrel, the oil price fell to below $30 in January 2016, a twelve-year nadir, and, although partially recovering since, the general consensus was that it would stay 'lower for longer'.[74] This trend vigorously pushed all GCC countries to embrace new economic strategies that would strongly point to diversification away from oil and gas dependence. The UK was widely considered as well-positioned to offer technical expertise and support to the Gulf allies as they attempt this historical transition. By the same token, it was reported that the UK Foreign Office had identified £30 billion worth of opportunities for British business in the region in areas including defence, education, healthcare, technology, energy and financial services.[75]

In Qatar, host of the FIFA World Cup in 2022, opportunities were in the infrastructure sector, including the construction of the first underground system, major roads, hospitality and sports facilities, but also in the organisation and management of the event.[76] Saudi Arabia, carrying on an all-encompassing diversification operation, has clearly expressed its interest regarding the FTA via a speech of its foreign minister Adel Al Jubeir to British parliamentarians and direct comments of the Saudi Deputy Crown Prince Mohammed bin Salman with Prime Minister Theresa May on the sidelines of the G20 summit in China.[77] Editorials in *The Times of Oman* pointed to the potential benefits of an FTA with the UK, the largest foreign investor in the sultanate.[78] The UAE Embassy in the UK endorsed comments that a UK–GCC deal was 'to fast track UAE diversification'.[79] Evidently, the deal might also encourage further investments from GCC SWFs in the UK, given that the SWFs were established with the clear intent of supporting diversification. In fact, between the end of 2016 and 2017, the relations between the UK and the GCC monarchies were marching ahead with full steam in geopolitical, security and economic terms once more.

Adding to the Brexit strategic shock, the June 2017 severe blockade of Qatar by its three closest neighbours (Saudi Arabia, Bahrain and the UAE) and Egypt, took the international community by surprise. It soon became apparent that the quartet wanted isolation not escalation, and a new norm in the Gulf seemed to be emerging. In this new world, external relations remained curiously unaffected. While, once upon a time, the British government would have been able to influence the dispute into settlement, on this occasion, London was never close to acting as an intermediary. Deemed to be permanently looking for opportunities to sell more 'UK PLC' goods and services to all of the monarchies, Britain was not seen as impartial by any side. Also, it had neither the clout to bring the sides together nor the spare bandwidth in a parliament gazing into the Gordianly complex Brexit abyss to launch any initiatives. Ultimately, the UK stood idly by as the Gulf faced its biggest crisis since the invasion of Kuwait in 1990, a testament to how, during the past decades, power relations between all sides have reshuffled.

Enduring engagement

A lot of water has gone under the bridge for the UK and its allies on the Arabian Peninsula. The colonial experience for the monarchies under British suzerainty was relatively positive. Certainly, the Crown was no attentive overarching power: London and Bombay cared more about regional stability than local development. But the leaderships of the monarchies were appreciative to London for anointing them – and not their rivals – as official leaders. Though such leaders in the smaller monarchies could and did drive a hard bargain with the Crown, there was no mistaking who was the preeminent partner in the nineteenth century and well into the twentieth century.

With the discovery of oil in the monarchies that was unusually cheap to produce, Britain's interest in the Gulf increased markedly, and London tenaciously sought to hive off as many local markets as it could. After the world wars, the oil-based importance of the region only increased, and Britain remained the Gulf protector until 1971. The Gulf and Britain then entered a new era of relations. The UK retained an importance in the region, particularly in matters of defence sales and training, but wider trade relations were diversified as the UK became just one of many viable partners, struggling amid stiff competition for contracts. Relations became a partnership of equals.

The liberation of Kuwait demonstrated that the UK was still a relevant actor, particularly in the defence space where the monarchies were evidently lacking. But it was the US that demonstrated its indispensability in 1990 and 1991. The UK certainly increased defence sales and training, but it was an add-on to American power. By the time of the 2003 Iraq invasion, the tables were beginning to turn. The monarchies were flush with cash, and looking for safe investment boltholes. London managed to attract the lion's share of investments. Along with increasing energy imports from the Gulf, notably LNG from Qatar, the monarchies were developing a real stake in the British economy. The opportunity cost for the monarchies to invest elsewhere was minimal: investing in Paris, Berlin, or Washington would equally do. But for the UK, losing such investment to Paris, Berlin, or Washington was a zero-sum game.

With the financial crisis at the end of the decade, Britain was one of many Western nations desperate for financial investment to prop up an ailing economy. This represented the tripping of the scales even more. The monarchies skilfully used their leverage for potential investment or potential defence acquisitions to extract a range of agreements from London relating to dampening criticism of human rights concerns, offering wider-ranging defence-orientated agreements, and subtle shifts in UK foreign policy towards antagonistic actors. Such an argument must not go too far. The UK still led the JCPOA, demonstrating that Downing Street would still drive through a foreign policy against the wishes of the monarchies. And monarchs in the Gulf had long extracted concessions from the British government going back to the early twentieth century.

Nonetheless there is a sense emerging that, particularly with Britain's large-scale defence-led reorientation to the Gulf, captured by Hammond's phrase 'your security is our security' and in British national security documentation, tactical concessions are heading towards strategic ones. It is certainly to Britain's benefit to safeguard the Gulf monarchies. In purely mercantile terms, the energy and investment are just too big to ignore and is worthy of securing. But restoring a 'permanent' military base in Bahrain and significantly deepening military cooperation with other monarchies must be decisions being made for the right reasons. After all, a permanent military base is the sort of architecture that, just like the grand embassies across the GCC capitals, can send messages about the current and future nature of the relations between London and the Gulf.

If these policies are cool and calculated decisions by British leadership to safeguard Britain's long-term future, then this is less problematic. But if such decisions are emanating from a short-term reflex for more investment at the behest of headstrong monarchies, then this is a grim comment on the nature of British policymaking, and is unlikely to undergird stable long-term relations.

Notes

1 J. E. Peterson, 'Britain and the Gulf', in *The Persian Gulf in History*, ed. Lawrence G. Potter (New York; Basingstoke: Palgrave Macmillan, 2009), 278–9.
2 Lawrence G. Potter, 'Introduction', ibid., ed. Lawrence G. Potter (New York; Basingstoke: Palgrave Macmillan, 2009), 13.
3 J. E. Peterson, 'Britain and the Gulf', ibid., ed. Lawrence G. Potter (New York; Basingstoke: Palgrave Macmillan, 2009), 279–80.
4 See James Onley, *The Arabian Frontier of the British Raj: Merchants, Rulers, and the British in the Nineteenth-Century Gulf* (Oxford: Oxford University Press, 2007).
5 Rosemarie Said Zahlan, *The Making of the Modern Gulf States: Kuwait, Bahrain, Qatar, the United Arab Emirates and Oman*, Updated ed. (Reading: Ithaca Press, 1998), 22.
6 Onley, *The Arabian Frontier of the British Raj: Merchants, Rulers, and the British in the Nineteenth-Century Gulf*.
7 Khaldoun Hasan Naqeeb, *Society and State in the Gulf and Arab Peninsula: A Different Perspective* (London: Routledge, 1990), 59.
8 David E. Long, *The United States and Saudi Arabia: Ambivalent Allies* (Boulder; London: Westview Press, 1985), 10–16, 33–6, 73–5, 101–7.
9 Barry Rubin, *The Great Powers in the Middle East 1941–1947* (London: Frank Cass, 1980), 18–34.
10 Anoushiravan Ehteshami, *Dynamics of Change in the Persian Gulf: Political Economy, War and Revolution* (London: Routledge, 2013), 26–9.
11 W. Fain, *American Ascendance and British Retreat in the Persian Gulf Region* (New York: Palgrave Macmillan, 2008), 45–77.
12 On the nationalisation of industries see Onn Winckler, 'Gulf Monarchies as Rentier States: The Nationalization Policies of the Labor Force', in *Middle East Monarchies: The Challenge of Modernity*, ed. Joseph Kostiner (Boulder: Lynne Rienner, 2000).
13 James Onley, 'Britain's Informal Empire in the Gulf 1820–1971', *Journal of Social Affairs* 22, no. 87 (Fall 2005): 29–45.
14 See examples in Qatar and Kuwait Jill Crystal, *Oil and Politics in the Gulf: Rulers and Merchants in Kuwait and Qatar* (Cambridge: Cambridge University Press, 1995), 62–6, 112–33.
15 Malcolm Yapp, *The Near East since the First World War* (Harlow: Lomgman Inc., 1991), 205.
16 Clive Jones and John Stone, 'Britain and the Arabian Gulf: New Perspectives on Strategic Influence', *International Relations* 13, no. 4 (1997): 2–6.
17 Mark Phythian, *The Politics of British Arms Sales since 1964: To Secure Our Rightful Share* (Manchester University Press, 2000), 202–66.
18 Jones and Stone, 'Britain and the Arabian Gulf: New Perspectives on Strategic Influence', 11–16.
19 Phythian, *The Politics of British Arms Sales since 1964: To Secure Our Rightful Share*, 260.
20 Quoted in Jones and Stone, 'Britain and the Arabian Gulf: New Perspectives on Strategic Influence', 7.
21 'Britain and the Arabian Gulf: New Perspectives on Strategic Influence', 7–8.
22 F. Gregory Gause III. *The International Relations of the Persian Gulf* (Cambridge University Press, 2009), 182.
23 Onn Winckler, 'Can the GCC Weather the Economic Meltdown?' *Middle East Quarterly* 17 (June 2010).
24 Rory Miller, *Desert Kingdoms to Global Powers* (Yale University Press, 2016), 140.
25 Qatar was a source of at least £20 billion worth of investments into Britain in the period 2005–13, see Francesca Astorri, 'Qatar Said to Mull New $23bn UK Investments', *Arabian Business*, 20 June 2013. In 2016, the Saudi Minister of

Commerce and Investment Majid bin Abdullah Al-Qassabi declared that total Saudi investments in Britain amounted to £60 billion, see 'Saudi Investments in Britain Reach 60 billion Pounds', *Arab News*, 24 July 2016, http://www.arabnews.com/node/958591/economy
26 Paul Vallely, 'A Royal Welcome for the 50bn Emir Buying Britain Brick by Brick', *The Independent*, 26 October 2010, http://www.independent.co.uk/news/uk/home-news/a-royal-welcome-for-the-16350bn-emir-buying-britain-brick-by-brick-2117471.html
27 'Strengthening a Long Friendship: David Cameron, UK Prime Minister, on Trade Links with the GCC', *Oxford Business Group*, 29 November 2012, http://www.oxfordbusinessgroup.com/news/strengthening-long-friendship-65-david-cameron-uk-prime-minister-trade-links-gc
28 Roberts, David B. 'British National Interest in the Gulf: Rediscovering a Role?.' *International Affairs* 90, no. 3 (2014): 663–77.
29 Energy consumption in the UK (London: Department of Energy and Climate Change, July 2013).
30 'Physical Imports and Exports of Gas', DUKES (London: Department of Energy and Climate Change, July 2013). Andrew Ward and David Shappard, 'Qatar Diplomatic Spat Reignites UK Gas Supplies Fears', *The Financial Times* 12 June 2017.
31 Rosemarie Said Zahlan, *The Creation of Qatar* (London; New York: Croom Helm 1979), 65.
32 House of Commons Foreign Affairs Committee, 'The UK's Relations with Saudi Arabia and Bahrain'. Fifth Report of Session 2013–14, Vol. 1, 22 November 2013. www.parliament.ul/business/committees-a-z/commons-select/foreign-affairs
33 'UK Relations with the GCC Region: A Broadening Partnership', speech of Foreign Office Minister Lord Howell at the 'GCC and the City Conference' on 20 June 2012, Foreign & Commonwealth Office website, https://www.gov.uk/government/speeches/uk-relations-with-the-gcc-region-a-broadening-partnership
34 See Leech, Philip, and Jamie Gaskarth. 'British Foreign Policy and the Arab Spring.' *Diplomacy & Statecraft* 26, no.1 (2015): 139–60.
35 Gareth Stansfield and Saul Kelly, 'On the Right Side of History? The Dilemmas of British Policy Towards the Gulf Arab States', in Niblock T., Hook S. (eds) *The United States and the Gulf: Towards a Reassessment of Gulf Commitments and Alignments* (Berlin: Gerlach, 2015).
36 Nicholas Watt, 'Cameron Says UK Prejudiced for Believing Muslims Cannot Manage Democracy', *The Guardian*, 22 February 2011, https://www.theguardian.com/politics/2011/feb/22/david-cameron-uk-muslims-democracy
37 International transfers of major weapons 2011–16. Source: SIPRI Arms Transfers Database (20 February 2017).
38 'United Kingdom Strategic Export Controls Annual Report 2012', Stockholm International Peace Research Institute, 12 July 2013, https://www.sipri.org/node/2563
39 Emily Duggan, 'Britain Accused of Hypocrisy Over Arab Arms Sales', *The Independent*, 15 January 2012, http://www.independent.co.uk/news/uk/home-news/britain-accused-of-hypocrisy-over-arab-arms-sales-6289847.html
40 Frank Gardner, 'Saudi Arabia "Insulted" by UK Inquiry', 15 October 2012, www.bbc.co.uk/news/uk-politics
41 House of Commons Foreign Affairs Committee, 'British Foreign Policy and the "Arab Spring"'. Second Report of Session 2012–13, 19 July 2012, www.parliament.ul/business/committees-a-z/commons-select/foreign-affairs
42 FAC report, 'The UK's relations with Saudi Arabia and Bahrain', 76.
43 Government response to the House of Commons Foreign Affairs Committee's fifth report of session 2013–2014 (HC88), Foreign and Commonwealth Office, 22 January 2014, https://www.gov.uk/government/publications/government-response-to-the-house-of-commons-foreign-affairs-committees-fifth-report-of-session-2013-2014-hc88

44 FAC report, 'The UK's Relations with Saudi Arabia and Bahrain'. Oral evidence taken before the Foreign Affairs Committee on Tuesday 22 January 2013, Q1, witness: Jane Kinninmont, Senior Research Fellow, Chatham House.
45 FAC report, 'The UK's Relations with Saudi Arabia and Bahrain'.
46 Toby Matthiesen, *Sectarian Gulf: Bahrain, Saudi Arabia, and the Arab Spring that Wasn't* (Stanford University Press, 2013).
47 David B. Roberts, 'Mosque and State: The United Arab Emirates' Secular Foreign Policy', *Foreign Affairs* (18 March 2016).
48 Eugenio Dacrema. 'New Emerging Balances in the Post-Arab Spring: The Muslim Brotherhood and the Gulf Monarchies', *ISPI Analysis* 155 (2013): 1–3.
49 Abubakr al-Shamahi, 'UK Safe Haven No More?' *The New Arab*, 5 November 2014, https://www.alaraby.co.uk/english/features/2014/11/6/uk-safe-haven-no-more
50 Stephen Ulph, 'Londonistan', *Terrorism Monitor* (The Jamestown Foundation), I, no. 12 (25 Feb 2004): 3.
51 Abubakr al-Shamahi, 'UK Safe Haven No More?'.
52 Ramesh Randeep, 'UAE told UK: Crack Down on Muslim Brotherhood or Lose Arms Deals', *The Guardian*, 6 November 2015, https://www.theguardian.com/world/2015/nov/06/uae-told-uk-crack-down-on-muslim-brotherhood-or-lose-arms-deals
53 Randeep, Ramesh, 'UAE Told UK: Crack Down on Muslim Brotherhood or Lose Arms Deals'.
54 Raissa Kasolowsky and Daniel Fineren, 'BP's UAE Rebuff Shows British Lustre Faded in the Gulf', *Reuters*, 30 August 2012, http://in.reuters.com/article/bp-uae-sidelined-idINL6E8JSF6420120830
55 Sean Farrell, 'BAE Systems Fails to Win £6bn Contract to Supply Typhoon Fighters to UAE', *The Guardian*, 19 December 2013, https://www.theguardian.com/business/2013/dec/19/bae-systems-fails-contract-typhoon-figthers-uae
56 Rory Donaghy, 'Muslim Brotherhood Review: A Tale of UK–UAE Relations' *Middle East Eye*, 17 December 2015, http://www.middleeasteye.net/news/muslim-brotherhood-review-tale-uk-uae-relations-378120043
57 House of Commons, 'Muslim Brotherhood Review: Main Findings', 17 December 2015, https://www.gov.uk/government/uploads/system/uploads/attachment_data/file/486932/Muslim_Brotherhood_Review_Main_Findings.pdf
58 Julian Borger, 'British Embassy in Iran Reopens', *The Guardian*, 23 August 2015, https://www.theguardian.com/politics/2015/aug/23/british-embassy-iran-tehran-reopens,
59 'Cameron Steps in After Barclays Blocks Trade Deals with Iran', *The Week*, 14 March 2016, http://www.theweek.co.uk/70542/cameron-steps-in-after-barclays-blocks-trade-deals-with-iran
60 David Blair, 'Britain's Ambitions in the Gulf Suffer Blow as UAE Rejects Typhoon Deal', *The Telegraph*, 20 December 2013, www.telegraph.co.uk/news/worldnews/middleeast
61 Andrew Critchlow, 'David Cameron's Debacle a Sign of Britain's Declining Arabian Influence', 19 December 2013, *The Telegraph*, www.telegraph.co.uk/finance/newsbysector/industry/defence
62 David Cameron, François Hollande, and Angela Merkel, 'Cameron, Hollande and Merkel: Why We Support the Iran Deal', *The Washington Post*, 10 September 2015.
63 'UK not Aligning with Tehran, Deal Keeps Iran From Nukes — Cameron', *The Times of Israel*, 18 July 2015, http://www.timesofisrael.com/uk-not-aligning-with-tehran-deal-keeps-iran-from-nukes-cameron
64 Stansfield, Gareth, and Saul Kelly. 'A Return to East of Suez?' Briefing Paper, Royal United Service Institute, April 2013.
65 Richard Spencer, 'Britain Returns "East of Suez" with Permanent Royal Navy Base in Gulf', *The Telegraph*, 6 December 2014.

66 Moign Khawaja, 'UK, UAE Enter Defence Partnership, Discuss Other Deals', *ArabianGazette*, 6 November 2012, http://www.arabiangazette.com/Britain-uae-defence partnership
67 HM Government, 'National Security Strategy and Strategic Defence and Security Review 2015 First Annual Report 2016', December 2016.
68 Dominic Webb and Matthew Keep, 'In Brief: UK–EU Economic Relations', Briefing Paper Number 06091, House of Commons Library, 13 June 2016.
69 'Theresa May's Brexit Speech: A Global Britain', *The Spectator*, 17 January 2017, https://blogs.spectator.co.uk/2017/01/theresa-mays-brexit-speech-global-britain
70 Speech by Dr. Raghavan Seetharaman, CEO of Doha Bank, at the International Banking Summit 'IABS 2017', 2 May 2017, London Hilton, London, UK.
71 Foreign and Commonwealth Office, Foreign Secretary speech: 'Britain is back East of Suez', 9 December 2016, https://www.gov.uk/government/speeches/foreign-secretary-speech-britain-is-back-east-of-suez
72 Foreign and Commonwealth Office, 'Gulf Co-operation Council – United Kingdom, First Summit: Joint Communiqué', 7 December 2016.
73 Aruba Khalid and Omar Shariff, 'Brexit: An Opportunity for the GCC', *Gulf News*, 15 January 2017, http://gulfnews.com/opinion/thinkers/brexit-an-opportunity-for-the-gcc-1.1962211
74 Jillian Ambrose, 'Oil Prices may Have "Bottomed Out", Says IEA', *The Telegraph*, 11 March 2016, http://www.telegraph.co.uk/business/2016/03/11/iea-oil-prices-may-have-bottomed-out/ ; Gawdat Bahgat, 'Lower for Longer: Saudi Arabia Adjusts to the New Oil Era', Middle East Policy Council, 9 September 2016, http://www.mepc.org/lower-longer-saudi-arabia-adjusts-new-oil-era
75 Maher Ghanma and Daniel Jones, 'A New Chapter for UK–Gulf Trade and Investment', *DLA Piper*, 22 December 2016, https://www.dlapiper.com/en/uk/insights/publications/2016/12/a-new-chapter-for-uk-gulf-trade/
76 Satish Kanady, 'Post-Brexit Trade: Qatar & UK Plan Joint Committee', *The Peninsula*, 29 March 2017, https://thepeninsulaqatar.com/article/29/03/2017/Post-Brexit-trade-Qatar-UK-plan-joint-committee
77 Omar Bahlaiwa, 'Britain has a Golden Opportunity to Leapfrog the EU and Secure a Free Trade Deal with the Gulf States', *City A.M.*, 10 October 2016, http://www.cityam.com/250987/britain-has-golden-opportunity-leapfrog-eu-and-secure-free
78 Syed Haitham, 'Oman Needs to Push for Free Trade Pact with UK in Post Brexit Era', *Times of Oman*, 30 April 2017, http://timesofoman.com/article/108007/Business/Oman-needs-to-push-for-free-trade-pact-with-UK-in-post-Brexit-era
79 'UK's Post-Brexit GCC Deal "To Fast Track UAE Diversification"', Embassy of the United Arab Emirates in London website, 13 April 2017, http://www.uae-embassy.ae/Embassies/uk/news/2017/04/13/9710

5 French policy in the Gulf
The other Western ally

Jean-Loup Samaan

Although the United Kingdom (UK) and the United States (US) are the traditional Western powers described as the key external players in the Arabian Peninsula, France has also been nurturing close ties, for several decades, with the monarchies of the Gulf. Because of common disinterest, the regional policy of France has not attracted a significant amount of scholarship compared to that dedicated to the British and American influences in the area.[1]

This limited academic literature does not fully capture the extent of this French presence. In fact, from military cooperation to economic and cultural exchanges, successive French governments have built significant relations with the members of the Gulf Cooperation Council (GCC), which competed with, and in some cases, even surpassed those of its old colonial rival, the United Kingdom. Furthermore, despite regional changes, the partnerships that France forged in the Peninsula have endured.

In recent years, as Arab regimes feared for their survival in light of the 2011 wave of uprisings (Tunisia, Egypt, Libya, Syria, and Bahrain), these French–GCC relations did not weaken but in fact have grown stronger. This contrasted with the misfortunes of the US administration during the same period. Under the Obama presidency, the diplomatic dialogue between the US administration and its Gulf counterparts significantly deteriorated as a result of Gulf discontent on issues such as the engagement with Iran, the pivot to Asia, or support for post-Mubarak Egypt. Whereas American–Gulf relations turned bitter, those with France deepened. This was in large part the result of common security interests and similar diplomatic positions – whether on the Syrian civil war or the Iranian nuclear issue. But if these diplomatic and economic relations have persisted, they have also generated increased controversy domestically in France, where the purpose of these partnerships is misunderstood and increasingly challenged by politicians, journalists, and intellectuals.

Against that backdrop, this chapter offers a comprehensive assessment of French presence in the Gulf. It first traces the origins of this presence back to the early seventies, and its relation to French Arab policy. The second section details the ties with three of the Gulf countries – Saudi Arabia, Qatar, and the United Arab Emirates – which constitute the main partners of France in the area. In the third section, we observe the impact of Arab revolutions on French–Gulf relations. In this regard, we look at the issues such as the civil war in Syria and the Iranian nuclear conundrum where diplomatic agendas have been converging. The fourth section exposes how this policy proximity translated into cooperation in multiple sectors including trade, cultural initiatives and educational partnerships. Finally, in the fifth section, we evaluate the widening – and rather preoccupying – gap between these diplomatic arrangements and the domestic views on the Gulf inside France.

Paris' *politique arabe* and the origins of French presence in the Gulf

Prior to the 1970s, the French presence in the Gulf was very limited. This absence was mainly due to its competition with the colonial powers – Portugal, and then the United Kingdom – which dominated the region, through their early presence and treaties signed with the local emirates. Attempts were made to enhance French access to these territories. There had been French explorers, such as Jean-Baptiste Tavernier and Jean Chardin, who visited the Peninsula, starting in the seventeenth century. A consulate was even built in Muscat in 1795 but was closed in 1920 (Beguin-Billecoq 1994). Meanwhile, in what is known as modern-day Saudi Arabia, France opened its first diplomatic representation at the consulate level in Jeddah in 1841 as the country was under Ottoman rule. Subsequently, relations with the Saud family arose before the declaration of the Kingdom of Saudi Arabia in 1932: a year before, France had signed a "Treaty of understanding and friendship between the Republic of France and the Kingdom of Hijaz, Najd and other provinces" (*Traité d'entente et d'amitié entre la République française et le royaume du Hedjaz, Nedj et autres dépendances*).

In spite of these early initiatives, it was only in the late 1960s, and more significantly in the 1970s, that France would become a significant interlocutor for the Gulf kingdoms. A key event during this period was the decision in 1968 by the UK government of Harold Wilson to remove all British military forces from territories "east of Suez" – a decision based on the unsustainable financial burden of the Empire overseas (Dockrill 2002). Wilson's withdrawal led the French governments of President Charles De Gaulle (1958–69), and, later, of George Pompidou (1969–74), to assess that the vacuum left by the British government could benefit France. They then started courting the newly independent states (Kuwait, Oman, Bahrain, Qatar, and the United Arab Emirates) in addition to Saudi Arabia.

De Gaulle's foreign policy was influenced by the fallout from the Suez war in 1956 – during which France fought alongside the British and Israeli forces against the Egyptians – as well as by the end of the Algeria war in 1962. Both conflicts left a very negative image of France in the Arab world (Papamstamkou 2007, 186). Additionally, the governments of the Fourth Republic (1946–58), which preceded De Gaulle, had developed close military cooperation with Israel – including on its clandestine nuclear program (Levey 1997, 55).

In the mid-1960s, France started distancing itself from Israel and realigning its strategy towards Arab countries. De Gaulle and his successor George Pompidou designed the so-called "Arab policy of France" (*politique arabe de la France*) that was to constitute an alternative to American and British positions frequently perceived as too pro-Israel in the Arab world (Youssef 2003).

After De Gaulle, a key architect of this new policy was Michel Jobert, French foreign minister (1973–4) under the Pompidou presidency. After the 1973 war and the subsequent oil embargo by Arab monarchies, Jobert called for the establishment of a Euro–Arab dialogue gathering the League of Arab States and the European Economic Community. This dialogue aimed at building a diplomatic framework for exchanges between European and Arab countries, but it also directly, and intentionally, challenged US diplomatic primacy in the region. It infuriated Henry Kissinger, then US secretary of state, who publicly opposed Jobert's project (Bourrinet 1979). This Euro–Arab dialogue never materialized due to multiple factors. The French government failed to overcome the disagreements among its European allies regarding the mandate and goals of the dialogue; the European Economic Community proved itself unable to supervise a diplomatic initiative that remained highly politicized; finally, the American opposition undermined the efforts to Europeanize a policy towards the Arab world (Miller 2014). Nevertheless, the idea of this dialogue enhanced French visibility in the Arab world and eventually strengthened its ties with Gulf monarchies.

The "*politique arabe*" of France led governments in Paris to move closer to Arab authoritarian regimes. In Libya, France started building relations with the new ruler, the young Colonel Muammar Gadhafi. In December 1969, President Pompidou expressed his support for the revolution led by Gadhafi and called for the reinforcement of the ties between the two countries. Only a month later, in January 1970, France agreed to sell 105 Mirage fighter aircraft to Libya. Ties remained solid until the following decade when both countries found themselves on opposite sides in the civil war in Chad.

Similarly, in the late 1970s and 1980s, French governments supported Saddam Hussein's Iraq through nuclear cooperation, arms sales, and trade deals (Styan 2006). In 1975, Jacques Chirac, then prime minister of France, hosted Saddam – who was at that time the vice-president of the Revolution Command Council of Iraq – and went as far to call him a "personal friend" (Laurenson 2003). Despite Saddam's nationalization of the Iraq Petroleum Company, the French company Total did not lose its share in the new entity. The French–Iraqi relationship became a pillar of Paris' Arab policy, and as Iraq and Iran entered an eight-year war in 1980, French support to Baghdad increased. For Paris, Iraq was perceived as a counterweight to the Islamic regime of Ayatollah Khomeini.

The Gulf states shared this view and were also invested in the Iraqi regime in its war against Iran. This strategy brought the monarchies closer to France. The slow rapprochement between Paris and the Arab kingdoms in the Peninsula was therefore the result of two factors: the French tactic to present itself as a Western alternative to American and British patronage, combined with the development of common interests in the Middle East (in Lebanon or vis-à-vis revolutionary Iran).

If these relations were forged in the 1970s as a way for France to capitalize on the declining British influence in the area, they deepened after the Iraqi invasion in 1990, as part of the GCC members' increasing reliance on Western security support (Gause 2010). For Gulf officials, France frequently played the role of a balancer vis-à-vis both the United Kingdom and the United States, for instance on arms sales. For the emirates historically tied to the former British Empire, the relations with France were perceived as a means to diversify their interactions with Western powers that were eventually perceived as necessary allies for the stability of their newly established regimes (Hasbani 2014). Even after the American military and economic footprint in the Peninsula increased, in particular following the Gulf War of 1990–1, the rationale of balancing security relations between several external protectors was maintained, with France playing a significant role.

Eventually, three Gulf states became close partners of France in the region: Saudi Arabia, Qatar, and the UAE. The other Gulf countries (Kuwait, Oman, and Bahrain) developed diplomatic and trade relations, but over the following years these relations never reached the level of partnership enjoyed with the other three.

France's strategic triangle in the Gulf

Saudi Arabia, Qatar, and the United Arab Emirates constitute what can be called the "strategic triangle" of France in the Gulf. French relations with these three states trump, by far, those with the rest of the Gulf in all fields: political, military, and economic. At the same time, a triangle does not equal a regional alliance: the word stresses the fluctuating nature of France's ties with these countries and their competitive dimension.

The building of the French–Saudi partnership is usually traced back to 1967 with the first official visit to Paris of King Faisal bin Abdulaziz Al Saud, during which he met with President De Gaulle. The close personal relations between both heads of state combined with a convergence of regional interests, in particular on the Palestinian file (Almejfel 2014, 51). Later, in 1973, President Pompidou signed a series of economic and cultural agreements that broadened the scope of the bilateral exchanges (Bauchard 2015, 112).

In 1979, these relations took a new dimension. Facing the seizure of the Grand Mosque in Mecca by insurgents led by Juhayman al-Otaybi, the kingdom deployed its special forces in the holy city. After an initial and failed attempt from CIA operatives to launch the assault, Saudi commanders turned to French troops (Menoret 2008, 129). Three policemen from the Intervention Group of the National Gendarmerie headed by Captain Paul Barril were hired as coordinators and played a decisive role in defeating the terrorist group.

French support to the operation impressed the Saudi leadership and came to symbolize the closeness between the countries in the aftermath of the crisis. Following this event, Prince Sultan bin Abdulaziz, Saudi Arabia's minister of defense for 48 years (1962–2011), became the closest ally of France within the royal family (Chesnot, Malbrunot 2016, 133). Prince Sultan later proved instrumental in the strengthening of military ties between the countries. Starting in 1982, the French armed forces intensified their cooperation with their Saudi counterpart through training courses, joint exercises, and acquisition of French defense materials such as the Sawari I and Sawari II programs, which included frigates, missiles, and oil tankers commissioned by the Saudi Navy (Almejfel 2014, 98). Prince Sultan would choose French companies for arms deals – carefully balancing these sales with simultaneous American and British purchases – while leading Saudi delegations to conclude a strategic partnership in 1996 and a decade later, a defense cooperation agreement.

The latter coincided with a new reshuffling of power plays within the Saudi Kingdom that caused some troubles for the supporters of the Saudi–French relationship. The French overreliance on Prince Sultan and the Sudairi branch of the Al Saud family put Paris in a delicate position vis-à-vis King Abdullah who acceded to the throne in 2005. As relations between Abdullah and Prince Sultan were reportedly tense, French access to the royal court became more difficult (Chesnot, Malbrunot 2016, 134).

Additionally, personal relations mattered. President Nicholas Sarkozy (2007–12) enjoyed a much less friendly relationship with King Abdullah than his predecessor, Jacques Chirac. Sarkozy was perceived in Riyadh not only as a close ally of the US and Israel but, maybe more importantly, as a friend of Sheikh Hamad bin Khalifa Al Thani, then emir of neighboring Qatar. Furthermore, Sarkozy's character, usually described as impulsive, was eyed with caution by Saudi rulers (Bauchard 2015, 112). In 2011, the death of Prince Sultan, a paramount actor of the bilateral relations, left France without a strong supporter in the inner circle of the royal family. The successor to Sarkozy, Francois Hollande, elected in 2012, revived the relationship by traveling extensively to Riyadh (four times in five years). Hollande and King Salman built a close relationship that translated into new Saudi investments in French armaments – under the framework of the Saudi–French Military Contract that includes a wide range of weapon systems – and coordination on several regional issues, especially Egypt and Lebanon (Jauvert 2016).

With regards to the emirate of Qatar, its relations with France started following the independence of Doha from the United Kingdom in 1971. By 1972, a Qatari embassy was opened in Paris and two years later, the ruler, Sheikh Khalifa, visited the French capital. In 1980, Doha decided to buy French Mirage fighter aircrafts. A defense agreement was signed in 1994 and paved the way for cooperation similar to that with Saudi Arabia, which included the training of Qatari armed forces, the organization of common exercises, and multiple arms sales such as the Mirage 2000–5, MICA missiles, and Apache cruise missiles. A year later, when Sheikh Khalifa was deposed by his son Hamad, French authorities displayed their neutrality. The change of ruler did not jeopardize the nascent relationship, but it was only 12 years later that France–Qatar relations would experience a kind of golden age under the Sarkozy presidency. It lasted during Hollande's mandate as well. In particular, Hollande signed a major contract for 24 Rafale fighter aircraft purchased by the Qataris, worth 6.3 billion euros.

If French relations with Saudi Arabia and Qatar have sometimes faced challenges, the relationship with the UAE has remained stable since the creation of the federation in 1971. Political relations between French presidents and

Sheikh Zayed, the founding president of the UAE, emerged in a similar context to those with Qatar. The French–Emirati rapprochement was initially a marriage of convenience. The leadership of the newly established Arab state wanted to balance the reliance on British patronage by diversifying its security cooperation. In Paris, this posture fit well with the French plan to increase its footprint in the Peninsula.

The relationship soon focused on energy – French company Total was present in Abu Dhabi since 1939 – and defense, as evidenced by the defense agreements, signed first in 1995 and again in 2009. According to French newspaper *Le Figaro*, the clause of solidarity included in the 2009 document implied a French commitment through "all military means it has to defend the United Arab Emirates if they were under attack" (Lasserre 2009). In theory, this suggests that French authorities may extend the benefits of their nuclear deterrence to the UAE – although it was never confirmed by officials.

That same year, France announced the building of a new military base in Abu Dhabi – a first since the presidency of Charles De Gaulle. This military footprint provided evidence of the closeness between the two countries. The creation of the base also has to be put into perspective with the negotiations over the renewal of Total's oil concession for forty years. In other words, the military presence reflected France's commitment to the long-term stability of the federation (Boulanger 2011). The capital of the UAE, Abu Dhabi, also hosts two emblematic French brands. The Sorbonne University opened a campus in Al Reem Island in 2006 and the Louvre opened in November 2017.

All in all, French Gulf policy has been mostly a policy directed towards this triangle composed of Saudi Arabia, Qatar, and the UAE. Over the years, French diplomats designed a tailored policy towards these countries that emphasized common security interests. Interestingly, this policy was not affected by the Arab revolutions of 2011; on the contrary, the events triggered a strengthening of the relations. This is reflected by the contemporary convergence of their strategic agendas.

The contemporary French diplomatic agenda in the Gulf

Since the end of the Cold War, crises in the Middle East have not altered the nature of France's relations with Gulf partners, whether the Gulf war in 1991 or the Arab uprisings of 2011. In fact, they even strengthened them. On security issues, French diplomacy proved to be one of the most assertive voices among the Western partners of the GCC countries. For example, on topics such as the Iranian nuclear issue and the Syrian conflict, French officials – whether during the Sarkozy presidency or Hollande's mandate – adopted a hard line which concurred with the Gulf positions (Samaan, May 2013).

Like other Western governments, France did not anticipate the 2011 uprisings in the Arab world and found itself in a fragile position as it supported political regimes such as Zine El Abidine Ben Ali's in Tunisia. President Sarkozy promptly condemned Libya's Gadhafi and Syria's Bashar al-Assad but remained cautious on the troubles within the Kingdom of Bahrain. The French authorities initially suspended exports to Bahrain – which were insignificant to begin with – following the regime's use of violence against protestors (AFP 2011). Since then, the Ministry of Foreign Affairs in Paris has only issued occasional statements expressing its "concern" over the latest developments. This caution may have been driven by the French government's desire not to condemn a regime that was increasingly supported by Saudi Arabia (Mikail 2011).

In Libya, it was the activism of Gulf kingdoms within the Arab League, and in particular Qatar, that paved the way for the military intervention led by France and the United Kingdom in March 2011. Later, the UAE and Qatar contributed to NATO's Unified Protector operation, with ground and air support. With regards to Syria, GCC and European leaders have been working closely to provide support to the rebels fighting President Bashar al-Assad's regime. France quickly condemned the repression of demonstrators by Bashar al-Assad and urged the Syrian ruler to step aside. It also condemned Iranian military and political support for the Assad regime, which the French government blamed for intensifying hostilities. As the conflict escalated, France became a strong supporter of Syrian rebels, hosting numerous conferences in Paris and backing the newly established Syrian National Coalition, a coalition of Syrian opposition groups that was founded in Qatar in November 2012.

When Gulf countries started transferring weapons to the armed groups in Syria, France pushed its partners within the European Union to deliver weapons to the rebels as well. Paris eventually failed to reach a consensus on the issue (Samaan, March 2013). But during this same period, President Hollande backed the British plan to insert the military wing of Hezbollah, the Lebanon-based, Iranian-backed organization, on the EU list of terrorist organizations. When Foreign Minister Laurent Fabius confirmed the decision, he underlined Hezbollah's role alongside the Assad regime in Syria. Additionally, the French government initially opposed Iran's participation in talks over the Syrian crisis, blaming Tehran for its involvement in the military crackdown. This reflected a growing consensus between French and Gulf allies that Hezbollah had to be condemned for its involvement in Syria.

In late August 2013, following revelations over the use of chemical weapons in Syria, French officials expressed by far the strongest determination to retaliate against Bashar al-Assad's regime. President François Hollande rapidly pledged to "punish" the regime. The rhetoric used by the French mixed principles of "responsibility to protect" with the necessity to restore the "taboo" on the use of chemical weapons. While the White House cautiously weighed its options, French Foreign Minister Laurent Fabius suggested that the UN Security Council could be bypassed in case of Russian and Chinese vetoes (*Le Monde* 2013). The French stance was warmly welcomed by its Gulf partners who had been calling for stronger pressure on the Assad regime for months. It is worth noting that in the middle of the crisis, the French Defense Minister Jean-Yves Le Drian traveled to Qatar and the United Arab Emirates to hold close consultations. According to a source revealed by French magazine *Le Point*, "the President of the Republic wished for Jean-Yves Le Drian to conduct political talks exclusively on the Syrian crisis with Qatar and the Emirates" (AFP 2013).

The Syrian issue was not the only topic where French and Gulf positions converged. A few months after the crisis over the Syrian chemical weapons, negotiations between Iran and the P5+1 related to Tehran's nuclear program took place in Geneva. The Obama administration had expressed its strong will to reach an interim deal but after several days of exchanges, the talks failed to produce an agreement, following the decision of France to object to the conditions of the document. Here too, French wariness of the deal was greeted warmly by Gulf monarchs. Saudi Arabia, in particular, expressed fears that a nuclear deal would leave the GCC countries alone to face their disputes with the Iranian regime. Moreover, as the Iranian military presence in the region – in Syria, Iraq, and Yemen – intensified, the rulers in the Arabian Peninsula believed a nuclear deal would embolden the regime in Tehran. After the conclusion of an agreement in 2015, French officials and pundits remained cautious and underlined the temporary nature and limitations of the agreement, rejecting its depiction as a major breakthrough as the Obama administration did in the US (Tertrais 2015). Official statements reflected this French skepticism too. In his 2016 speech to the conference of Ambassadors, President Hollande underlined that "if Iran wants to achieve [its reintegration into the regional system], it has to contribute to the reconciliation in the region." He then added that "France is ready to facilitate this process with Gulf States, everyone knows the relations of trust we built with these countries" (Hollande 2016).

Likewise, France's support for the regime of Field Marshall Abd al-Fattah al-Sisi in Egypt followed the same logic of Gulf allies in Riyadh and Abu Dhabi: the leadership in the three countries estimated that strengthening the ability of Sisi to fight against terrorism in Egypt prevailed over other governance issues. In particular, the sale of twenty-four Rafale fighter aircrafts and two Mistral helicopter carriers in 2015 was not only supported by the Gulf allies of Sisi, Saudi Arabia, and the UAE, but directly financed by Riyadh (Nkala 2016). In his 2016 Speech to the Conference of Ambassadors, President Hollande described Egypt as "an essential actor for the stability of the region" (Hollande 2016).

Finally, on Lebanon, France, and the Saudi kingdom worked closely together to strengthen the Lebanese Armed Forces (LAF). In 2014 Saudi Arabia signed the Donas contract, which amounted to 2.4 billion euros and aimed to finance French training support to the LAF. Nevertheless, as the tensions grew between Riyadh and Beirut over the influence of Hezbollah within the Lebanese military, Saudi participation in Donas was suspended in February 2016 (Merchet 2016).

All in all, France and the Gulf countries shared many similar views on their diplomatic agendas over the last three decades. This convergence has an obvious limitation: the French ability to act decisively on its own, whether on the Syrian or the Iranian issue. Although Gulf leaders appreciate their relations with France, they fully recognize its status as a middle power. Notwithstanding this fact, the rapprochement was reinforced after the Arab Spring. The presence of President Francois Hollande as the first Western head of state in 2015 to attend a GCC summit (Sailhan 2015) was evidence of such proximity. However, this proximity has been increasingly called into question by commentators. In their critical investigation *Nos très chers Emirs* (*Our Very Dear Emirs*), journalists Christian Chesnot and Georges Malbrunot depict the French Gulf policy as a "Sunni diplomacy under the influence of Gulf oil", a description implying that Paris fully embraced the Gulf sectarian view of a cultural war with Shia Iran, mainly because of the economic prospects (Chesnot, Malbrunot 2016, 145). In the next section, we measure the significance of the commercial dimension within French–Gulf relations.

The economics of French–Gulf relations

The first way to explain France's rapprochement with Gulf monarchies is through the lens of energy imports from the region. But this idea of a French dependency on Gulf oil is more complicated than what observers tend to describe. True, Saudi Arabia is today the largest supplier of French oil imports with 20.7% in 2016 but it is worth remembering that before 2013, it was Russia. Moscow's share decreased as a result of the sanctions issued by the European Union, following the Russian annexation of Crimea in 2014. The second-largest supplier is not a Middle Eastern country but Kazakhstan (13.3%). Other partners such as Qatar and the UAE only represent a very low share (below 2%) of French oil consumption. Likewise, in the field of gas, Qatar's share amounts to 1.8%, far below the level of Norway (38.1%) and Russia (12%) (Connaissance des Energies 2016).

Overall the trade relationship between France and the Gulf is important. The UAE is the most significant partner in the region with French exports to the federation reaching 3.8 billion euros in 2015 (French Ministry of Foreign Affairs 2017). Saudi Arabia follows with 3.1 billion euros. The Emiratis are also the largest Gulf investors in France with 4.9 billion euros in foreign direct investment for the year 2013. Today, around fifty French companies are held partially or mainly by Emirati assets (Chesnot, Malbrunot 2016, 78).

Beyond the oil dimension, French–Gulf exchanges include a wide variety of domains, arms sales being the key one. As the Arabian Peninsula represents one of the biggest markets for defense industries, French companies like Airbus, Dassault, and Thales have been very active in the region. According to the 2016 Ministry of Defense Report to the French Parliament on arms sales, three out of the top six purchasers of French arms were from the Gulf for the 2015–16 period: Saudi Arabia is by far the first, followed then by Qatar, and the UAE is the sixth (French MoD 2016, 6). For example, the 2015 sale of twenty-four Rafale combat aircraft to Qatar is worth 6.3 billion euros (Sailhan 2015).

This dependence of the French defense industry on Gulf markets has been the subject of growing controversy arising from France's civil society. In particular, non-governmental organizations such as Amnesty International and Human Rights Watch have blamed the French government – alongside the US and the British – for providing weaponry to regimes whose track record in the field of human rights remains poor. To tackle these criticisms, governments in Paris frequently emphasized the positive consequences of these sales for the French job market. For instance, in October 2015, former Prime Minister Manuel Valls revealingly tweeted after a visit to Riyadh, "France-Saudi-Arabia: 10 billion euros worth of contracts! The government is committed to our companies and jobs" (Chesnot, Malbrunot 2016, 47). In other words, decision-makers emphasize the economic advantages for France while downplaying the political controversy.

Inside France, Gulf investments target mostly the real estate sector, and to a much lesser extent, tourism and aerospace fields. They usually operate through sovereign wealth funds such as the two giants of Abu Dhabi, Mubadala and Abu Dhabi Investment Authority (ADIA), or Qatar Investment Authority. The purchases are concentrated in Paris, Lyon, and the Provence region. Some of the properties are highly visible such as prestigious hotels in the Champs Elysée district and other luxurious areas of the French capital.

Qatar's investments increased significantly during the Sarkozy presidency. According to French media, more than 12 billion euros have been invested by Qatari funds into France's economy between 2008 and 2015 (Editorial, *Le Parisien* 2015). Not only was the level of these investments high, but their high visibility suddenly made French citizens aware of a new distant country. Qatar's soft power offensive in France was now obvious not only to experts but to the public as well. In real estate, Qatari funds purchased the Printemps Haussmann, a luxury mall in the center of Paris. High-quality hotels have also been the target of Qatar. Katara Hospitality now owns the Royal Monceau, Hyatt Regency, Concorde Opera, Hotel du Louvre, as well as the Hotel Lambert. This investment strategy also targeted sites outside of Paris, especially in the south of the country, where Doha purchased the Carlton and Martinez hotels in Cannes and the Palais de la Méditerranée in Nice.

But the most significant investments were in the sports and media sectors. On May 31, 2011, Qatar Sports Investments bought a 70% stake in Paris Saint-Germain, the football team of the French capital. Citizens with no knowledge at all of this small faraway emirate, suddenly discovered its financial power and its ability to turn the football club of the French capital into a serious contender in European competition. A year later, the TV channel BeIn Sports appeared on French programs and eventually bought the broadcasting rights of French national football championship, the Champions' League, and the 2014 World Cup.

Cultural and educational programs also play a significant role in the French–Gulf cooperation. The Sorbonne University opened a campus in Abu Dhabi in 2006 while renowned business schools HEC and INSEAD established regional sites, respectively in Qatar and the UAE. French architects also played a key role in the construction of new Gulf museums. Jean-Michel Wilmotte designed the interior of Doha's Islamic Art Museum while Jean Nouvel built the National Museum of Qatar and the Louvre Abu Dhabi. The Louvre Abu Dhabi may be the most iconic project the French government has conducted in the Peninsula. The initiative started with a government-to-government agreement on 6 March 2007 between France and the UAE. It relies on the collections of the Louvre and most of the prestigious cultural centers in France: Centre Pompidou, Orsay museum, Versailles Castle, and the Rodin museum, among others. Designed as a universal museum, the Louvre Abu Dhabi aims to position the emirate as the epicenter of a dialogue between east and west. It also reflects the intensity of the cooperation between Paris and the federal capital of the UAE.

In addition to this cultural cooperation between Paris and Abu Dhabi, both countries launched an international initiative to defend cultural heritage against terrorist fanaticism in 2016. This translated into the creation of a specific fund to support programs such as building temporary safe havens for emergency transfers of cultural goods if a country considers that they are under immediate threat. As the drivers of the initiative, France at US$30 million and the UAE at US$15 million are the biggest donors so far. (Emirates News Agency 2017) This initiative highlighted the resolve of both France and the UAE to play a role in counterterrorism efforts that goes beyond military responses.

Some other projects failed. After years of talks, the project of establishing Saint-Cyr Qatar – a local branch of the French military school equivalent to Sandhurst and Westpoint – was abandoned. In the nuclear field, French company Areva faced a major, and rather unexpected, defeat in December 2009 when the UAE announced the selection of a South Korean consortium (including Korea Electric Power Corp., Westinghouse Electric, Hyundai Engineering and Construction, Samsung C&T Corp, and Doosan Heavy Industries) to supply four nuclear plants. Competition for this US$20 billion dollar contract had been closely monitored by the French government which supported the proposal of the Areva team. In Saudi Arabia, French companies experienced similar setbacks. In 2011, a consortium which included Altstom and SNCF lost a bid against a Spanish competitor for the construction of a metro in Mecca – a contract worth 6.7 billion euros. This loss came after high expectations that the contract would be granted, thanks to the French government's support and the companies' expertise in the transport field. It was followed by numerous controversies within the political establishment regarding what was assessed as an inappropriate influence strategy (Guillemard 2011).

Overall, the strategic and economic projects that shape the relationship between France and its Gulf allies reveal a significant convergence of interests. This wide array of projects involving Paris and its local allies created a complex web of interdependent interests. The geopolitical and commercial aspects of this relationship are now so intertwined that it would be hard to simply point out which one drives the other. However, these interests are not immune to reactions in France's public opinion and the general perception of French citizens towards the Arabian Peninsula.

The domestic challenge to France's Gulf policy

Like the United Kingdom and the United States, French governments face internal criticisms regarding their relations with Gulf countries. The last decade witnessed an escalation in Gulf-bashing rhetoric, both among politicians and journalists in Paris. For a long time, French relations in the Peninsula did not produce any meaningful debate but the spectacular rise of Gulf investments in the country, and in particular, those of Qatar under the Sarkozy presidency have recently triggered a public reaction.

Representatives of the main leading political parties initially tried to keep the issue of French–Gulf relations at bay to avoid diplomatic repercussions. Meanwhile, books and documentaries negatively portraying Gulf countries grew in earnest during this period. Over the 2014–17 period, no less than five books on Qatar were released by major publishing houses in Paris. The titles of these best-sellers are revealing: *The French Republic of Qatar* (Bonte 2017), *Our Very Dear Emirs* (Chesnot, Malbrunot 2016), *Qatar: The secrets of the safe-deposit box* (Chesnot, Malbrunot 2014), *France under influence: When Qatar turns our country into its playground* (Pean, Ratignier 2014), *The Little Bad Qatar: This Friend who wants to hurt us* (Beau, Bourget 2013).

This Gulf-bashing trend in French politics has to be put into context. First, it is more specifically a Saudi-bashing and a Qatari-bashing trend, which largely ignores the other GCC members. Paradoxically, the UAE, which accounts for more than the double of Qatar's trade relations with France, does not stir any particular controversy. This may relate to the low-key Emirati approach in contrast with the flamboyant Qatari strategy.

Despite its massive investments, the Qatari strategy reached its limit when in 2011, the small emirate designed a specific fund amounting to 50 million euros targeting the population in the French suburbs. The amount represented 10% of the annual budget of the French Ministry of the City (*le Ministère de la Ville*) in charge of urban development and aimed to sponsor local projects in poor neighborhoods (Frayer 2012). The announcement was ill-timed: France was entering the campaign for the May 2012 presidential election. Shortly after, Marine Le Pen, leader of the far-right party, the National Front, portrayed the fund as a "Trojan horse of Islamism." She accused the Gulf country of sectarian investment, seeing in this investment a way to strengthen the French Muslim community (Malbrunot, March 28, 2012).

The far-right movement was not the only one expressing anger. Socialist and conservative politicians also publicly shared their criticisms of the initiative. As a result, the project was suspended and redesigned. It is now named "Future French Champions" and the reference to the suburbs has been removed. Instead, it provides financial support to small- and medium-sized French companies exporting in the field of research, agriculture, and healthcare.

In addition to this controversy over Qatar's fund for the suburbs, in March 2012 President Sarkozy blocked the visit to France of the controversial Sheikh Youssef al-Qaradawi, living in Doha. An Islamic theologian and an influential voice for the Muslim Brotherhood, al-Qaradawi had been perceived as an instrumental actor for Qatar in the support of Islamist forces in Egypt and Tunisia. In a public interview, President Sarkozy argued that al-Qaradawi's "speeches are not compatible with the Republican ideal" (Malbrunot, March 26, 2012).

Although the presidency of Francois Hollande (2012–16) aimed to calm tensions, the Qatar-bashing rhetoric increased. It reached a new level with the waves of terrorist attacks that the country suffered in 2015–16. Although the terrorists at Charlie Hebdo or the Bataclan claimed allegiance to Al Qaeda and the Islamic State, the events triggered a soul-searching debate within France on its relations with the Arab world, and in particular with the Gulf monarchies.

This new debate had intellectual foundations. On November 20, 2015, only a week after the simultaneous attacks in Paris, the Algerian writer Kamel Daoud wrote an op-ed for *The New York Times* titled "Saudi Arabia, a Daesh which succeeded." A winner of the prestigious French Goncourt Prize, Daoud made the case that Saudi Arabia and the Islamic State were two faces of the same phenomenon: "Daesh has a mother: the invasion of Iraq. But it also has a father: Saudi Arabia" (Daoud 2015). Daoud's piece was widely shared and discussed in France. It touched upon a sensitive topic and reflected a common perception. For influential French scholars like Gilles Kepel, the radicalization of the terrorists behind the 2015–16 attacks was rooted in Salafi ideology, and its most extreme form, Wahhabism, Saudi Arabia's official religion. For Kepel, this ideology encouraged by Saudi Arabia did not automatically lead to jihadism but it created the opportune conditions for radicalization (Kepel 2016).

Kepel's thesis became salient within the French media. In a way that was reminiscent American debates after the 9/11 attacks, French politicians and journalists looked at France's relations with Saudi Arabia and Qatar as a root cause for the terrorist attacks. Such a view transcended the traditional left–right divide. "Jihadi terrorists do not come from planet Mars, they come from the Saudis" asserted Pierre Lellouche, a former conservative minister, in 2015 (Sailhan, 2015). Socialist Prime Minister Manuel Valls then called for a united front to fight against "islamo-facism" (Editorial, *Le Monde* 2015).

At the same time, the government was trapped in its own policies. In March 2016, the government of Francois Hollande generated much anger on social networks when it delivered the *Legion d'honneur* – an honorific award – to Mohammed bin Nayef, minister of interior and crown prince of Saudi Arabia. The domestic context – only four months after the terrorist attacks – was very sensitive, but Mohammed bin Nayef was considered a key supporter of French interests in Riyadh and an essential actor in the Saudi fight against terrorism.

Finally, during the latest presidential campaign in 2017, far-right media spread rumors that candidate Emmanuel Macron received funding from Saudi Arabia in a deliberate attempt to damage his image (Sénécat 2017). In the debate leading to the run-off of the election, Marine Le Pen repeatedly accused Macron of close ties with both Saudi Arabia and Qatar. Although she did not provide substantial evidence, the accusation revealed, alongside the numerous rumors, how Gulf-bashing had now become a common tactic to shame a rival in French politics.

Conclusion

French policy in the Gulf has significantly evolved since the late 1960s when President De Gaulle reoriented the country towards the Arab world and used the British withdrawal from the Trucial States as an opportunity to increase France's influence in the Peninsula. Over the following decades, Paris deepened the scope of its relations with Arab monarchies. It increased the level of military cooperation and signed defense agreements that bound France to the stability of these regimes. Meanwhile, the close political relationships with local rulers allowed French governments to win major contracts – from arms sales to construction projects and education projects – while Gulf countries poured money into the French economy.

Interestingly, the latest *French White Paper on Defense and National Security*, published in April 2013, described Gulf security as the fourth "strategic priority" of the French government.[2] The official document stated explicitly that "Iran's race to acquire nuclear-armed capabilities" was the biggest challenge to this "strategic priority" (Livre Blanc 2013, 56). Through that process, it confirmed the strategic convergence between the Arab kingdoms and Paris. Moreover, it indicated the intention of French authorities to formalize this relationship in an official long-term document. In other words, the White Paper claims that French partnerships in the Gulf will remain steady over the next fifteen years This contrasts with France's purpose in the 1970s, which was mainly to exploit the British military withdrawal from the area.

At the same time, given the increased visibility of Saudi, Qatari, and Emirati investments in France, the politics of Gulf-bashing in Paris is unlikely to disappear in the near future. Increasingly, French governments may find themselves cein a difficult position to sustain their regional policy in the Peninsula, mixing military action with commercial deals, while defusing the risk of a backlash at home. But eventually, the ability of French decision-makers to navigate their way through this environment will also depend on the security context in the Gulf itself.

Notes

1 The only available study of France in the Gulf in the English language is an edited volume from the Abu Dhabi-based Emirates Center for Strategic Studies and Research. 2008. *France and the Arabian Gulf*. London: I.B. Tauris.
2 The White Paper lists five "strategic priorities": "- protect the national territory and French nationals abroad, and guarantee the continuity of the Nation's essential functions; - guarantee the security of Europe and the North Atlantic space, with our partners and allies; - stabilise Europe's near environment, with our partners and allies; - contribute to the stability of the Middle East and the Persian Gulf; - contribute to peace in the world." (Livre Blanc 2013, 47).

Bibliography

Agence France Presse. 2011. "Britain France Halt Security Exports to Bahrain & Libya." February 19, 2011.
Agence France Presse. 2013."Syrie: Le Drian au Qatar et aux Emirats." *Le Point*, August 26, 2013.
Almejfel, Faisal. 2014. *Les relations entre la France et l'Arabie Saoudite de 1967 à 2012*. Paris: L'Harmattan.
Bauchard, Denis. 2015. "La France et les émirats et monarchies du Golfe: un partenariat d'intérêt mutuel." *Pouvoirs* 152 (1): 107–20.

Beau, Nicolas and Jacques-Marie Bourget. 2013. *Le vilain petit Qatar: cet ami qui nous veut du mal*. Paris: Fayard.
Beguin-Buillecoq, Xavier. 1994. *Oman*. Paris: Relations internationales et culture.
Bonte, Bérengère. 2017. *La République Française du Qatar*. Paris: Fayard.
Boulanger, Philippe. 2011. "Le positionnement géostratégique de la France dans le golfe Arabo-Persique: la base interarmées d'Abu Dhabi." *Outre-terre* 3 (29): 531–37.
Bourrinet, Jacques (Ed.) 1979. *Le dialogue euro-arabe*. Paris: Economica.
Chesnot, Christian and Georges Malbrunot. 2016. *Nos très chers Emirs*. Paris: Michel Lafon.
Chesnot, Christian and Georges Malbrunot. 2014. *Qatar, les secrets du coffre-fort*. Paris: Michel Lafon.
Connaissance des Energies. 2016. "Quel est le montant de la facture énergétique française?" January 15, 2016. http://www.connaissancedesenergies.org/le-gaz-consomme-en-france-vient-principalement-de-russie-120222.
Daoud, Kamel. 2015. "L'Arabie saoudite, un Daesh qui a réussi." *The New York Times*, November 20, 2015.
Dockrill, Saki. 2002. *Britain's Retreat from East of Suez: The Choice between Europe and the World*. New York: Palgrave.
Editorial. 2013. "Syrie: la France promet une 'reponse proportionnee' et imminente." *Le Monde*, August 26, 2013.
Editorial. 2015. "Manuel Valls prône l'unité pour combattre 'l'islamo-fascisme'." *Le Monde*, February 16, 2015.
Editorial. 2015. "Immobilier, sport et luxe: les investissements du Qatar en France." *Le Parisien*, December 3, 2015.
Emirates News Agency. 2017. "UAE and France reunite for the establishment of the international alliance for protection of heritage in conflict areas." March 20, 2017. http://wam.ae/en/details/1395302604067.
Frayer, Arthur. 2012. "Après le PSG, le Qatar au chevet des banlieues françaises." *Le Monde*, January 5, 2012.
French Ministry of Defense. 2016. *Rapport au Parlement 2016 sur les exportations d'armement de la France*. http://www.defense.gouv.fr/actualites/articles/rapport-au-parlement-sur-les-exportations-d-armement-2016.
Gause III, F. Gregory. 2010. *The International Relations of the Persian Gulf*. Cambridge: Cambridge University Press.
Guillemard, Véronique. 2011. "Le TGV de la Mecque échappe au duo Alstom-SNCF." *Le Figaro*, October 26, 2011.
Hasbani, Nadim. 2014. *Géopolitique des achats d'armements des Emirats Arabes Unis*. Sarrebruck: Presses académiques francophones.
Hollande, Francois. 2016. "Discours du Président à l'occasion de la semaine des ambassadeurs," Présidence de la République, August 30, 2016. http://www.diplomatie.gouv.fr/fr/le-ministere-et-son-reseau/evenements-et-actualites-du-ministere/actualites-du-ministere-de-l-europe-et-des-affaires-etrangeres/article/discours-du-president-de-la-republique-a-l-occasion-de-la-semaine-des.
Jauvert, Vincent. 2016. "France-Arabie saoudite: une si étroite amitié." *Le Nouvel Observateur*, January 4, 2016.
Kepel, Gilles. 2016. *La Fracture: Chroniques 2015–2016*. Paris: Gallimard.
Laurenson, John. 2003. "Ties with Iraq: French Industry Stands to Lose." *The New York Times*, March 7, 2003.

Lasserre, Isabelle. 2009. "Moyen-Orient: la France se donne les moyens de riposte." *Le Figaro*, June 16, 2009.
Livre Blanc. 2013. *Défense et Sécurité Nationale*. http://www.defense.gouv.fr/portail/enjeux2/politique-de-defense/le-livre-blanc-sur-la-defense-et-la-securite-nationale-2013/livre-blanc-2013.
Lazar, Mehdi. 2013. "France-Qatar: une relation complexe, privilégiée et ancienne." *Atlantico*, April 6, 2013. http://www.atlantico.fr/decryptage/france-qatar-relation-complexe-privilegiee-et-ancienne-mehdi-lazar-688159.html.
Levey, Zach. 1997. *Israel and the Western Powers, 1952–1960*. Chapel Hill: University of North Carolina Press.
Malbrunot, Georges. 2012. "Sarkozy contre la venue de Youssef al-Qaradawi." *Le Figaro*, March 26, 2012.
Malbrunot, Georges. 2012. "Banlieues françaises: le Qatar gèle son aide financière." *Le Figaro*, March 28, 2012.
Menoret, Pascal. 2008. "Fighting for the Holy Mosque" In *Treading on Hallowed Ground*, edited by C. Christine Fair and Sumit Ganguly, 117–39. Oxford: Oxford University Press.
Merchet, Jean-Dominique. 2016. "Contrat Donas: ça se complique encore plus." *L'Opinion*, November 6, 2016.
Mikail, Barah. 2011. *France and the Arab Spring: An Opportunistic Quest for Influence*. Madrid: FRIDE.
Miller, Rory. 2014. "The Euro-Arab Dialogue and the Limits of European External Intervention in the Middle East, 1974–77." *Middle Eastern Studies* 50 (6): 936–59.
Nkala, Oscar. 2016. "Egypt, France to Sign Arms Deal Mid-April." *Defense News*, April 6, 2016.
Papastamkou, Sofia. 2007. "La France au Proche-Orient, 1950–1958. Un intrus ou une puissance exclue?" *Bulletin de l'Institut Pierre Renouvin* 25: 177–88.
Ratignier, Vanessa and Pierre Péan. 2014. *Une France sous influence: Quand le Qatar fait de notre pays son terrain de jeu*. Paris: Fayard.
Sailhan, Michel. 2015. "Experts: French Courtship of Gulf Nations Is Risky." *Defense News*, May 6, 2015.
Samaan, Jean-Loup. 2013. "The European Dilemmas on Arming Syrian Rebels." *Al Monitor*, March 27, 2013.
Samaan, Jean-Loup. 2013. "The Limits to Europe's Pivot to the Gulf." *Al Monitor*, May 23, 2013.
Sénécat, Adrien. 2017. "Macron 'financé par l'Arabie saoudite': une intox massivement relayée par l'extrême droite." *Le Monde*, March 2, 2017.
Styan, David. 2006. *France and Iraq: Oil, Arms and French Policy-Making in the Middle East*. London: I.B. Tauris.
Tertrais, Bruno. 2015. "Iran: An Experiment in Strategic Risk-Taking." *Survival* 57 (5): 67–73.
Youssef, Ahmed. 2003. *L'Orient de Jacques Chirac: La Politique arabe de la France*. Paris: Editions du Rocher.

6 A rising economic agenda
Assessing current Brazil–GCC relations

Vânia Carvalho Pinto

A little-researched but increasingly significant relationship

Relations between Brazil and the Gulf Cooperation Council (GCC) countries continue to be an under-explored topic in academic research.[1] Various reasons account for this lack of engagement. The absence of controversial political matters with which to attract media and scholarly attention is certainly one of them. To this, one may add the geographical distance between the two regions, a factor that also explains the traditional lack of interaction between the area studies disciplines of Latin America and Gulf studies.

Brazilian foreign policy towards the Middle East is described as not being particularly active. Guided by Brazil's traditional foreign policy principles of non-intervention and peaceful resolution of conflicts, the former mainly consists of observation, following-up and analysis of information.[2] These main principles of engagement were not altered with the events of the Arab Spring, as the latter did not bring about much change to Brazilian policy (Brazilian Diplomat D, 2017).[3] According to Tadeu Valadares, former Brazilian ambassador in Doha (2012–14), its impacts were certainly taken into account from a 'realistic and pragmatic' point of view, but they created neither new relevant opportunities nor insuperable obstacles for the country's policies (Valadares, 2017). In fact, the main axis of the recent insertion of Brazil into the Middle East is the economy, and 2011 was not seen as changing that (Brazilian Diplomat A, 2017). Therefore, the gist of Brazil's engagement with the Middle East, in particular with the Gulf, must be sought not within the domain of 'grand' politics, but within the former's increasing economic relevance for the Gulf states, particularly in terms of food security. Conversely, the Gulf states are becoming an important arena for Brazilian companies looking for new markets and opportunities, which in some cases leads to them being the ones 'pushing' the state into forging new (or renewed) diplomatic relations as was the case with the establishment of the Brazilian company Vale in Oman.

The growth of Brazil's economic insertion into GCC trade links is not exclusive to the former. The rise in trade between the countries of Latin America and those of the Gulf is already widely known. Economic exchanges have risen from around $7 billion in 2006 to $16 billion[4] in 2015, accounting for 1% of GCC exports and 2% of imports. When viewed in absolute terms, these numbers are certainly unimpressive, and they do pale in comparison to other more meaningful trade (and diplomatic) relationships espoused by all the countries concerned. However, when these interactions are looked at in closer detail, it becomes apparent that the two regions rely on each other for essential products, such as food and agricultural produce from Latin America and hydrocarbons and fertilizer from the GCC. In 2015, for instance, Latin America supplied nearly half the meat imports into the GCC and 36% of the region's total sugar imports. Within the Latin American group, Brazil is by far the GCC's greatest trading partner. The country was the source of 77% of the GCC's imports from the region (worth $11 billion), and it received 65% of its exports (worth $5.6 billion) (The Economist Intelligence Unit, 2016, pp. 3–5, 10). From 2005 onwards, Brazil's trade with the GCC increased rapidly from $3.8 billion in 2005 to $13 billion in 2013, the highest level to date. The bulk of Brazil's exports to the GCC consist of meat and derivatives, cereals, seeds, sugar and minerals, and importations are comprised of mainly hydrocarbons and fertilizers (Ministério da Indústria, Comércio Exterior e Serviços, n.d.a).

As elaborated upon later in the chapter, relations were boosted first by then-President Luiz Inácio Lula da Silva's 2003 visit to several Middle Eastern countries – the first by a Brazilian head of state since Emperor Pedro II toured the Ottoman Empire in the nineteenth century – as well as by the 2005 establishment of the Arab–South America Summit, (ASPA as per the Portuguese and Spanish acronym). Despite criticisms that have been leveled at this body's performance, it should be appreciated that this inter-regional mechanism has offered an unprecedented institutionalized setting for leaders and businesspersons from both regions to get together every three years (See, e.g., Carvalho Pinto, 2015, pp. 100–20).

Adopting a political–economic perspective, this chapter presents an overview of relations between Brazil and the GCC states, highlighting not only the opportunities and difficulties hampering greater interactions but also the areas that offer more promise at the time of writing. The Brazilian government's perspective of the Qatar blockade is also addressed. The chapter concludes with a summing up of the argument and the laying out of directions for future research.

Given the dearth of secondary literature on this topic, I draw heavily on interviews, which were conducted with diplomats from Brazil and from the countries of the GCC who are based in Brasília. Some of the interviews were anonymized upon request. The insights and information obtained through these conversations were complemented with newspaper articles mainly from Brazilian newspapers, as well as with materials garnered from Brazilian official websites and documents. All translations from Portuguese are my own.

An overview of relations and promising areas of engagement

> When a representative of the Brazilian government travels to the Arabian Peninsula, the indication is to visit all the countries as part of the government's policy of keeping good relations with all.
>
> (Diplomat A, 2017)[5]

Saudi Arabia, Kuwait and Bahrain

Saudi Arabia is Brazil's main commercial partner in the Middle East and its second largest oil supplier after Nigeria (Ministério das Relações Exteriores, n.d.-a). It is the fifth-largest destination in the world for Brazilian agribusiness products, thus accounting for 2.4% (Ministério da Agricultura, Pecuária e Abastecimento (ASPA), 2017, pp. 2–4).

Both countries established diplomatic ties in 1968 and embassies were opened in their respective capitals in 1973. Then-President Lula da Silva was the first Brazilian head of state to visit Saudi Arabia in May 2009 (Ministério das Relações Exteriores, n.d.-a). They set up a joint commission, which has only met twice: in 1981 and in 2015. In this latter meeting, areas of discussion included the importation of Brazilian beef, air services, sports and diplomatic cooperation (Carrieri, 2015).

As a result of increased interactions from the ASPA meetings, trade with Saudi Arabia experienced a sharp increase from 2005 onwards. Whereas from 2000 to 2003 trade varied between $1.3 billion and $1.5 billion; in 2006, it reached $3 billion. It reached the highest level to date in 2011 with $6.5 billion. Brazil holds 82.1% of the Saudi Arabian chicken market, and 61.4% of the refined sugar market (Comex do Brasil, 2016). In addition to foodstuff, Brazilian exports since 2005 also started including planes from the company *Embraer* (Ministério das Relações Exteriores, n.d.-a). From 2012 onwards there has been some decrease in the economic exchanges between both countries that can be attributed to the suspension of the importation of beef by Saudi Arabia in 2012 due to a case of mad cow disease (Custódio, 2014). Exports of beef were resumed in 2016 but were again partly suspended due to suspicions as regards quality and safety uncovered within the context of the Brazilian police investigation entitled *carne fraca* (weak meat) (Oswald, 2017).

In 2016, Saudi Arabia was Brazil's eighteenth-largest trade partner, a number which in itself is not particularly impressive (Ministério de Relações Exteriores, 2016b, p. 4). These overall small numbers – not only of trade with Saudi Arabia but with other Gulf states – have motivated assessments throughout the years that contended that links between the regions were still essentially aspirational (See, e.g., World Politics Review, 2017). It may well be so, but if these numbers are placed within a broader comparative perspective their analysis would deliver an altogether different assessment. If we view trade with Saudi Arabia side by side with that of Brazil with several of its Latin American neighbors, such as Colombia and Peru, economic exchanges with Saudi Arabia *surpass* those conducted with these two countries (Brazilian Diplomat B, 2017). In 2016, for example, trade with Peru stood at a little more than $3 billion. The highest value was in the year 2013 with $3.9 billion. Trade with Colombia in 2016 totaled $3.1 billion, having reached the highest level in 2014 with $4 billion (Ministério da Indústria, comércio exterior e serviços, n.d.b). Given that long distance was often presented as an important reason for low trade, adding these two examples would surely deliver some fresh reassessment of this *problematique*, particularly within Latin America area studies.

A rising economic agenda 93

Relations with Kuwait were also established in 1968 when the Embassy of Brazil in Cairo started to also represent Brazil to the Kuwaiti authorities. Diplomatic representations in both capitals were opened in 1975 (Ministério das Relações Exteriores, n.d.-b).[6] Also, in this case, trade began increasing steadily from 2003 onwards, reaching its peak value in 2014 with $1.4 billion. It decreased in 2015 and 2016, standing in the latter year at $485 million (Ministério da Indústria, comércio exterior e serviços, n.d.-b). Like Saudi Arabia, Kuwait had also suspended the importation of Brazilian beef in 2012 but the embargo was set to be lifted in 2017. Also in 2017, Brazil began exporting live cattle to the country (Rocha, 2017). Further cooperation and investment opportunities have been precluded due to the fact that the Brazilian Congress has yet to approve the 2010 Amendment to the Cooperation Agreement between Brazil and Kuwait, originally signed in 1975. The amendment replaces four articles of the original agreement so as to adapt the text to the current rules of the WTO (Câmara dos Deputados, 2017). There are other agreements concerning air services, technical cooperation, among several others that are stalled in the Brazilian Congress since 2010.

In his final management report, Brazilian Ambassador to Kuwait and Bahrain Antônio Carlos do Nascimento Pedro (2013–16) stated that there were wide opportunities for cooperation between the countries. As a way to intensify relations between them, he makes several suggestions of which I highlight two: to ratify all agreements already signed with Kuwait; and to settle issues regarding double taxation and the legal framework for the protection of investments (to be developed below). Finally, the ambassador refers to the severe budget and personnel restrictions on the Brazilian Embassy in Kuwait, which precludes a more concerted effort towards economic and cultural cooperation (Pedro, n.d.). This embassy also represents the country's interests in Bahrain. The latter has no mission in Brasília, and dealings with Brazil are conducted via Bahrain's Washington embassy. With diplomatic ties established in 1980 (Ministério das Relações Exteriores, n.d.-c), Bahrain is the Gulf country with which Brazil has the least contact (Brazilian Diplomat B, 2017). As of 2016, there are no agreements signed between the two countries (Pedro, n.d.), and trade with Bahrain reached its highest value in 2011 at $707 million, dropping to $348 million in 2016 (Ministério da Indústria, comércio exterior e serviços, n.d.-b). As regards the 2011 protests in Bahrain, Brazil reaffirmed its usual position of supporting the search for dialogue and a peaceful resolution of the dispute. The Ministry of Foreign Affairs issued two notes: one on the 17 February 2011, and the second exactly one month later. In both, the government cautioned against the use of force and reaffirmed the need to uphold civil and political rights as well as Bahrainis' rights to peacefully express themselves (Ministério das Relações Exteriores, 2011a; Ministério das Relações Exteriores, 2011b). The following year, Brazilian Ambassador to the UN Maria Nazareth Azevêdo delivered an address emphasizing similar points at the 20th Session of the UN Human Rights Council on the situation in Bahrain. (Ministério das Relações Exteriores, 2012).

UAE

The UAE is Brazil's second-largest commercial partner in the region. Relations were formally established in 1974, and embassies were opened in 1978 in Abu Dhabi and in 1991 in Brasília. This was the emirates' first diplomatic representation in Latin America. Bilateral relations evolved rapidly throughout the past two decades, both politically and economically. Approximately thirty Brazilian companies have commercial offices in the country, using it as an export platform to the region. The Brazilian Trade and Investment Promotion Agency (APEX-Brazil) keep an office in Jebel Ali to assist companies wishing to establish themselves in the emirates. Between 2000 and 2016, trade between the countries increased 785% from $300 million to $2.6 billion. Emirati investments in Brazil total about $5 billion (Ministério das Relações Exteriores, 2017a; Ministério das Relações Exteriores, n.d.-d). The highest value of trade, amounting to $3.3 billion, was recorded in 2014 (Ministério da Indústria, comércio exterior e serviços, n.d.-b). Again, foodstuff dominates Brazilian exports as the country accounts for 76.8% of the UAE's chicken *in natura* market, and 70.3% of the refined sugar one (Comex do Brasil, 2016).

Current relations with the UAE are described as being quite dynamic. The Emirati Embassy is showing signs that it intends to deepen relations as there are programmed visits with investors who are interested in agribusiness as well as in renewable energies (Brazilian Diplomat A, 2017). In April 2017, a delegation from Dubai opened an office of the Dubai Chamber of Commerce in the city of São Paulo (ANBA, 2017). This is one of only eight such offices worldwide, and the ceremony was emphasized as a means of expanding relations (Brazilian Diplomat B, 2017). Indeed, underlying this move is the Dubai Chamber of Commerce's aim of doubling Latin America's share of Dubai's total trade in three years (from 3% to 6%) and to reach double digits by 2022 (*Arabian Business*, 2017). This strong commercial interest springs at least partly from the perceived stability and reliability of Brazil. According to Emirati Ambassador to Brazil Hafsa al-Ulama, Brazil has always managed to maintain stability, despite having extensive borders and having undergone changes of regime, an achievement that she states the UAE appreciates. In her view, despite the current political crisis, the country still attracts foreign direct investment, which means that there is confidence that Brazil is a good place to invest. She finds that there are many opportunities for both countries, and the strategic and interaction potential is much higher than it is now in areas such as humanitarian aid and agriculture. The agreement to waive non-diplomatic visas for Brazilians is moving fast through Congress but in the ambassador's opinion, in order for closer cooperation to come to fruition some fundamental changes of laws in Brazil must take place (al-Ulama, 2017). She is supposedly referring to two rather thorny issues that have been hampering cooperation between Brazil and the GCC states, not just the UAE. These are the lack of accord as regards agreements on preventing double taxation as well as the framework governing the promotion and protection of investment. At the root of these issues is Brazil's legal framework and political traditions. As regards double taxation, Brazil's fiscal authority (*Receita Federal*) does not sign such agreements with countries that have a very favorable taxation system (Brazilian Diplomat C, 2015). Exceptions do exist, but conversations with the UAE on this matter are still ongoing (Brazilian Diplomat A, 2017).

As regards the agreements on the promotion and protection of investment, also called Bilateral Investment Treaties (BITs), these have historically been polemical in Brazil. In the 1990s, the country signed BITs with 14 states but these were strongly opposed by both the Congress and the Judiciary. None was ratified, and Brazil became known as one of the few top economies without BITs or an investment agreement model (Morosini and Badin, 2015). Seen both as limiting and as not adequately fulfilling the country's interests, the Brazilian government developed a new model entitled Agreement on Cooperation and Facilitation of Investments (*Acordo de Cooperação e Facilitação de Investimentos* – ACFI). Enacted in 2015, Brazil has already signed ACFIs with Angola, Chile, Colombia, Malawi, Mexico, Mozambique and Peru (Ministério da Indústria, comércio exterior e serviços, n.d.-b).

Being the only model that is accepted by Congress, this is the agreement that Brazil has been offering to all its partners. Given that it is something new, countries are still familiarizing themselves with it, and the UAE appears to have found it quite interesting (Brazilian Diplomat A, 2017). Nevertheless, this is an impasse that has been going on for years. Already in 2015, Brazilian diplomat C expressed his frustration with these matters. In his view, since Brazil would never sign such agreements, the UAE should be more accommodating. He recognized, however, that such flexibility would generate similar demands from other countries. Such a standoff was in his perspective attributable to the fact that the Brazilian government did not have a proactive policy geared towards presenting Brazil as more than just a developing country. In his opinion, Brazil ought to show that it is an important international actor, one that has been present in every major international event, from the formation of the League of Nations and Bretton Woods to the UN (Brazilian Diplomat C, 2015).[7]

Qatar

Even though relations were established in 1974, these only started developing in the past decade. Embassies in the respective capitals were opened in the 2000s; in 2005 in Doha and two years later in Brasília. Positive personal rapport between former President Lula and the former Qatari Emir Sheikh Hamad al-Thani (al-Hayki, 2017) as well as Qatari royals' fondness of Brazil (Brazilian Diplomat C, 2015) led to a quick expansion of contacts. Sheikh Hamad's visit to Brazil in January 2010 jump-started relations. About fourteen agreements were signed covering a wide range of fields such as education, civil aviation, library archives, technical trade and waiving of diplomatic visas, among others (al-Hayki, 2017). An increase in trade accompanied these political trends as economic exchanges rose from $199 million in 2007 to more than $1 billion in 2012, 2014 and 2015, a growth of around 435%. It should be mentioned also that with Qatar there has been a decrease in economic exchange and that in 2016, it stood at $910 million (Ministério da Indústria, comércio exterior e serviços, n.d.-b).

The Qatar Foundation has also been quite active in promoting educational opportunities to deprived children and youngsters in poor zones such as in Rio de Janeiro's shantytowns (*favelas*) and in indigenous areas. There were also plans to set up a cultural center in Rio de Janeiro in 2013, but the mayor of that time, Eduardo Paes, was deemed uncooperative. Plans were dropped, but the current mayor, Marcello Crivella, is said to be seeking rapprochement and has demonstrated intentions of an official visit to Rio for Sheikha Moza bint Nassr, the wife of the former emir of Qatar and co-founder and chair of the Qatar Foundation. Until 2014, she was undertaking yearly visits to Brazil to follow up on these projects (al-Hayki, 2017).

In addition to the rising diplomatic and economic interactions, Qatar will also enter Brazil's emerging private liquefied natural gas (LNG) market through the Ocean LNG company, which is a joint venture operated by Qatar Petroleum (70%) and the North American ExxonMobil (30%). But in order to understand the significance of this participation, some background information is in order. Brazil has an agreement with Bolivia for the supply of natural gas for twenty years, from 1999 to 2019. In 2006, the Bolivian government decided to nationalize its gas and oil production, forcing foreign companies' such as Brazil's Petrobrás to either renegotiate existing contracts or leave the country (Folha Online, 2006). Fearing that the continuous and reliable stream of gas to the south and southeast regions of Brazil could be at risk – since Bolivia was then the sole supplier – the government at the time anticipated projects for the importation of LNG and for the diversification of sellers. Energy security was then considered a top priority.

Therefore, still in 2006, the Brazilian National Council of Energetic Policy approved Resolution No. 4, establishing guidelines and recommendations for the construction of terminals of regasification of LNG. After 2006 and especially between 2008 and 2009, with the beginning of the operations of the first (public) terminals of regasification of LNG in Brazil, the sources of importation of natural gas began to be diversified. LNG was acquired in the spot market, which decreased dependence on Bolivian imports. Qatar was among several countries, such as Norway and Spain, from which Brazil acquired this product (Ministério de Minas e Energia, 2017, pp. 27–9). In parallel, legal changes were made to the rules concerning the production and distribution of natural gas that had awarded the state company Petrobrás the monopoly on conducting those activities.[8] As a result of these policies and also due to the domestic generation of energy (Clara, 2015),[9] there was a gradual reduction of Brazilian imports of gas from Bolivia. Whereas in 2007 Bolivia was Brazil's sole supplier of gas, in 2015 the former accounted for a little over half of the country's gas needs, at 60% (Ministério de Minas e Energia, 2017, pp. 27–9). Whether the agreement with Bolivia will be renewed or not and if so in what terms is still unclear (Fariello, 2016). Furthermore, there are doubts as regards Bolivia's capacity to continue feeding the Brazilian market at sufficient levels. The perspective is thus that the importation of LNG will intensify through the operation of private companies (Clara, 2015). It is within this context that on the 10 November 2016, Ocean LNG signed a long-term agreement with the Electric Centrals of Sergipe (CELSE) towards the supply of the product to the first private terminal of regasification that is due to be completed in 2020. When ready, this will be the biggest gas power plant in Latin America. It can generate up to 1.5GW of power, allowing it to supply 15% of the energy requirements of the whole northeast region of Brazil, which corresponds to about 18% of the national territory (Governo do Brasil, 2009). Qatar will supply 1.3 million tons of LNG a year, but the values of the contract are not available (Lage, 2016; Brasil Energia, 2016). The cost of both the terminal and of the power plant are estimated at approximately $1.3 billion. The main energy company in Paraná Compel – Companhia Paranaense de Energia – is also in the process of expanding the sources of supply of LNG (Agência de notícias do Paraná, 2017), and has demonstrated an interest in Qatar's LNG (al-Hayki, 2017).

As was the case with the Arab Spring, the recent diplomatic crisis in the Gulf that resulted in the blockade imposed on Qatar by Saudi Arabia, the UAE, Egypt and Bahrain, did not bring about significant changes to Brazil's Gulf relations. According to Brazilian Diplomat A (2017), all of the Gulf countries presented their views on the crisis to the government, but there was no particular expectation that Brazil would take sides. Brazilian companies that trade with the Gulf countries did express some concern as regards possible retaliations in case they continued to do businesses with both parties. The position that was conveyed to them by the Brazilian government was that all was to remain the same. On this matter, the government released two notes: one from 6 June 2017 concerning the crisis itself; and the second on the 14 July asserting Brazil's support for the emir of Kuwait's mediation role (Ministério de Relações Exteriores 2017b; Ministério de Relações Exteriores 2017c). Both diplomatic notes stated the habitual traditional principles of Brazilian foreign policy, thus emphasizing dialogue and the peaceful settlement of disputes. The government's concern in this matter was basically to keep good relations with all the countries from the region (Brazilian Diplomat A, 2017). According to Tadeu Valadares (2017), there would not be any space for Brasília to play any sort of relevant role in diminishing tensions in the region, assuming that the current government would even be interested in taking up such a role. He stated:

> the Brazil of today, so different from the Brazil from the period [of] Lula-Dilma,[10] wouldn't have conditions, or the willingness or the interest to get involved in what would be considered by the current government an adventure already in the territory or in the limit of irresponsibility.[11]

Indeed, the Qatar blockade brought no immediate effects to Brazil. It is worth mentioning that Qatar did become more publicly vocal as regards its interest in diversifying suppliers and imports (Brazilian Diplomat A, 2017). This also included buying foodstuff such as meat and food oils directly from Brazilian companies rather than importing them through Saudi Arabia and the UAE, as used to be the case. Indeed, in September 2017 a very large Qatari delegation traveled to Brazil seeking to do precisely that (Lopes, 2017). Even though it still cannot be empirically observed, maybe one of the effects of the blockade will be Qatar's increase in food importations from Brazil.

Oman

Relations with Oman are quite new and began developing from 2007 onwards. In that year, the Brazilian mining company Vale established itself in the industrial area of the port of Sohar in Oman, which led to the opening of a Brazilian Embassy in Muscat in 2008. Previously, interests in Oman were represented by the embassy in Saudi Arabia.

Vale is in the business of supplying pellets to clients located in Asia and the Middle East (Vale, 2017) and its current investments in Oman exceed $3 billion (Brazilian Diplomat B, 2017). Still under-researched, this investment would be a very interesting case study of how an economic private actor is spearheading relations between the two countries. It would, additionally, offer a differing view from existing works that essentially favor a state-centric view (Funk, 2016, pp. 11–36). Indeed, more than driving relations forward, the establishment of Vale in Oman can be seen as having almost inaugurated relations between the two countries, as fifteen years ago there were basically no bilateral relations (Brazilian Diplomat B, 2017). Attesting to the scarcity of interactions between the countries, the first visit by a Brazilian member of government to Oman was in 2005 (Ministério das Relações Exteriores, n.d.-e). Nowadays, Brazil is the only Latin American country with an embassy in Oman, and Brasília hosts the only Omani Embassy in South America.

As a result of increased contacts, trade began swelling steadily from 2005 onwards. In 2006, it stood at $60 million; by 2015 it had reached $656 million, an increase of more than 980% (Ministério das Relações Exteriores, 2016). In 2013 economic exchanges reached their highest value at $1.1 billion. Similar to the other Gulf states and for the same reasons highlighted previously, trade decreased in the past three years; it stood at $587 million in 2016 (Ministério da Indústria, comércio exterior e serviços, n.d.-b). The success of President Michel Temer's visit to Oman in 2013, then in his capacity as vice-president, was another important landmark in relations. It led to the first bilateral agreements signed between the two countries (Ministério das Relações Exteriores, n.d.-e) and to the establishment of the Brazil–Oman joint commission in April 2013. The first meeting occurred in 2016 and issues such as investment promotion and cooperation in the areas of mining, agriculture, education and air services were addressed (Ministério das Relações Exteriores, 2016a). On this occasion, both countries signed a memorandum of understanding in the field of investment, whose contents are indicative of the recentness of relations. In its Article 1, they establish the obligation to inform one another of opportunities for investment and to provide information on publications that clarify each country's investment environment (Ministério das Relações Exteriores, 2016a).[12]

As mentioned above, agriculture is one of the fields of interest. Oman is seeking to increase agricultural production and asked for an agreement on this matter.

The agreement offered by the Brazilian government would involve the company *Embrapa*, a public research institution linked to the Ministry of Agriculture, which has the necessary know how to conduct the process. The issue has still not moved further (Brazilian Diplomat A, 2017). It should also be added that similar to relations with the UAE, disagreements on issues surrounding double taxation as well as the model base agreement for the protection of investments are also looming over further cooperation.

Oman has also demonstrated a strong interest in becoming the hub for the distribution of Brazilian products to Asia, a role that has hitherto been played by the UAE. The country's geographical proximity to Iran has been presented to the Brazilian government as its greatest advantage (Brazilian Diplomat B, 2017). Indeed, in the Omani ambassador's words, his country has many resources that can attract foreign investors such as social stability, security, and friendliness to foreigners (al-Abry, 2017). Currently, in the wake of the blockade crisis – and the closing off of the Jebel Ali free trade zone to products destined to Qatar – Oman is already partially playing that role by redirecting Brazilian shipments to the country.

Concluding remarks and directions for future research

> In my personal evaluation, there is no understanding of the potential that exists, of how much the Gulf economies and the Brazilian one are complementary. ... the issue of food security, everything is complementary ... now the parties are being able to deal with it in a better way and exploring its potential. Energy, food, there is no negative agenda. They are relations that are being built. It's construction not maintenance.
>
> (Diplomat B, 2017)[13]

The absence of a negative agenda in Brazil–GCC relations (Brazilian Diplomat B, 2017) is indicative of a still growing relationship unencumbered and untested by major conflicting interests. Indeed, in 2015, an *Arab News* editorial stated that the strength of the relationship lay precisely in the distance between the two regions, as there were no disputes among them (Arab News, 2015).

For now, the synergies between these countries' economies have been an important driver for the deepening of relations. Indeed, this piece has shown that if one looks for 'grand' diplomatic engagements in the relationship between Brazil and the GCC countries, such an undertaking will surely deliver disappointment. The country's policies towards the Middle East are characterized more by continuities within the normal wording and functioning of international law and institutions, rather than by ruptures, big or small. The Brazilian government's reactions to the events of the Arab Spring and to the Qatar blockade thoroughly reflect that traditional positioning. By this token, it seems far more promising to look at selected bilateral relationships, particularly in its economic dimension, with a keen eye on the role of Brazilian private economic actors. The establishment of Vale in Oman stands as an interesting case study of a private actor practically inaugurating state-to-state relations; the investigation of this would be a welcome contribution to existing studies that favor a state-centric view. Furthermore, the restructuring of Brazil's energy market may see more Gulf companies participating in the former's supply, and the Gulf States' pursuit of food security may see these governments buying more stakes in Brazilian foodstuff companies. Such was the case with Saudi Arabia's purchase of 20% of the company Minerva that deals in beef and derivatives (Brazilian Diplomat A, 2017).

But a focus on the economy should not be seen as the sole valid perspective with which to assess these relationships. Another interesting angle is the Brazilian government's diplomatic discourse towards the Arab countries, one crafted around the commonality of values and on "family closeness" between itself and the Middle East. In my view, such a discourse has generated a superficial level of cultural comfort that has facilitated interactions (Carvalho Pinto, 2015, pp. 100–20). It is based on the presence of an Arab diaspora of Lebanese descent in Brazil, one whose ancestors migrated to the country in the early twentieth century. Several publications have mentioned the facilitating roles played by this diaspora, particularly of those involved with the Arab–Brazilian Chamber of Commerce (See, e.g., Brun 2012; 2016). From the organization of meetings and seminars for businesspersons from both regions, to the easing of the logistics of international trade, to the tips on appropriate cultural behavior when dealing with Arab customers, this chamber deserves a far greater examination than it has hitherto received. Indeed, with the exception of John Tofik Karam's book (2007) on this topic – an anthropological work that is already a decade old – within international relations, these relationships remain suggested rather than thoroughly researched and theorized.

In sum, the data presented here clearly shows the existence of a very interesting yet overlooked dynamic that merits closer attention. Thus, adding the Gulf countries as an area of interest to the study of Brazilian foreign policy and vice-versa would refresh analysis of the contemporary foreign relations of all the countries concerned. Until now these have been characterized by an almost exclusive focus on their respective regional neighborhoods as well as on relations with traditional allies in Europe and the US. Indeed, Brazil does not make headlines anymore as regards its Middle Eastern engagements, but that does not mean that there are not interesting developments worth examining.

Notes

1 Exceptions include Brun (2013, pp. 143–72) and Carvalho Pinto (2016, pp. 1–18). On relations between other Latin American states and the GCC countries, see, e.g., the edited volume by A. Galindo (2013).
2 Other traditional elements of Brazilian foreign policy include pragmatism as well as "the importance of autonomy, universalist action, and destiny, the idea that the country will one day come to occupy a place of greater distinction in international politics." See Saraiva (2011, pp. 53–66). For a historical overview of Brazilian policy towards the Middle East see Feres (2009).

3   For more on the Brazilian government's position as regards the interventions in Libya and Syria – the topics that attracted more attention domestically – see Casarões (2012, pp. 47–50) and Galindo, Baeza and Brun (2014, pp. 125–54).
4   All figures throughout are in US dollars, unless otherwise noted.
5   Original in Portuguese: "Quando um representante do governo brasileiro viaja para a península arábica, a indicação é a de que se visitem todos os países como parte da política do governo de manter boas relações com todos."
6   The Brazilian government website further adds that "Kuwait's invasion by Iraq (1990) and the subsequent Gulf War deeply changed the panorama of bilateral relations: focused on the economic- commercial aspect until that time, dialogue between the two countries gained greater political density, in particular in the periods 1993–1994 and 1998–99, when Brazil held a non-permanent seat in the UN Security Council." Unfortunately, I could not find more information about this more heightened dialogue and to my knowledge, there is no work on this topic. It remains as an outstanding theme for future research.
7   On the issue of Brazil's historical self-perception, see Burges (2012, pp. 109–19).
8   Law n. 11.909, of 4 March 2009 (Presidência da República, 2009) replaced Law n. 9.478 of 1997 (Presidência da República, 1997).
9   In 2007, light oil was discovered in the Brazilian pre-salt. This discovery has altered the industry's prospects as regards oil and natural gas, but there are doubts regarding how that will develop.
10 Luiz da Silva (2003–11) and Dilma Rousseff (2011–16) were former presidents of Brazil.
11 Original in Portuguese: " o Brasil de hoje, tão diferente do Brasil do período Lula-Dilma, não teria condições, nem ânimo e interesse para se envolver no que seria muito possivelmente considerado, pelo governo atual, aventura já no território ou no limite da irresponsabilidade."
12 The memorandum is available here: http://www.itamaraty.gov.br/images/notas_a_imprensa/20160203-Oman-MdE-Coop-Invest-triling.pdf
13 Original in Portuguese: "Na minha avaliação pessoal não se percebe o potencial que existe. O quanto as economias do golfo e a brasileira são complementares. ... A questão da segurança alimentar, tudo é complementar. Agora as partes estão a saber encaminhar isso um pouco melhor e a explorar o seu potencial. Energia, alimentos, não existe uma agenda negativa propriamente dita. São relações que estão a ser construídas. É construção, não manutenção."

Bibliography

Agência de notícias do Paraná (2017). Copel e Shell firmam parceria para expandir gás natural no Paraná [online]. 16 October. Available at: http://www.aen.pr.gov.br/modules/noticias/article.php?storyid=95866

ANBA (2017). Câmara de Dubai abre escritório em São Paulo [online]. 18 April. Available at: http://www.ccab.org.br/pt/noticias/camara-de-dubai-abre-escritorio-em-sao-paulo

Arab News (2015). Editorial: ASPA highlights isolation of Iran [online]. 13 November. Available at: http://www.arabnews.com/editorial/news/834576

Arabian Business (2017). Dubai's next frontier: Latin America [online]. 4 July. Available at: http://www.arabianbusiness.com/the-next-frontier-677927.html

Brasil Energia (2016). Celse fecha acordo para terminal de GNL [online] GasNet. 17 November. Available at: http://www.gasnet.com.br/conteudo/18986/Acesso-a-terminais-de-GNL-depende-de-mudanca-em-leilao-de-energia

Brun, É. (2016). Brazil's Relations with Middle Eastern Countries: A Diplomacy in Search for Constancy (2003–2014). In: M. T. Kuri, ed., *Latin American Foreign Policies towards the Middle East. Actors, Contexts, and Trends*, 1st ed. New York: Palgrave, pp. 37–58.

Brun, É. (2013). Relations between Brazil and the Arab Countries of the Gulf: Renewed Context, Persistent Objectives. In: A. Galindo, ed., *The Gulf and Latin America: An Assessment of Expectations and Challenges*, 1st ed. Cambridge: GRC, pp. 143–172.

Brun, É. (2012). La diplomacia brasileña hacia el Medio Oriente: una estrategia oscilante. Araucaria. Revista Iberoamericana de Filosofía, Política y Humanidades, 14(28), pp. 73–90.

Burges, S. W. (2012). Brazil. Making Room at the Main Table. In: B. J. C. McKercher, ed., *Routledge Handbook of Diplomacy and Statecraft*, 1st ed. London and New York: Routledge, pp. 109–119.

Câmara dos Deputados (2017). CREDN discutirá acordo de cooperação bilateral com o Kuwait [online]. Available at: http://www2.camara.leg.br/atividade-legislativa/comis soes/comissoes-permanentes/credn/noticias/credn-discutira-acordo-de-cooperacao-bilateral-com-o-kuwait

Carrieri, M. (2015). Sauditas e Brasil fazem acordos em comissão mista [online]. ANBA. 14 April. Available at: http://www.anba.com.br/noticia/21867419/diplomacia/sauditas-e-brasil-fazem-acordos-em-comissao-mista/

Carvalho Pinto, V. (2016). Latin America and the Gulf: Assessment of Current and Future Trends [online]. *Gulf Yearbook 2015–1026*. Jeddah: GRC, pp. 1–18. Available at: http://grc.net/index.php?frm_module=contents&frm_action=detail_book&frm_type_ id=&pub_type=23&publ_id=&sec=Contents&publang=&frm_title=Gulf%20Year book&book_id=87093&p_id=&frm_pageno=&op_lang=en

Carvalho Pinto, V. (2015). The ideational elements of Brazil's Arab Strategy: An Assessment (2002–2010). *Journal of Middle Eastern and Islamic Studies (in Asia)*, 9 (4), pp. 100–120.

Casarões, G. (2012). Construíndo pontes? O Brasil diante da Primavera Árabe [online]. *Ciência e Cultura*, 64(4), pp. 47–50. Available at: http://dx.doi.org/10.21800/S0009-67252012000400018

Clara, Y. (2015). O mercado de GNL do futuro: risco ou oportunidade para o Brasil? [online]. Blog Infopetro. 21 September. Available at: https://infopetro.wordpress.com/ 2015/09/21/o-mercado-de-gnl-do-futuro-risco-ou-oportunidade-para-o-brasil/

Comex do Brasil (2016). Apex-Brasil identifica oportunidades para exportações de frutas e alimentos para países árabes. 28 September. Available at: https://www.comexdobrasil. com/apex-brasil-identifica-oportunidades-para-exportacoes-de-frutas-e-alimentos-para-paises-arabes/

Custódio, F. (2014). Arábia Saudita suspende as importações de carne bovina do Brasil," Notícias agrícolas. 19 May. Available at: https://www.noticiasagricolas.com.br/noti cias/carnes/139461-arabia-saudita-suspende-as-importacoes-de-carne-bovina-do-brasil.html#.WfsOhq1OreQ

Fariello, D. (2016). Negociação de acordo de gás com a Bolívia deixa Petrobras de lado [online]. O Globo. 5 February. Available at: https://oglobo.globo.com/economia/nego ciacao-de-acordo-de-gas-com-bolivia-deixa-petrobras-de-lado-18612765#ixzz4x 6SoeQIW

Feres, S. T. (2009). *O pragmatismo do petróleo. As relações entre o Brasil e o Iraque*. Curitiba: Juruá Editora.

Folha Online (2006). Bolívia ocupa Petrobras e nacionaliza exploração de petróleo e gás [online]. 1 May. Available at: www.folha.uol.com.br

Funk, K. (2016). How Latin America Met the Arab World: Toward a Political Economy of Arab-Latin American Relations. In: M. T. Kuri, ed., *Latin American Foreign Policies Towards the Middle East. Actors, Contexts, and Trends*, 1st ed. New York and Basingstoke: Palgrave, pp. 11-36.

Galindo, A., Baeza C., and Brun, É. (2014). Diversity Behind Unity: Latin America's Response to the Arab Spring. In: R. Mason, ed., *The International Politics of the Arab Spring. Popular Unrest and Foreign Policy*, 1st ed. New York and Basingstoke: Palgrave, pp. 125-154.

Galindo, A. (Ed.) (2013). *The Gulf and Latin America: An Assessment of Expectations and Challenges*. Cambridge: GRC.

Governo do Brasil (2009). Território nacional tem cerca de 8,5 milhões de quilômetros quadrados [online]. Available at: http://www.brasil.gov.br/governo/2009/11/territorio

Karam, J. T. (2007). *Another Arabesque. Syrian-Lebanese Ethnicity in Neoliberal Brazil.* Philadelphia: Temple University.

Lage, A. (2016). Uma usina única em Sergipe [online]. Galileu. 12 December. Available at: http://revistagalileu.globo.com/Caminhos-para-o-futuro/Energia/noticia/2016/12/uma-usina-unica-em-sergipe.html

Lopes, F. (2017). Comitiva do Catar se reúne com empresas brasileiras [online] Valor Econômico. 26 September. Available at: http://www.valor.com.br/agro/5134582/comitiva-do-catar-se-reune-com-empresas-brasileiras

Ministério da Agricultura, Pecuária e Abastecimento (2017). Balança Comercial do Agronegócio – Março/2017 [online]. Secretaria de Relações Internacionais do Agronegócio. 10 April. Available at: www.agricultura.gov.br/noticias/..agronegocio..8..marco/nota-marco-2017.docx

Ministério da Indústria, Comércio Exterior e Serviços (n.d.a). ACFI [online]. Available at: http://www.mdic.gov.br/comercio-exterior/negociacoes-internacionais/218-negociacoes-internacionais-de-investimentos/1949-nii-acfi

Ministério da Indústria, Comércio Exterior e Serviços (n.d.b). Balança comercial brasileira: Países e Blocos [online]. Available at: http://www.mdic.gov.br/index.php/component/content/article?id=87

Ministério das Relações Exteriores (n.d.a). Reino da Arábia Saudita [online]. Available at: http://www.itamaraty.gov.br/en/ficha-pais/6020-kingdom-of-saudi-arabia

Ministério das Relações Exteriores (n.d.b). Estado do Kuwait [online]. Available at: http://www.itamaraty.gov.br/en/ficha-pais/11216-state-of-kuwait

Ministério das Relações Exteriores (n.d.c). Reino do Bahrain [online]. Available at: http://www.itamaraty.gov.br/templates/padraogoverno01/pesquisa-postos/index.php?option=com_content&view=article&id=4853&Itemid=478&cod_pais=BHR&tipo=ficha_pais&lang=pt-BR

Ministério das Relações Exteriores (n.d.d). Emirados Árabes Unidos [online]. Available at: http://www.itamaraty.gov.br/pt-BR/ficha-pais/5103-emirados-arabes-unidos

Ministério das Relações Exteriores (n.d.e). Sultanato de Oman [online]. Available at: http://www.itamaraty.gov.br/index.php?option=com_content&view=article&id=5615&Itemid=478&cod_pais=OMN&tipo=ficha_pais&lang=pt-BR

Ministério das Relações Exteriores (2017a). Nota 77: Visita do ministro dos Negócios Estrangeiros e Cooperação Internacional dos Emirados Árabes Unidos ao Brasil – Brasília, 16 de março; São Paulo, 21 de março de 2017, 14 de março de 2017 [online]. 14 March. Available at: http://www.itamaraty.gov.br/pt-BR/notas-a-imprensa/15880-visita-do-ministro-dos-negocios-estrangeiros-e-cooperacao-internacional-dos-emirados-arabes-unidos-ao-brasil-brasilia-16-de-marco-sao-paulo-21-de-marco-de-2017

Ministério das Relações Exteriores (2017b). Nota 176: Situação no Golfo e na Península Arábica [online]. 6 June. Available at: http://www.itamaraty.gov.br/pt-BR/notas-a-imprensa/16427-situacao-no-golfo-e-na-peninsula-arabica

Ministério das Relações Exteriores (2017c). Nota 229: Situação no Golfo e na Península Arábica [online]. 14 July. Available at: http://www.itamaraty.gov.br/en/press-releases/16854-situation-in-the-gulf-and-the-arabian-peninsula

Ministério das Relações Exteriores (2016a). Nota 42: I Reunião da Comissão Mista Brasil-Omã – Brasília, 4 de fevereiro de 2016 [online]. 2 February. Available at: http://www.itamaraty.gov.br/pt-BR/notas-a-imprensa/13073-i-reuniao-da-comissao-mista-brasil-oma-brasilia-4-de-fevereiro-de-2016

Ministério de Relações Exteriores (2016b). BRASIL-ARÁBIA SAUDITA BALANÇA COMERCIAL [online]. DPR/DIC. December. Available at: https://investexportbrasil.dpr.gov.br/arquivos/../web/pdf/INDArabiaSaudita.pdf

Ministério das Relações Exteriores (2012). Nota 162: 20ª Sessão do Conselho de Direitos Humanos da ONU sobre a situação no Bahrein – Pronunciamento da Embaixadora do Brasil, Maria Nazareth Farani Azevêdo - Genebra, 28 de junho de 2012 [online]. 28 June. Available at: http://www.itamaraty.gov.br/pt-BR/notas-a-imprensa/3083-20-sessao-do-conselho-de-direitos-humanos-da-onu-sobre-a-situacao-no-bareine-pronunciamento-da-embaixadora-do-brasil-maria-nazareth-farani-azevedo-genebra-28-de-junho-de-2012

Ministério das Relações Exteriores (2011a). Nota 64: Situação no Bahrain [online], 17 February. Available at: http://www.itamaraty.gov.br/pt-BR/notas-a-imprensa/2475-situacao-no-bareine

Ministério das Relações Exteriores (2011b). Nota 102: Situação no Bahrain [online]. 17 March. Available at: http://www.itamaraty.gov.br/pt-BR/notas-a-imprensa/2513-situacao-no-bareine-marco

Ministério de Minas e Energia (2017). Panorama da Indústria de Gás Natural na Bolívia [online]. Empresa de Pesquisa Energética. 22 June. Available at: http://www.epe.gov.br/Petroleo/Documents/EPE%202017%20-%20Panorama%20da%20Indústria%20de%20Gás%20Natural%20na%20Bol%C3%ADvia%2022jun17.pdf

Morosini, F. and Badin, M. (2015). The Brazilian Agreement on Cooperation and Facilitation of Investments (ACFI): A new formula for international investment agreements? [online]. Investment Treaty News. Available at: https://www.iisd.org/itn/2015/08/04/the-brazilian-agreement-on-cooperation-and-facilitation-of-investments-acfi-a-new-formula-for-international-investment-agreements/

Oswald, V. (2017). Arábia Saudita suspende importações de quatro frigoríficos brasileiros [online]. O Globo. 23 March. Available at: https://oglobo.globo.com/economia/arabia-saudita-suspende-importacoes-de-quatro-frigorificos-brasileiros-21102634

Pedro, A.C.N. (n.d.). Relatório de gestão [online]. Embaixada do Brasil no Estado do Kuaite. Available at: www.senado.leg.br/atividade/materia/getTexto.asp?t=197390

Presidência da República (2009). LEI Nº 11.909, DE 4 DE MARÇO DE 2009. [online]. Casa Civil. Subchefia para Assuntos Jurídicos. Available at: http://www.planalto.gov.br/ccivil_03/_ato2007-2010/2009/lei/l11909.htm

Presidência da República (1997). LEI Nº 9.478, DE 6 DE AGOSTO DE 1997 [online]. Casa Civil. Subchefia para Assuntos Jurídicos. Available at: http://www.planalto.gov.br/ccivil_03/leis/L9478.htm

Rocha, A. (2017). Kuwait libera importação de gado vivo do Brasil [online]. ANBA. 16 May. Available at: http://www.anba.com.br/noticia/21875025/agronegocio/kuwait-libera-importacao-de-gado-vivo-do-brasil/

Saraiva, M. G. (2011). Brazilian Foreign Policy: Causal Beliefs in Formulation and Pragmatism in Practice. In: G. L. Gardini and P. Lambert, eds., *Latin American Foreign Policies Between Ideology and Pragmatism*, 1st ed. New York: Palgrave, pp. 53–66.

The Economist Intelligence Unit (2016). Bridging the Gulf: LatAm–GCC trade and investment [online]. A report by The Economist Intelligence Unit. Available at: https://perspectives.eiu.com/sites/default/files/EIU-Dubai%20Chamber%20Bridging%20the%20Gulf.pdf

Vale (2017). Businness [online]. Available at: http://www.vale.com/oman/EN/business/mining/iron-ore-pellets/pelletizing-plant/Pages/default.aspx

World Politics Review (2017). Latin American–Gulf economic ties are still largely aspirational. [online]. 3 April. Available at: https://www.worldpoliticsreview.com/trend-lines/21731/latin-american-gulf-economic-ties-are-still-largely-aspirational

Interviews

al-Abry, Ahmed, Omani ambassador in Brasília, Brasília, 5 October 2017.
Brazilian Diplomat A, Brasília, 4 October 2017.
Brazilian Diplomat B, Brasília, 4 October 2017.
Brazilian Diplomat C, Brasília, 10 June 2015.
Brazilian Diplomat D, Brasília, 27 September 2017.
al-Hayki, Mohammed, Qatari ambassador in Brasília, Brasília 6 October 2017.
al-Ulama, Hafsa, Emirati ambassador in Brasília, Brasília, 24 September 2017.
Valadares, Tadeu, Former Brazilian ambassador in Doha, Brasília, 17 October 2017.

7 Between geopolitics and economics

Turkey's relations with the Gulf

Birol Başkan

Introduction

The prime objective of this chapter is to give an analytical account of Turkey's changing relations with the six Arab states of the Gulf since the founding of the Republic in 1923.[1] The chapter divides this history into two major eras: simply the pre- and the post-1980 periods. While Turkey had been indifferent towards the Gulf in the pre-1980 period, it has been eager to develop stronger economic relations with the Gulf in the post-1980 period.

This is not to suggest that the relations between Turkey and the Gulf Cooperation Council (GCC) member states have not undergone any drastic change after the current ruling party in Turkey, the Justice and Development Party (JDP), came to power in 2002. Like their predecessors, the JDP leaders continued to view the Gulf primarily as a market for Turkish products and as a source of capital.

While economics has primarily driven Turkey's relations with the Gulf in the latter period, after the Arab Spring, Turkey began to act in ways that risked its economic interests, especially with Saudi Arabia and the UAE, by then Turkey's largest trading partners in the Gulf. To be more specific, with the eruption of the Arab Spring in late 2010, Turkey dropped its earlier cautious rhetoric and instead adopted a more radical one as it came to demand political change in the region. Turkey's changing rhetoric and attempts to develop strong relations with post-revolution Egypt were a disturbing development in the Middle East and thus harmed Turkey's otherwise good relations with the Gulf.

Turkey has by and large avoided a total collapse in its relations with the Gulf. It has even forged a special relationship with Qatar in the aftermath of the military coup in Egypt in Summer 2013, which overthrew the Muslim Brotherhood (MB)-affiliated president, Muhammed Morsi. This special relationship with Qatar has involved Turkey in the security of the Gulf. How this new role will change Turkey's relations with the other Gulf states is yet to be seen.

It must be stated at the outset that Turkey's relations with the Gulf have not evolved in a geopolitical vacuum. Because Turkey and the Gulf are not in each other's immediate geographical neighborhood, they do not pose direct security risks for each other, unlike larger neighbors such as Iran, Egypt, and Iraq. When Turkey or the Gulf have faced a common security risk or a geographical rival, they found each other to be natural diplomatic allies. It must also be added that Turkey has not nurtured geopolitical ambitions beyond its immediate neighborhood. The Gulf therefore seemed well beyond its reach. This was to change, as noted above, after the Arab Spring.

The pre-1980 period: Turkey's indifference towards the Gulf

Prior to 1980, Turkey had long been absent in the Gulf. Its predecessor, the Ottoman Empire, had already begun to withdraw from the region before the First World War and lost its last territory, Hijaz, by the end of it.[2] Following the Independence War (1919–22), Turkey adopted a peaceful international posture and pursued a policy of isolationism and neutrality so that it could fully devote its attention and energy to its own domestic problems, and focus instead on recovering from the great economic and human losses of the preceding decade.

Illustrative of this broader foreign policy is a phrase by Mustafa Kemal Atatürk, the founder and the first president of the Republic of Turkey: "Peace at Home, Peace in the World." It is also noteworthy that Atatürk made no foreign visit during his tenure in office until his death in 1938. His successor, İsmet İnönü, pursued more or less the same policy and successfully kept Turkey out of the Second World War despite the strong sympathies many in the military and civilian bureaucracy felt towards Germany.

At the end of the war, however, Turkey began to perceive the Soviet Union as a threat and sought allies to thwart any Soviet aggression.[3] Turkey therefore dropped its former isolationism and neutrality and firmly took its place within the Western bloc. Turkey even sent troops to the Korean War on the side of the US and in return was rewarded membership in NATO in 1952.

In this new period, Turkey was also alarmed by developments in the Middle East, especially the rise of pan-Arab nationalism in the form of Nasserism in Egypt and Baathism in Syria and Iraq. It shared this concern with Saudi Arabia, which was similarly aligned with the US-led Western bloc. This geopolitical motivation could have pushed the two states to develop much stronger relations, but relations between the two remained quite limited by the 1980s. Even though Turkey was among the first countries that recognized the Kingdom of Najd and Hejaz – later the Kingdom of Saudi Arabia – and opened its embassy in 1926, it did not have much incentive to develop stronger relations with Saudi Arabia. Saudi Arabia was far away and literally quite poor, as oil was to turn Saudi Arabia into a capital-rich country only after the 1950s.

Similarly, Saudi Arabia had few incentives to pursue closer relations with Turkey. Even though Saudi Arabia opened its embassy in Ankara in 1945, the two countries did not exchange any high-level visit until 1966. In that year King Faisal of Saudi Arabia visited Turkey as a part of his diplomatic initiative to form a broad anti-Nasserite front in the Middle East. Turkey joined King Faisal's initiative, the Organization of the Islamic Conference as a member when it was founded in 1969, albeit with some reluctance since it viewed membership in such an organization to be against its secular character. Turkey would not reciprocate the king's visit until the 1980s.

Because the other Gulf states – Kuwait, Bahrain, Qatar, and the Trucial states, later the United Arab Emirates (UAE) – had left their foreign policies in the hands of the British until their independence, Turkey could not have direct relations with them. After their independence, Turkey established diplomatic relations, but opened its embassies later, in Kuwait in 1970, in the UAE in 1979, in Qatar in 1980, in Oman in 1985, and finally in Bahrain in 1990. The Gulf states reciprocated, but later than Turkey, save Kuwait. Kuwait opened its embassy in Ankara in 1970, the UAE in 1983, Qatar in 1992, and finally Bahrain in 2008.

Reflecting the general weakness of relations between Turkey and the Gulf in the first seven decades of the Republic, Turkey's trade with the Gulf was quite negligible. Only in the 1950s did Turkey begin to trade with Saudi Arabia, the first trade statistics coming from the year 1952. Turkey began to trade with the other Gulf countries even much later: the first statistics on Turkey's trade with Kuwait come from 1969, Bahrain from 1970, the UAE from 1980, and Qatar and Oman from 1982.[4] Turkey's exports to each of these countries began quite modestly and then rose systematically. Turkey's exports to Saudi Arabia, for example, were worth $382,000 in the period between 1952 and 1959, with an annual average of $47,000. In the period between 1975 and 1979, however, Turkey's exports were worth $78.2 million with an annual average of $15.6 million. Turkey's imports from these three countries had also increased in the same period. Turkey had recorded a substantial trade deficit with them, importing at a much higher volume than it exported. From 1975–79, for example, Turkey's imports from Saudi Arabia were worth double its exports, an imbalance that can be explained by the sudden jump in oil prices in the 1970s (Table 7.1).

Table 7.1 Turkey's trade statistics with the Gulf, 1950–79

	1952–59	*1960–69*	*1970–74*	*1975–79*
Exports to the Gulf (in thousands of dollars)				
Saudi Arabia	382	1,726	7,399	78,237
Kuwait	NA	524	21,463	64,159
Bahrain	NA	NA	316	4,211
UAE	NA	NA	NA	NA
Qatar	NA	NA	NA	NA
Oman	NA	NA	NA	NA
Imports from the Gulf (in thousands of dollars)				
Saudi Arabia	96,598	91,533	416,973	150,339
Kuwait	NA	176	48,623	130,415
Bahrain	NA	NA	13,602	32,018
UAE	NA	NA	NA	NA
Qatar	NA	NA	NA	NA
Oman	NA	NA	NA	NA

Source: Turkish Statistical Authority Data Base, http://tuik.gov.tr

The post-1980 period: Turkey's developing relations with the Gulf

The 1980s

In 1980, the Turkish Armed Forces staged a coup and took over the government. In the succeeding three years, the Armed Forces not only redesigned the political system but also introduced neo-liberal economic reforms. With the latter Turkey switched from an import substitution strategy to an export promotion strategy, resulting in the search for new markets and foreign direct investment.

The oil-rich Gulf was a natural choice that would serve both ends. In the 1980s Turkey began to pay multiple visits to the Gulf at the highest levels for the first time in the history of the Republic. Turkish President Kenan Evran, for example, visited Kuwait three times in 1982, 1987 and 1988, Saudi Arabia in 1984, the UAE in 1985, and Qatar in 1986. Turgut Özal, the name most associated with Turkey's transition to a neo-liberal economy, also made official visits to the Gulf, visiting Saudi Arabia five times as the prime minister and in 1990 as the president, Bahrain in 1986 as the prime minister, the UAE in 1990 as the president and Qatar in 1990 as the president. Some Gulf states reciprocated these visits: the UAE's president, Zayed bin Sultan Al Nahyan, in 1984; Qatar's emir, Khalifa bin Hamad al Thani, in 1985; and Kuwait's emir, Jaber al Ahmed Al Sabah, in 1991.

In the 1980s Turkey's trade with the Gulf increased. Turkey began to trade now with all the Gulf countries at a greater volume, although trade was limited somewhat due to a decline in energy revenues for the Gulf states. Turkey's exports to Saudi Arabia, for example, increased from $78.2 million between 1975 and 1979 to $1.3 billion from 1980 to 1984, increasing again to $1.9 billion from 1985 to 1989. Imports also increased from a total of $150.3 million in the period from 1975 to 1979 to $1.5 billion between 1980 and 1984, before decreasing to $1 billion over the next five-year period (Table 7.2).

What is noteworthy is that Turkey tipped the trade balance in its favor for the first time in the 1980s, recording trade surplus with Bahrain in the first half of the 1980s, Saudi Arabia and Kuwait in the second half, and throughout the decade with the UAE, Qatar, and Oman. Moreover, the share of Turkey's trade with the Gulf rose in the 1980s. Turkey's exports to the Gulf had constituted less than 1% of Turkey's total trade until the first half of the 1970s and 1.5% in the second. The share of total exports to the Gulf jumped to a historic 7% in the first half and then slightly decreased to 6.5% in the second half of the 1980s.

Although economics began to drive Turkey's efforts to develop stronger relations with the Gulf, geopolitics facilitated them. In the 1980s, the Gulf states began to face revolutionary Iran as their new geopolitical rival. Previously an ally against the pan-Arabist movement, Iran changed course after its revolution, which resulted in an anti-US regime in Teheran and led to a new political activism among the Shia populations across the Gulf. This directly affected Saudi Arabia, Kuwait, and Bahrain, all of which have significant Shia populations. Turkey was also wary of Iran's revolutionary rhetoric and its agenda to export the revolution to other countries. Hence both Turkey and the Gulf found

Table 7.2 Turkey's trade statistics with the Gulf, 1980–89

	1980–84	1985–89
Exports to the Gulf (in thousands of dollars)		
Saudi Arabia	1,331,627	1,919,364
Kuwait	403,344	850,656
Bahrain	9,075	12,377
UAE	74,475	323,123
Qatar	19,612	54,680
Oman	3,764	18,684
Imports from the Gulf (in thousands of dollars)		
Saudi Arabia	1,519,793	1,010,652
Kuwait	596,727	551,412
Bahrain	5,874	30,302
UAE	67,603	208,020
Qatar	8,099	8,018
Oman	8,419	381

Source: Turkish Statistical Authority Data Base, http://tuik.gov.tr

themselves facing the same geopolitical challenge, which brought the two sides closer together.

The 1990s

Turkey's priorities changed from economics back to security in the 1990s, as Turkey began to face a stronger and more aggressive Kurdistan Workers' Party (PKK), a Kurdish separatist organization that terrorized Turkey in the second half of the 1980s. By the early 1990s, the PKK was Turkey's greatest security threat, especially after the First Gulf War created a vacuum in Northern Iraq from which the PKK benefitted. This changing focus on domestic security priorities influenced Turkey's Gulf policy.[5]

Turkey enlisted Iranian and Syrian cooperation in fighting the PKK, and after failing to gain European support, turned to Israel. Throughout the 1990s Turkey decisively and systematically developed extensive relations with Israel, sharing intelligence, undertaking joint-military training and exercises, and granting huge military contracts to Israeli firms.[6] This relationship became a concern to Iran and its Arab neighbors, especially in the second half of the 1990s. Both the Arab League and the Organization of Islamic Conference strongly condemned Turkey for developing close ties with Israel. The Arab league also strongly criticized Turkey for the military incursions it made into Iraq to destroy PKK bases.[7]

Despite its cooling relations with the broader Arab world, Turkey still sought to develop closer ties to the Gulf states. President Süleyman Demirel continued in his predecessor's footsteps and paid critical attention to the Gulf. As prime minister he toured the Gulf in 1993, visiting Qatar, Kuwait, Saudi Arabia, Bahrain,

Table 7.3 Turkey's trade statistics with the Gulf, 1990–99

	1990–94	1995–99
Exports to the Gulf (in thousands of dollars)		
Saudi Arabia	2,570,653	2,276,779
Kuwait	406,510	523,885
Bahrain	46,310	56,959
UAE	561,838	1,295,817
Qatar	30,633	55,357
Oman	31,914	100,326
Turkey's Total		
Imports from the Gulf (in thousands of dollars)		
Saudi Arabia	6,946,110	5,358,906
Kuwait	283,851	537,301
Bahrain	45,248	79,626
UAE	1,565,571	150,304
Qatar	5,675	95,444
Oman	876	947
Turkey's Total		

Source: Turkish Statistical Authority Data Base, http://tuik.gov.tr

and the UAE, and he visited again as president, first traveling to Kuwait, the UAE, and Oman in 1997, and then Bahrain and Qatar in 1999.[8] Helping Turkish outreach to the Gulf states was its strong stance against Iraq's invasion of Kuwait, condemning Iraq and declaring full support for Kuwait. Turkey also suspended the transport of Iraqi oil through the Kirkuk–Incirlik pipeline and joined the international coalition that expelled Iraq from Kuwait. However, these positive diplomatic overtures were undermined by the Turkish–Israeli relationship.[9]

Overall, however, Turkey's trade with the Gulf was mostly unaffected. In the first half of the 1990s Turkey's exports to and imports from Saudi Arabia, Bahrain, the UAE, and Oman increased, while its volume of trade with Kuwait and Qatar decreased.[10]

The Gulf's share in Turkish total exports decreased in the 1990s. While exports to the Gulf constituted 6.5% in the second half of the 1980s, they constituted 4.8% in the first half of the 1990s and 3.46% in the second. The Gulf's share in Turkey's total imports, however, first increased to a historic 7.44% in the first half of the 1990s, but then decreased to 2.9% in the second half. Due to the increase in Turkey's imports, the Gulf's share in Turkey's total trade increased in the first half of the 1990s and then decreased in the second half (Table 7.3).

The 2000s[11]

In the beginning of the 2000s economic concerns again overtook security. The Turkish Armed Forces' heavy-handed measures minimized the PKK threat to Turkey. The capture of its leader, Abdullah Ocalan, in Kenya in 1991 further boosted the Turkish military and demoralized the PKK. However, this success came with an economic cost, as the 1990s were a lost decade for Turkey. The economy was highly unstable with gross national product fluctuating between 9.4% in 1990 to −6.1% in 1994. Inflation fluctuated between a historic high of 106% in 1994 to 50% in 1999, and the ratio of domestic debt to gross national product rose from 2.5% in 1990 to 12.4% in 1999. Worse was to come in 2001 when a major financial crisis hit Turkey hard. In that year gross national product shrank by 9.5% and the ratio of domestic debt to gross national product reached a historic high of 13.3%.[12]

Weak coalition governments and petty fights among leading politicians aggravated the economic crisis in Turkey. The electorate severely punished all parties in the parliament with none passing the electoral threshold of 10% in November 2002 national elections. Only two parties entered the parliament, one of which was the newly founded JDP, which formed a government. The coming to power of the JDP effectively ended a period beset by political instability and economic crisis (Tables 7.4 and 7.5).

By the time the JDP came to power Turkey had already developed a thriving export-oriented economy thanks to the neoliberalization program that had been pursued since the early 1980s. Furthermore, Turkey had already managed to increase its exports worldwide, starting immediately after it initiated its neoliberal economic reforms in 1980. The value of Turkey's total exports jumped from a total of $9.6 billion in the period 1975–9 to a total of $26.2 billion in the next five-year period. In the second half of the 1990s, on the other hand, Turkey exported $124.6 billion worth of goods and services. Once in power, the JDP leaders set out set out to increase Turkey's trade with a renewed dedication and energy, resulting in $500 billion in exports in the second half of the 2000s (Table 7.6).

Table 7.4 The Gulf's share in Turkey's total exports and imports

	To/from the Gulf	Turkey's total	Share (%)
Turkey's exports (in thousands of dollars)			
1950–59	382	2,658,522	0.01
1960–69	2,250	4,337,359	0.05
1970–79	175,785	14,662,947	1.19
1980–84	1,841,897	26,220,464	7.02
1985–89	3,178,884	48,891,492	6.50
1990–94	3,647,858	74,718,318	4.88
1995–99	4,309,123	124,683,754	3.45
Turkey's imports (in thousands of dollars)			
1950–59	96,598	3,653,994	2.64
1960–69	91,709	6,359,469	1.44
1970–79	791,970	34,876,706	2.27
1980–84	2,206,515	45,677,395	4.83
1985–89	3,178,884	66,677,395	2.71
1990–94	6,222,529	118,918,584	7.44
1995–99	3,384,187	214,487,038	2.90

Table 7.5 Turkey's trade statistics with the Gulf, 2000–09

	2000–04	2005–09
Exports to the Gulf (in thousands of dollars)		
Saudi Arabia	2,951,833	7,402,392
Kuwait	749,256	1,354,936
Bahrain	137,932	575,721
UAE	3,000,082	17,773,796
Qatar	84,651	2,237,529
Oman	138,166	524,064
Imports from the Gulf (in thousands of dollars)		
Saudi Arabia	2,373,618	3,630,630
Kuwait	749,256	1,354,936
Bahrain	137,932	575,721
UAE	502,771	2,386,877
Qatar	53,788	391,784
Oman	2,996	57,513

Source: Turkish Statistical Authority Data Base, http://tuik.gov.tr

Table 7.6 The Gulf's share in Turkey's total exports and imports

	To/from the Gulf	Turkey's total	Share (%)
Turkey's exports (in thousands of dollars)			
2000–04	7,061,920	205,588,201	3.43
2005–09	29,868,439	500,452,642	5.97
Turkey's imports (in thousands of dollars)			
2000–04	3,384,187	314,335,159	1.08
2005–09	7,222,801	769,305,035	0.94

Source: Turkish Statistical Authority Data Base, http://tuik.gov.tr

The JDP leaders paid special attention to the Gulf, evident in the numerous visits by Recep Tayyip Erdoğan, Turkey's prime minister, made to the region. Both as prime minister and president, Erdoğan made multiple visits throughout the decade, as did former President Abdullah Gul during his time in office (2007–14). These visits were reciprocated by Gulf leaders, and political and diplomatic meetings boosted trade relations. Turkey's exports to and imports from all Gulf countries increased over the decade, with Turkey recording a trade surplus with each of the Gulf countries in the 2000s.

The share of Turkey's exports to the Gulf in relation to its total volume of worldwide exports also increased from 3.43% to 5.97%. Remarkably, however, the share of Turkey's imports from the Gulf as a percentage of Turkey's total worldwide imports decreased first to 1.08% in the first half of the 2000s and then to a historic 0.94% in the second half. This decrease was partly due to the fact that Turkey's gas and oil imports from Russia and Iran, the Gulf's two main competitors, skyrocketed between 2000 and 2010. While Turkey's imports from Russia increased almost six-fold from $3.8 billion in 2000 to $21.6 billion in 2010, its imports from Iran increased more than nine-fold from $815 million in 2000 to $7.6 billion in 2010.

Turkey also succeeded in attracting foreign capital from the Gulf. Four of the six GCC countries – Saudi Arabia, the UAE, Qatar, and Kuwait – were among the top 20 sources of foreign direct investment into Turkey in the period between 2002 and 2010. As a group, the Gulf states were the fourth-largest foreign investor in Turkey, behind the Netherlands, the US, Greece, and Belgium. Among the Gulf countries the UAE had been the largest investor, followed by Saudi Arabia, then Kuwait and finally Qatar.[13]

Turkey also sought to diversify its links with the Gulf in the 2000s. In 2004, Turkey was instrumental in launching a NATO initiative, known as the Istanbul Initiative, which aimed to develop cooperation in the field of security with the Middle East. Although all Gulf states were invited, only four, Bahrain, Qatar, Kuwait, and the UAE, responded positively.[14] Another major step in relations came in May 2005. Turkey and the Gulf states signed a Memorandum of Understanding (MoU) in Manama, Bahrain, to support economic cooperation, encourage the exchange of technical expertise and information, improve economic relations, and initiate negotiations to establish free trade zones.[15] A milestone in relations came, however, on September 2, 2008, when the GCC foreign ministers declared Turkey a strategic partner.[16] The GCC also signed another MoU with Turkey, calling for the establishment of a comprehensive and regular consultation mechanism on political, economic, defense, security, and cultural matters. In this vein, both sides agreed to hold a joint annual meeting of foreign ministers.[17] The first joint ministerial meeting was held in Istanbul on July 8, 2009. The sides decided to improve cooperation in "all economic, commercial and technical fields," seek new prospects of cooperation "in the field of energy, including oil, gas, renewable energy and mineral resources," coordinate the activities of security authorities "in the fields of countering terrorism, sources of terror funding, money laundering, drug trafficking, and organized crime," establish "mechanisms to increase cooperation among institutions of research and higher education, national archives and cultural institutions," and "promote and facilitate educational and cultural exchange programs as well as exchanges of young diplomats for language and on-the-job training."[18]

Reflecting the overall progress made in relations in the 2000s, Saudi Arabia awarded the "King Faisal International Prize for Service to Islam" to Recep Tayyip Erdoğan, Turkey's then prime minister, in 2010. The press release announcing the prize stated that Erdoğan "set an example of judicious leadership in the Islamic world," and thanks to his "unyielding position on various Islamic and global issues, gained the respect of the entire Islamic nation and the rest of the world." Finally, Erdoğan was claimed to have "rendered an outstanding service to Islam by fiercely defending the rights and just causes of the Islamic nation, particularly the rights of the Palestinian people."[19] Following Saudi Arabia, Kuwait awarded Erdoğan the "Outstanding Personality in the Islamic World Award" in January 2011.

Geopolitics also contributed to stronger Turkey–GCC relations. In the 1990s, Iran dropped its earlier radical rhetoric and adopted a more pragmatic policy towards the Gulf after a change in leadership. This was to change, however, in the aftermath of the September 11, 2001 attacks, as Iran came to be perceived as a major beneficiary of the US's invasions of Afghanistan and Iraq. With the ascension to the throne of King Abdullah in 2005, Saudi Arabia set out to reverse what it saw as a shift in the balance of power towards Iran by bringing together a broad coalition of states which shared similar concerns about the rise of Iran. Among them were Egypt and Jordan.

Turkey seemed to be less concerned by Teheran and sought to avoid entanglement in what some called the new Cold War in the Middle East.[20] Turkey even worked to develop stronger relations with Iran. In this vein, Turkey paid numerous visits to Iran: President Ahmet Necdet Sezer visited Iran twice in 2002 and 2003, President Abdullah Gul visited in 2009 and Turkey's Prime Minister Recep Tayyip Erdoğan visited in 2004, 2006, 2009, and 2010. Turkey's trade with Iran also expanded in the 2000s. Turkey's exports to Iran, for example, increased from $235 million in 2000 to $3 billion in 2010, and Turkey's imports from Iran increased from $815.7 million in 2000 to $7.6 billion in 2010. For Iran, Turkey even put its strategic interests with the United States, the European Union, and the Arab World at great risk by engineering the Nuclear Fuel Swap Deal in May 2010. One month after the deal, Turkey voted against further UN sanctions on Iran as a non-permanent member of the Security Council.

In the 2000s, in short, Turkey hedged between Iran and the GCC, pursuing relations on both sides of the deepening rift. This approach was challenged by the Arab Spring.

The Arab Spring

Turkey's reactions to the Arab Spring were not uniform across all affected countries and even exhibited certain inconsistencies and contradictions. Yet Turkey did not waver in its reactions in one critical way and this found its clearest expression in the very first statement Turkey's prime minister, Recep Tayyip Erdoğan, made on the Arab Spring when he declared that Turkey demanded "democracy, prosperity, justice, freedom for … our fellow nations."[21] Turkey thereafter maintained this position and repeatedly expressed its full, unconditional support for the demands of the protesters, be it in Egypt, or in Libya or in Syria or even in Bahrain.[22]

This stance had the potential to put Turkey in disagreement or conflict with the Gulf countries, especially with regards to its positions on Bahrain and Egypt. More worrisome for Saudi Arabia, the UAE, and Kuwait was the rise of political parties, especially in Tunisia and Egypt, which were ideologically akin to the ruling JDP in Turkey. The Islamist Al Nahda movement in Tunisia and the Freedom and Justice Party (FJP) in Egypt scored critical victories in the first parliamentary elections in Tunisia in October 2011 and Egypt in November and December 2011 and January 2012 respectively and signaled that Islamists would be prominent in these countries.[23] The FJP scored an even more important victory in June 2012 when its presidential candidate, Muhammed Morsi, became the first democratically elected president of Egypt. The ruling JDP in Turkey itself hailed from the political Islam tradition and had strong historical and ideological ties to the Muslim Brotherhood movement. Even before Morsi's election, Turkey had already taken steps to develop stronger relations with post-Mubarak Egypt.

Turkey's then-president, Abdullah Gul, visited Egypt soon after Mubarak stepped down. In September 2011, Turkey's prime minister paid a visit to both Egypt and Tunisia, signing the Friendship and Cooperation Treaty with Tunisia and a framework that was to become the High Level Strategic Cooperation Council with Egypt. Turkey's foreign minister, Ahmet Davutoğlu, gave an interview to *The New York Times* in which he indicated that Turkey's leaders were aspiring to form a partnership with Egypt that would represent a new axis of power. Davutoğlu said, "This will not be an axis against any other country – not Israel, not any other country, this will be an axis of democracy, real democracy," forming an axis "of the two big nations in our region, from the north to the south, from the Black Sea down to the Nile Valley in Sudan."[24]

When Morsi was elected, more concrete steps were taken, including an extension of financial aid to Egypt, mutual high-level visits and signing of cooperation treaties. Turkey and Egypt came to be perceived as so strongly allied that King Abdallah of Jordan would tell Jeffrey Goldberg of *The Atlantic* magazine, "I see a Muslim Brotherhood crescent developing in Egypt and Turkey."[25] The king was concerned as in his view "wolves in sheep's clothing" were running the Brotherhood and had to be prevented from coming to power across the region.

Saudi Arabia, the UAE, and Kuwait had similar reasons to worry. The Arab Spring and the rise to political prominence of Muslim Brotherhood-affiliated political parties and figures emboldened and inspired Islamists in Saudi Arabia, the UAE, and Kuwait, a scenario that had occurred before in the aftermath of the Iranian revolution. Furthermore, Islamists in the Gulf could now seek the powerful backing of the two most populous countries in the region, Turkey, and Egypt. The three other GCC countries had less to worry about. In Oman, there was almost no Muslim Brotherhood network. In Bahrain there was, but it was a staunch ally of the ruling family.[26] Qatar had nurtured cordial relations with both the local and transnational Muslim Brotherhood movement, and as such, its leaders were not alarmed by the rise of the Muslim Brotherhood, and in fact saw in its rise an opportunity to expand Qatar's sphere of influence. Like Turkey, therefore, Qatar had become a major financial and diplomatic supporter of Egypt under Morsi.

The formation of a potentially powerful axis among Turkey, Egypt, and Qatar was cut short when the Egyptian military staged a coup against Morsi and took over the government in Egypt on July 3, 2013. The Muslim Brotherhood actively opposed the coup, organizing a series of street protests. In reaction, the Egyptian military unleashed a crackdown on the movement, after which many Brotherhood figures escaped Egypt and found refuge in Turkey and Qatar. Turkey immediately condemned the coup and continued to express its criticisms of the crackdown. Relations between Turkey and Egypt inevitably deteriorated and eventually

Between geopolitics and economics   117

collapsed in November 2013. Qatar was silent about the coup and even congratulated the interim president. It was also less vocal on the crackdown but still voiced some criticisms. Saudi Arabia, the UAE, and Kuwait, on the other hand, welcomed the coup, immediately recognized the new regime in Egypt, and thereafter became its major diplomatic and financial supporters. The rift within the Gulf, pitting Qatar against Saudi Arabia and the UAE, became public in March 2014 when the two countries, along with Bahrain, withdrew their ambassadors from Doha.

Turkey was able to avoid a dramatic escalation and minimize the harm that the episode could have inflicted on its relations with Saudi Arabia, the UAE, and Kuwait, its three major Gulf trading partners. This was achieved by Ankara's attempts to act as a mediator and its refusal to take an outright pro-Qatar position. Turkey–GCC trade relations remained stable, and its exports to all Gulf countries – except interestingly Qatar – increased. Exports to Saudi Arabia, for example, doubled from $7.4 billion from 2005–09 to $14.8 billion in the period 2010 to 2014. Exports to Qatar, however, almost halved from $2.2 billion to $1.2 billion during the same period.

In the meantime, the Gulf's share in Turkey's total exports continued to increase, first to 6.33% in 2010–14 and then to 6.8% in 2015–16. The Gulf's share in Turkey's total imports recovered from historical lows in the 2000s to 2.49% in 2010–14 and to 2.68% in 2015–16 (Table 7.7 and 7.8).

Yet, there were also signs of tension. For example, the fifth joint ministerial meeting of the Turkey–GCC High Level Strategic Dialogue was not held in 2012, although the sides had agreed to hold it in Bahrain.[27] It was also rumored that Saudi Arabia, along with Egypt, had led a campaign in 2014 against Turkey's candidacy for a non-permanent membership seat in the UN Security Council.[28] Foreign direct investment statistics better reflect the changing relations between

Table 7.7 Turkey's trade statistics with the Gulf, 2010–16

	2010–14	2015–16
Exports to the Gulf (in thousands of dollars)		
Saudi Arabia	14,896,350	6,646,835
Kuwait	1,690,099	913,899
Bahrain	944,112	418,576
UAE	24,836,486	10,088,404
Qatar	1,196,806	862,207
Oman	1,477,459	568,370
Imports from the Gulf (in thousands of dollars)		
Saudi Arabia	9,911,187	3,952,449
Kuwait	1,250,283	252,128
Bahrain	808,878	232,251
UAE	14,581,914	5,709,842
Qatar	1,893,038	632,062
Oman	400,630	109,256

Source: Turkish Statistical Authority Data Base, http://tuik.gov.tr

Table 7.8 The Gulf's share in Turkey's total exports and imports

	To/from the Gulf	Turkey's Total	Share (%)
Turkey's exports (in thousands of dollars)			
2010–14	45,040,311	710,664,619	6.33
2015–16	19,498,291	286,384,818	6.80
Turkey's imports (in thousands of dollars)			
2010–14	28,846,930	1,156,769,516	2.49
2015–16	10,887,988	405,850,498	2.68

Source: Turkish Statistical Authority Data Base, http://tuik.gov.tr

Table 7.9 Foreign direct investment (in million dollars)

	2002–10	*2011–16*
Saudi Arabia	1,424	525
The UAE	3,621	549
Kuwait	856	725
Qatar	208	1,298

Source: Turkey Minister of Economy, http:www.economy.gov.tr

Turkey and the Gulf. While total foreign direct investment from the UAE, Saudi Arabia, and Kuwait decreased from the period 2002–10 to the period 2011–16, total foreign direct investment from Qatar increased in the same period (Table 7.9).

Despite these tensions, mutual interest in Syria contributed to Turkey–GCC ties remaining relatively stable. In the beginning of the Syrian crisis, Turkey openly called on Syrian President Bashar Al Asad to listen to the demands of the protesters and implement political reforms and became harshly critical of the regime's violence against the protesters. By the beginning of 2012, Turkey and Saudi Arabia were on the same page: the Asad regime had to go, by force if necessary. To this end both countries extended financial and military support to the rebel groups in Syria; the Free Syrian Army (FSA) served as their focal point to reach out to these rebel groups.[29] Turkey, having a long border with Syria, has also benignly neglected the activities of Syrian rebel groups, especially of Jihadi groups inside Turkey.[30] Other regional developments in 2014 were also critical in preventing a collapse in Turkey's relations with Saudi Arabia. The rise of the Islamic State in Iraq and Syria and of the Houthis in Yemen completely changed the security parameters in the region.

In the meantime, however, Qatar and Turkey have come to forge a special relationship in the midst of the regional isolation they find themselves in. This was evident especially in the signing of a ten-year military agreement between Turkey and Qatar in December 2014. The most consequential item of the agreement was that Turkey's Armed Forces could be deployed in Qatar's territories for educational purposes and military exercises.[31] As a part of this agreement Turkey even established a military base, named after the famous Berber commander, Tariq bin Ziyad, in Qatar in April 2016 and also sent some 100 military officers to the base.

Finally, in June 2017, Turkey passed a new law that allowed its military forces to be deployed in Qatar.[32] The law came just two days after Saudi Arabia, the UAE, Bahrain, and Egypt broke all diplomatic ties with Qatar. Even though Turkey claimed that the deployment was to serve the broader Gulf security, the move was clearly intended to show a strong support for Qatar against the four Arab states.

Whether this strong show in favor of Qatar will have any short- to long-term negative impact on Turkey's relations with Saudi Arabia and the UAE is yet to be seen. To say the least, however, Saudi Arabia, the UAE, Bahrain, and Egypt cited the closure of the Turkish military base in their list of demands submitted to Qatar to end the crisis. Moreover, the Syrian crisis that prevented a total collapse in relations in 2013 might not do the same as the intervention of Russia on the side of the Asad regime has decisively changed the balance of power in favor of the regime. As for Turkey–Qatar relations, the future is contingent on the popularity of Recep Tayyip Erdoğan, Turkey's powerful president. He is still popular among his constituency and seems to be secure in power. Yet, this is also a source of uncertainty: if Erdoğan sees Turkey's commitment to Qatar as a burden on his rule, he will likely change Turkey's policy.

Conclusion

Two prime drivers of Turkey's foreign policy have been security and economics. Depending on the domestic and regional context, one has trumped the other and set the course and tone of Turkey's foreign policy. The Gulf states are not in the immediate geographical vicinity of Turkey, say, like Greece, or Iran, Iraq, or Syria, and cannot pose an imminent security threat to Turkey. Therefore, economics had largely driven Turkey's relations with the Gulf until the Arab Spring. With the Arab Spring, Turkey began to act in ways that could seriously jeopardize its carefully nurtured relations with the Gulf.

In fact, by the end of summer 2013 Turkey had become almost totally isolated in the region. The only country in the region Turkey had good relations with was Qatar, which was likewise isolated. This regional isolation induced Turkey and Qatar to forge a special relationship, which has also acquired a military dimension. After 100 years, Turkey is militarily back in the Gulf. What Turkey wishes to gain from this entanglement in the Gulf crisis is not certain. The government has built Turkey's relations with Qatar in almost full secrecy and seems to desire to keep it that way. It is also unclear how the government will protect Turkey's vital interests with Saudi Arabia and the UAE. Turkey is torn apart in the Gulf and seems to have no strategy to make its foreign policy right again.

Notes

1 As far as I am aware there is no academic or popular book in English or in Turkish that focuses on Turkey–Gulf relations in the said period. For the post-2001 period, see Birol Başkan, *Turkey and Qatar in the Tangled Geopolitics of the Middle East* (New York: Palgrave MacMillan, 2016). However, this book focuses on Turkey–Qatar relations, not on the whole Gulf.

120 Birol Başkan

2 The Ottoman Empire extended its rule over the Gulf in the sixteenth century, but had lost it over the eastern part of the Peninsula starting in the mid-seventeenth century. In the late nineteenth century, the Ottoman Empire reasserted its rule and attached Kuwait, Qatar, Najd and Al Ahsa to the province of Basra. See Zekeriya Kurşun, *Necid ve Ahsa'da Osmanlı Hakimiyeti: Vehhabi Hareketi ve Suud Devletinin Ortaya Çıkışı* (Ankara: Türk Tarih Kurumu Yayınları, 1998); Frederic Anscombe, *The Ottoman Gulf: The Creation of Kuwait, Saudi Arabia, and Qatar* (New York: Columbia University Press, 1997).
3 Turkey began to perceive the Soviet Union as a threat because of the latter's territorial claims and request to change the status of the straits. See William Hale, *Turkish Foreign Policy Since 1774*, 3rd ed. (London: Routledge, 2013), chp. 4.
4 All trade data is available in Turkish Statistical Institute's data base at http://tuik.gov.tr. I made the calculations in the tables.
5 See Robert W. Olson, *The Kurdish Question and Turkish–Iranian Relations: From World War I to 1998* (Costa Meza: Mazda Publishers, 1998).
6 For more on Turkey–Israel relations in the 1990s, see Ofra Bengio, *The Turkish–Israeli Relationship: Changing Ties of Middle Eastern Outsiders*, 2nd ed. (New York: Palgrave Macmillan, 2009).
7 For more on Turkey–Iran relations in the 1990s, see Robert Olson, *Turkey–Iran Relations, 1979–2004: Revolution, Ideology, War, Coups and Geopolitics* (Costa Mesa: Mazda Publishers, 2004).
8 Muhammed Berdibek, "Türkiye-Ortadoğu İlişkilerinde Karşılıklı Üst Düzey Ziyaretler: (1923–2014)," *Akademik Ortadoğu* 10, no.3, (2016): 81.
9 Bengio, *The Turkish–Israeli Relationship: Changing Ties of Middle Eastern Outsiders*.
10 The decrease in Turkey's exports to and imports from Kuwait seems to be due to Iraq's invasion in 1990.
11 This section on Başkan, *Turkey and Qatar in the Tangled Geopolitics of the Middle East*, chp. 4.
12 Turkish Statistical Institute, *Statistical Indicators 1923–2004* (Ankara: Türkiye İstatistik Kurumu, n. d.), 575.
13 The data on Foreign Direct Investments are available in annual reports published by Turkish Minister of Economy, available at http://www.economy.gov.tr . Unfortunately I could not come across any statistics on which sectors the Gulf investment went to.
14 "Istanbul Cooperation Initiative," accessed October 14, 2017, http://www.nato.int/cps/en/natohq/topics_58787.htm?
15 "Türkiye Cumhuriyeti ve Körfez Arap Ülkeleri İşbirliği Konseyi Üyesi Ülkeler Arasında Ekonomik İşbirliğine ilişkin Çerçeve Anlaşma," accessed October 14, 2017, http://www2.tbmm.gov.tr/d23/1/1-0322.pdf
16 Mariam Al Hakeem, "GCC Names Turkey First Strategic Partner Outside the Gulf," *Gulf News*, September 3, 2008, http://gulfnews.com/news/gulf/uae/general/gcc-names-turkey-first-strategic-partner-outside-the-gulf-1.129631
17 Al Hakeem, "GCC Names Turkey First Strategic Partner Outside the Gulf."
18 "Joint Statement of the Joint Ministerial Meeting of the GCC-Turkey High Level Strategic Dialogue, 8 July 2009, Istanbul–Turkey," accessed October 14, 2017, http://www.mfa.gov.tr/joint-statement-of--the-joint-ministerial-meeting-of-the-gcc-turkey-high-level-strategic-dialogue-istanbul-_-turkey_-8-july-2009.en.mfa
19 "Press Release: Winners Announced: 2010/1431H King Faisal International Prize for Service to Islam," accessed October 14, 2017, http://kfip.org/wp-content/uploads/2013/09/SI-2010-PR.pdf
20 F. Gregory Gause III, "Beyond Sectarianism: The New Middle East Cold War," Brookings Doha Center Analysis Paper, No.11, July 2014, https://www.brookings.edu/wp-content/uploads/2016/06/English-PDF-1.pdf
21 "Erdogan to Mubarak: 'Listen to the Egyptians'," accessed October 14, 2017, http://www.setav.org/public/HaberDetay.aspx?Dil=tr&hid=63385&q=erdogan-to-mubarak-listen-to-the-egyptians

22 See Başkan, *Turkey and Qatar in the Tangled Geopolitics of the Middle East*, chp. 5
23 Egypt held the elections in three stages, each stage with a run-off. The elections lasted from 28 November to 11 January.
24 Anthony Shadid, "Turkey Predicts Alliance with Egypt as Regional Anchors," *International New York Times*, September 18, 2011, http://www.nytimes.com/2011/09/19/world/middleeast/turkey-predicts-partnership-with-egypt-as-regional-anchors.html?_r=0
25 The following excerpts are from Jeffrey Goldberg, "The Modern King in the Arab Spring," *The Atlantic*, March 18, 2013, http://www.theatlantic.com/magazine/archive/2013/04/monarch-in-the-middle/309270/
26 Ibrahim Hatlani, "Bahrain Between its Backers and the Brotherhood," Carnegie Endowment Sada Middle East Analysis, May 20, 2014, http://carnegieendowment.org/sada/55653
27 In September 2008, the GCC declared Turkey as a strategic partner in the annual meeting of ministers of foreign affairs of GCC states. In the same meeting, Turkey and the GCC agreed to hold joint ministerial meetings every year. The first meeting was held in Istanbul in July 2019. See "Joint Statement on Turkey–GCC High Level Strategic Dialogue 4th Joint Ministerial Meeting, 28 January 2012, Istanbul – Turkey," accessed October 14, 2017 http://www.mfa.gov.tr/joint-statement-turkey-gcc-high-level-strategic-dialogue-4th-joint-ministerial-meeting_-28january-2012_-istanbul-_-turkey.en.mfa
28 Benny Avni, "Turkey Loses U.N. Security Council Seat in Huge Upset," *Newsweek*, October 16, 2014, http://www.newsweek.com/venezuela-malaysia-angola-new-zealand-win-un-council-seats-277962
29 See Charles Lister, "The Free Syrian Army: A Decentralized Insurgent Brand," The Brookings Project on US Relations with the Islamic World, Analysis Paper, No.26, November 2016.
30 See Charles Lister, *The Syrian Jihad: Al-Qaeda, the Islamic State and the Evolution of an Insurgency* (New York: Oxford University Press, 2015).
31 For what Turkey seeks from the agreement, see Menekşe Tokyay, "What Does the Turkey–Qatar Military Deal Mean for Arab Conflicts," *Al Arabiya*, updated June 25, 2015, http://english.alarabiya.net/en/perspective/analysis/2015/06/25/What-does-Turkey-Qatar-military-deal-mean-for-Arab-conflicts-.html . For what Qatar seeks from the agreement, see Feyza Gümüşlüoğlu, "Katar'da 100 yıl sonra Türk askeri," *Star*, updated June 26, 2015, http://haber.star.com.tr/acikgorus/katarda-100-yil-sonra-turk-askeri/haber-1038052
32 The law does not specify how many troops will be deployed in Qatar. It is reported by Turkish news outlets that the military base in Qatar can host up to 5,000 troops. See "Türkiye Cumhuriyeti Hükümeti ile Katar Devleti Hükümeti Arasında Katar Topraklarında Türk Kuvvetlerinin Konuşlandırılmasına İlişkin Uygulama Anlaşması ile Anlaşmanın Tadili Hakkında Protokolün Onaylanmasının Uygun Bulunduğuna Dair Kanun Tasarısı," accessed October 14, 2017, http://www2.tbmm.gov.tr/d26/1/1-0800.pdf

8 India and the Gulf states

David Brewster and Kadira Pethiyagoda

Introduction

In many ways, the Gulf represents a natural economic, political and strategic hinterland for India. But despite India's size, geographic proximity and civilisational relationships, for many years it was not an active player in the region. This is changing. Economic relationships between Gulf Cooperation Council (GCC) states and India are now close and growing in intensity, and India is also increasingly taking a strategic interest in the Gulf. This is driven by concerns about the changing balance of power and India's growing confidence in its potential role as a regional security provider. GCC states too are increasingly seeing value in developing closer relations with India that go well beyond the economic sphere.

India's interests in the Gulf – an overview

Prior to any discussion of contemporary interests, it is important to note India's enduring cultural and historical ties to the Gulf region which provide Delhi's policymakers with insights and soft power that enhance its ability to pursue its interests. The shared history means that culture plays a more significant role in influencing India's image in the Middle East than it does for other extra-regional powers.

India had peaceful relations with Middle Eastern civilisations before the Mughals. The relationship between the two regions stretches back to antiquity. Indian Emperor Ashoka had received an ambassador from Ptolemy II of Egypt and even proselytised Buddhism to the region. There was trade and immigration from Arabia, particularly Yemen, as well as Persia, even prior to Islam, including in the first century CE along the coasts of Malabar, and then to the coast of Bengal.[1] From the seventh to tenth centuries, migrants from the south of the Gulf were settling in Gujarat. One of the first mosques in the world was built in Kerala by an Arab trader in 629 CE.[2] As such, India had its introduction to Islam directly from the Gulf, well before Mughal rule. Islam in India has influenced and was influenced by, Indian cultural values. The Turko-Afghan-Persian Mughals also imported values with regard to social structure, philosophy and the legal realm that were rooted in Islam.[3] Much of this occurred through the Sufis with their ability to attract the masses and engage with Hindus.[4] Islam perhaps made its most lasting impact on the cultural values of the majority of Indians indirectly, via developments occurring concurrently in Hinduism.[5] Ideals and precepts of Sufism influenced the thinking of Hindu reformers such as the Bhakti movement. The value that certain societal groups should be considered equal was a characteristic of Islam that stood in contrast to India's caste system. It helped attract large numbers of lower caste and outcaste Hindus, particularly in Bengal,[6] and likely helped influence Hindu reformers. This rich history of cultural exchange potentially places India in an advantageous position to pursue its contemporary interests.

India has wide-ranging and significant economic, political and strategic interests in the Gulf. However, its engagement with the Gulf has clearly been most successful in the economic sphere, increasingly making the GCC states what Prime Minister Manmohan Singh called India's "natural economic hinterland."[7] In 2016–17, India's bilateral trade with the GCC countries was US$97 billion (comprising Indian imports of US$55 billion and Indian exports of US$41 billion). This compared with US$71 billion in bilateral trade between India and the states of the Association of Southeast Asian Nations in the same period.[8] While both GCC–India imports and exports have been adversely impacted by recent falls in energy prices, the GCC collectively remains India's largest trading partner. Not surprisingly, India's imports from GCC states are overwhelmingly comprised of energy commodities. Perhaps more surprising is the level and composition of Indian exports to GCC states. Indian exports to Saudi Arabia and Oman are dominated by refined petroleum which is re-exported by India to the Gulf after processing, while gems and jewellery dominate the Indian export basket to the United Arab Emirates (UAE). The main exports to Kuwait are cereals, while major exports to Bahrain include iron and steel.[9]

The UAE acts as India's economic hub in the Gulf. India is the UAE's largest trading partner, with bilateral trade of around US$50 billion in 2015–16[10], which the countries aim to grow by 60% over the next five years.[11] Despite this relatively high level of bilateral trade, the volume of India–GCC investment has until recently been relatively underdeveloped. But Indian investment in GCC states is growing quickly from 4.7% of total foreign investment in GCC states in 2011 to 16% in 2016 (aggregating US$2.9 billion – the overwhelming majority of which is in the UAE).[12] Again, the UAE acts as the hub for India–GCC investment, with thousands of Indian companies operating in UAE.[13] There is also a target for US$75 billion in UAE investments in Indian infrastructure.[14]

With 25% of India's population (around 300 million people) still lacking electricity in 2014, assured access to energy will be fundamental to India's development. The average Indian uses around one-third of the energy used by the average person worldwide, and that is likely to grow.[15] With growth in India's economy comes a growing dependence on foreign energy imports. Demand for imported oil is predicted to grow much faster than domestic sources of supply, which face substantial constraints.[16] India's primary energy consumption more than doubled from 1990–2012.[17] By 2011 India was the fourth-largest consumer of energy in the world[18] and by 2040, the country will account for 25% of the rise in global energy use.[19] The largest growth will be in coal and oil.[20] India's high level of import dependence means that oil prices have an arguably greater impact on India's economy than on many other great or emerging powers.[21] India's net oil imports grew from 42% of total demand for oil in 1990 to an estimated 71% in 2012.[22] India's reliance on energy (most certainly for oil[23] and natural gas) sourced from overseas, including the Gulf, is projected to increase.

The increasing proportion of India's energy requirements being filled by imported energy gives the GCC relationship a strong strategic dimension.[24] This energy trade relies on the continuing firm political relationship with the Gulf which provides further impetus to policymakers to view Gulf relations through a strategic, rather than a purely commercial prism.[25] The geopolitics of energy is now firmly part of "daily business in India."[26] India has even acquired upstream hydrocarbon reserves in the Gulf in its bid to become energy secure.[27] Delhi has also made a deal with the UAE's Abu Dhabi National Oil Company (ADNOC) to have the company store crude oil in India's Mangalore strategic petroleum reserve.[28] ADNOC will use it as a wholesale storage facility and Indian refiners will be able to buy whenever required. On the other hand, India's high level of reliance on energy imports also creates an imperative for it to diversify its suppliers, which we saw in October 2017 when India for the first time began importing crude oil from the United States. As Winston Churchill once said, "safety and certainty in oil, lie in variety and variety alone."[29]

The Middle East has been important in helping both the Bharatiya Janata Party (now India's ruling party) and Congress in their main economic policy objectives – to increase prosperity and bring India's masses out of poverty. Foreign exchange remittances have also long played an important role in relieving India's balance of payments pressures. During India's financial crisis in the 1990s, foreign exchange via remittances played a significant role in supporting the economy. With a population set to be the world's largest within the next decade, India has an excess of manpower, which it seeks to export to the Gulf and elsewhere. India is the world's biggest recipient of foreign remittances and these form a key part of the economy, particularly amongst poorer households.[30] Over half of India's total remittances income in 2014 came from GCC countries.[31] The Gulf region alone hosts around 7 million Indians who in 2015–16 contributed approximately US$35.9 billion in remittances to the Indian economy.[32]

This mutually beneficial relationship has also helped accelerate the development of Gulf countries through providing cheap skilled and unskilled labour. The Indian state of Kerala has played a particularly important role. In 2014, the number of Keralite emigrants living overseas was 2.4 million out of a total state population of 33.9 million, the majority based in the Gulf.[33] Kerala has provided so much labour to the UAE that it is even referred to as the "Eighth Emirate of the UAE." During Modi's visit to the country, he spoke in Kerala's major language, Malayali, when announcing the UAE's setting aside of land to build the first Hindu temple in Abu Dhabi.[34]

For some years, Delhi sought to bring its economic and other relations with the Gulf within what it calls its "Look West" policy. This has now been rebranded

"Link West" as an indication of the Indian government's intention to develop more active and comprehensive relationships with the GCC states. Indian Prime Minister Narendra Modi has made several visits to the Gulf and broader Middle East since taking office and evinced a greater prioritisation of political ties with the region. This is timely, given that India's stakes in the Middle East have in recent years risen beyond merely commercial concerns to include the strategic realm.

Indian strategic perspectives on the Gulf

India's economic, energy and diasporic interests in the Gulf give it a major stake in security and stability of Gulf states. In the Gulf and throughout the wider Middle East there are considerable concerns about state fragility and the rising power of non-state actors and non-state sources of identity (including sectarianism and tribalism). These concerns have been exacerbated by Gulf states' responses to the volatile environment, including a potential arms race between Saudi Arabia and Iran. India's leadership sees the current powers involved in the region, including the United States, European powers, Russia and regional players like Turkey, as lacking the ability and will to facilitate stability.[35] While India has an interest in stability in all regional states due to its diaspora being spread across the region, many of these other powers have their own security interests and relationships that may sometimes be prioritised above the goal of overall regional stability. While Delhi currently lacks the capacity to shape regional politics to the same degree as some of these other powers, there may be an increasing impetus for Indian policymakers to act to support regional stability.

At first glance, it would seem natural that India, a growing power with a population of more than 1.2 billion people and one of the world's largest economies, would have a major strategic role in the neighbouring Persian Gulf. However, for many years this was not the case, and indeed for much of its modern history, India has 'punched below its weight' in the Gulf. It has been constrained from playing a significant strategic role in the Gulf through a combination of factors, including a lack of resources, ideological limitations, and adverse strategic alignments. Although India's perspectives, aspirations, and alignments are changing, some of these constraints continue to be obstacles in its potential role in the region.[36]

During the colonial era, British India played an important role in the Gulf, where Indian troops, administrators, and traders anchored Britain's strategic influence. However, in the decades after India's independence, India's role in the Gulf largely withered away. India lacked the resources to play a substantial strategic role beyond its immediate environs and for decades it was preoccupied with major security challenges both internally and with several of its immediate neighbours. India's rivalry with Pakistan, in particular, kept India largely preoccupied in South Asia right up to the turn of this century.

These constraints were reinforced by ideological limitations. During much of the Cold War, Nehruvian strategic doctrine and the principles of non-alignment formed a foundation of Indian foreign-policy thinking, including commitments to non-intervention and opposition to the use of military force not expressly authorised by the United Nations. From the 1970s, India publicly opposed the US alliance system in the Gulf or the idea that any extra-regional military presence was required to maintain security. But in practice, India saw its interests in the Gulf as largely limited to rhetorical efforts to minimise the influence of other major powers. After 1971, India's strategic alignment with the Soviet Union also did not endear India to conservative Gulf monarchies that substantially depended on the United States for their security.[37]

Changes in Indian strategic perspectives since the end of the Cold War have mitigated some of these constraints. India has gradually developed greater confidence in its potential role as what it calls a 'net provider of security' to its region.[38] While this term is not defined, it evinces India's long-term aspirations of being recognised as the leading security manager for its region, which could one day include the Persian Gulf. Since the turn of this century, India has claimed a much-expanded area of strategic interest beyond South Asia. The Indian Navy now sees itself as almost destined in the long term to be the predominant maritime security provider from the Red Sea to Singapore and having a significant security role in areas beyond.[39] The Indian Navy's Maritime Security Strategy includes the Persian Gulf and its littoral as one of India's primary areas of maritime interest.[40] The idea of an area of strategic interest extending from the Persian Gulf in the west to the Straits of Malacca in the east and beyond has broad political and bureaucratic support. Former Foreign Minister Jaswant Singh called the Persian Gulf part of India's *sphere of influence*,[41] and former Prime Minister Manmohan Singh said it was part of India's *strategic footprint*.[42] Singh argued that there is "no doubt that the Indian Navy must be the most important maritime power in this region."[43] As noted above, in 2013, Singh announced that India should henceforth be regarded as a "net security provider" to its region, a phrase that since has been frequently echoed by Indian defence officials and analysts.[44]

But India's aspirations towards being recognised as the leading power across a broad swathe of the Indian Ocean region have long been constrained by its material shortcomings, including the relatively meagre power projection capabilities of the Indian defence forces. This means that India has been overshadowed by the United States as the predominant military power in the region and will likely continue to be so for years to come. However, the Indian Navy is already the largest naval power among Indian Ocean states and its capabilities are expected to grow in line with growth in the Indian economy in coming decades. A recent PricewaterhouseCoopers report projected that between 2016 and 2050 India's GDP will grow by 533% in purchasing power parity terms and 1,244% in market exchange rate terms.[45] Such growth would give India the financial capabilities to fulfil its aspirations to play a leading security role across a broad area.

Despite changing perspectives and growing material capabilities, some ideological factors continue to constrain India's security role in the Persian Gulf. For one thing, there is a wide gap between India's rhetoric and strategic action and a longstanding hesitancy to use military force beyond South Asia. One well-known study of India's strategic culture in the early 1990s characterised Indian strategic thinking as being "defensive" and having a "lack of an expansionist military tradition."[46] Similarly, US analyst Stephen Cohen argues that India has a culture of "strategic restraint" that is deeply rooted in the Indian strategic psyche and is derived from a political culture that stresses disengagement, avoidance of confrontation and a defensive mind-set. He claims that this has been a major factor in Indian strategic behaviour throughout India's modern history, and will continue to be an important limiting factor in Indian strategic behaviour even as India gains the material resources to play a more active strategic role outside of South Asia.[47] Despite much rhetoric, India remains relatively defensive and cautious in its strategic behaviour. This caution will likely continue while the US maintains its current predominance in the Gulf. However, as discussed later, a significant change in the regional balance of power could force India to assume a more assertive role.

As a result of these constraints, some have criticised Delhi for not "taking a position" on Middle Eastern conflicts, accusing it of lacking a grand strategy, particularly attacking any continued support for a "non-aligned" approach.[48] In reality, despite its rhetoric, during the Cold War years, India's support for non-alignment led it to support radical regimes in Egypt in the 1950s and 1960s and Iraq in the 1970s and 1980s that did little to endear it to most GCC states. More recently, India's strongly non-interventionist policies on conflicts in Iraq, Libya and Syria were partly driven by its traditional values-based wariness of intervention. Beyond South Asia, India's foreign military deployments have been largely restricted to the provision of UN peacekeeping troops to low-intensity conflicts outside of the Middle East where there was no major international disagreement.

Despite some criticisms, India's non-interventionist traditions have also endowed Delhi with a relatively rare ability to seem non-threatening. In the long term, continuing its "neutral" stand strengthens India's image and could give Delhi a degree of leverage with the GCC and other major players. If Modi can maintain Delhi's positive "friend-to-all" image while harnessing and responding to the strategic opportunities and threats of an increasingly multipolar region, India could be a real player in the Gulf theatre. Connecting with the Middle East beyond economic interests at the strategic level fits well the popular narrative in India of a monumental historical correction taking place; one in which the once great Indian civilisation takes its rightful place on the global stage.

But there may be limits to this friend-to-all approach. Realists would argue that India's past policies of non-alignment reflected material weakness. It was a strategy in which India, as a weak state, sought to play off other major powers to the maximum extent possible without being in a position to positively project its own power.[49] But as India's material capabilities grow in future years there may well come a point when India will be expected by GCC states to back political and economic influence with hard military power.

India's contemporary security relationships in the Gulf

Relations with Gulf states

To what extent do these factors affect India's contemporary security relationships in the Persian Gulf? India may have many reasons to develop its security relationships in the region: its need to protect economic, energy and diasporic interests; a desire for regional stability; and a desire to balance Pakistan (and China's) influence in West Asia. However, India is acting cautiously and its security relationships are growing slowly. Although India is expanding its economic relationships with the GCC states, there still remain constraints on its security relations with Saudi Arabia and to a lesser extent with the smaller GCC states. India is also not inclined to take sides in the intense strategic rivalry between the Sunni Muslim regimes of the Gulf states and the Shia regime in Iran.

India's relationship with Saudi Arabia has improved in recent years, although the security relationship will likely be constrained for some time to come, involving limited cooperation on terrorism. India is keen on developing a productive relationship with Saudi Arabia not only to secure energy supplies but also to potentially act as a partial counterweight to Pakistan in India's relations with the Islamic world. Thus far, Islamabad has traditionally relied upon the Gulf as a source of economic and political support. Gulf states have in the past backed Pakistan in international fora, including when Islamabad criticises India's approach to Kashmir.[50] Weakening Islamabad's support base in the Gulf will greatly strengthen India's hand in relations with Pakistan. Interestingly, the anti-Islamic sentiment amongst segments of the Indian public that colours and politically constrains policymakers when dealing with Pakistan is less present when dealing with Gulf states.[51] Indians generally view the region through a more practical lens, underpinned by energy access and trade, and remittances.

India is also developing closer relationships with several smaller GCC states, including Oman, Qatar and the UAE. They share common interests in combating jihadist terrorism and they may also see India as a partial hedge against Saudi Arabia and Iran and their overwhelming reliance on the US for security. Gulf rulers might also see India as a potential source of support for their regimes against domestic opposition. As discussed above, the UAE acts as India's economic hub in the Gulf. India also has a good relationship with Qatar. India is a major purchaser of Liquefied Natural Gas from Qatar and in 2008 they signed an agreement relating to maritime security and intelligence sharing which, according to some speculative reports, included Indian security guarantees.[52] For some years, the Qatari regime has followed a somewhat quixotic foreign policy line while maintaining a close security relationship with the US. The agreement with India, which was reportedly concluded following the "persistent" efforts of Qatar, relates to maritime security and intelligence sharing. According to reports, Qatar wanted more "comfort" than was provided by its security arrangements with the US. One Indian official reportedly commented: that "We will go to the rescue of Qatar if Qatar requires it, in whatever form it takes.[53] The prominent Indian security analyst, Raja Mohan, claims that although Qatar was keen to see India develop a semi-permanent naval presence, India was cautious about taking actions that might upset others in the region.[54] However, US diplomats downplayed the significance of the arrangement, calling it more symbolic than substantive.[55]

The recent split that saw Saudi Arabia, Bahrain and the UAE cut off ties with Qatar in June 2017 could have significant implications for India. This is reflected in the prominence given to the Indian foreign minister when international media first covered the crisis. Minister Sushmita Singh was one of the first foreign leaders to make a statement on the situation, emphasising that India's priority was stranded Indian workers. The 600,000 Indians that live in Qatar represent 25% of the emirate's population and outnumber native Qataris. Past Gulf crises have cost India significantly, including during the Gulf Crisis when over two months in 1990, New Delhi evacuated over 110,000 of its nationals from Iraq and Kuwait via an airlift that included nearly 500 flights.[56]

India's closest security relationship in the Gulf region is with Oman, which for decades has used India as a partial hedge against its larger neighbours. Oman sits at the maritime chokepoint of the Strait of Hormuz, control over which the Indian Navy considers as one of its key strategic objectives.[57] India has deployed small naval and army training teams to Oman almost continuously since the sultanate gained independence in 1971.[58] Over the past several decades, there have been numerous security-related agreements on terrorism, information sharing and assistance, and there are annual naval and air exercises and regular military talks. The Indian Air Force has access to Oman's Thumrait airbase (which is operated by the US Air Force) in support of anti-piracy efforts, and the Indian Navy uses port facilities at Salalah. According to some reports, India also operates a signals intelligence facility near Rad al-Hadd in northeast Oman.[59] Oman sees India as having an important but nevertheless limited role in the region. As Oman's Deputy Prime Minister Sayyid Fahd bin Mahmoud Al Said reportedly explained to a US official in 2010, Oman wants to encourage India to engage in the region diplomatically and politically as part of a balance of power, but it does not believe that India requires a military presence in the region.[60] Oman's links with India are still overshadowed by Oman's ties with both the US and Pakistan.

The Iran–Arab factor and India

India's relationship with the Gulf has many potentially complicating factors, and one significant factor is the rivalry between the Gulf states and Iran. Thus far, India has increased ties with both Tehran and the GCC without them significantly impinging on Delhi's interests in either entity.

For much of the Cold War India and Iran were on opposite sides, with India aligned with the Soviet Union and Iran with the US. India reacted positively to Iran's Islamic Revolution in 1979, even though differences remained over the Soviet intervention in Afghanistan and the Iran-Iraq War (1980–8). In recent decades, the two countries worked towards a comprehensive relationship that included trade in energy, military and intelligence ties, and infrastructure development.[61] Two declarations, signed in 2001 in Tehran and 2003 in Delhi, provided the structure for economic and strategic cooperation.[62] Under Modi, this pragmatic pursuit of interests continued and accelerated. In May 2016, the prime minister visited Iran and signed twelve MoUs.[63] In line with Modi's initiative to allow individual Indian states to have a role in foreign relationships, the prime minister and his Iranian counterpart promoted cooperation between Iranian provinces and Indian states.

After Iran secured the nuclear deal with the US and other major powers in 2015, India's opportunity to expand its trade and strategic involvement in the region increased.[64] India's business leaders were enthusiastic about engaging in the region and the nuclear deal removed many obstacles from Washington that impeded trade and investment with Iran.[65] India was also able to enhance its strategic engagement, such as through the upgrading of the Chabahar Port. This project is important to India as it would facilitate overland access to Afghanistan and Central Asia without having to cross Pakistani or Chinese territory. The project also helps India to compete with China's Maritime Silk Route initiative along the Indian Ocean Rim which incorporates the Gwadar Port in Pakistan and port projects in countries such as Bangladesh, Myanmar and Sri Lanka. The nuclear deal also potentially opens the door for greater cooperation between India and Iran in Afghanistan, where the two countries have a common interest in curtailing the role of the Taliban.

India and Iran have proclaimed to domestic audiences that their relationship is one of a "strategic alliance" that binds the two countries.[66] However such publicly declared alliances may be more indicative of future possibilities than current reality.[67] As Christine Fair argues, the relationship has to do with India's Great Power aspirations and Delhi's agenda for the region.[68]

In a joint statement in 2016, Modi and Iranian President Hasan Rouhani reverted to the tone and substance of the language of the Non-Alignment Movement in defining the two countries' broad strategic alignment.[69] The two leaders highlighted their belief that "all countries must be able to pursue the aspirations of their people for peace and prosperity in the international system."[70] These announcements emphasise equal sovereignty, peace and non-interference. At a meeting of the Indian Ocean Rim Association in Chabahar, Iran, in May 2016, the two countries announced some new initiatives on maritime security. With a view to enhancing defence collaboration, Modi and Rouhani agreed to have regular institutional consultations on security, terrorism and organised crime, including their respective national security councils and other agencies. The two countries also agreed to have high-level engagement through regular visits and meetings between senior government personnel including strategic analysts of the two countries.[71] India's strategic involvement may be much more than what is seen overtly.[72] Strategically placed consulates and the presence of Indian military advisers in Iran, which enables India to monitor ship movement in the Persian Gulf and the Strait of Hormuz, indicates that Delhi has significant strategic access in Iran.[73]

As India's relations with both the GCC states and Iran evolve in a more strategic direction, continuing to be a "friend to all" could be more difficult. Mohammad bin Salman, who became crown prince of Saudi Arabia in 2017, has made an example of Qatar to demand that GCC states' foreign policies are characterised by unquestioning loyalty. Whether this will translate to Saudi relations with extra-regional powers like India remains to be seen. On the other hand, the split within the GCC and Qatar's move closer to Tehran and Turkey may increase Saudi Arabia's need to expand its extra-regional relationships. This may put India in a stronger position to resist any Saudi requests to curtail ties with Iran.

On the economic front, there seems to be a mixed outlook. Traditionally, Iranian crude oil has suited India's refineries and, prior to sanctions, Iran was India's second-largest oil supplier. More recently, however, there have been disputes in the relationship. While the May 2016 Joint Statement between the two countries told of aims for a commercial contract for Iran's Farzad B gas field and agreement that companies abide by a pre-agreed timeline, by April 2018 there was still no contract.[74] This led to India cutting oil purchases. Delhi's aforementioned agenda of diversifying its energy sources and import partners will also impact ties.

The changing balance of power and India's security role in the Gulf

Indian perspectives on the changing balance of power and its strategic role in the Gulf

India's current, relatively constrained security role in the Gulf could change substantially if there is a significant change in the regional balance of power that is perceived to threaten India's interests.

Pakistan may, to some extent, be a driver for India's relationships with GCC states, but it is also one of the biggest factors that limit India's security relationships in the Gulf. The security threats presented by Pakistan long kept India strategically preoccupied in South Asia and unable or unwilling to project its influence beyond. While India is successfully transcending the India-Pakistan rivalry in other regions, Pakistan continues to be a significant constraint among GCC states. In the decades after independence, Pakistan was able to largely politically marginalise India in the Persian Gulf area. The CENTO alliance, which joined the US, UK and Pakistan together with Iran, Iraq and Turkey, provided a structure that was sometimes used by its members to give informal support to Pakistan in its disputes with India, including during the 1965 and 1971 wars. Although the 1971 war was a military victory for India in South Asia, it damaged most of India's relationships in the region and further focused Pakistan's energies on building security relationships in the Gulf.[75]

Pakistan now maintains close political and military ties with several GCC states. Since the early 1970s, Pakistan has provided training and manpower throughout the region, as newly wealthy Gulf states sought to diversify their previous reliance on Britain. Pakistan currently maintains an active army, air force and, to a lesser extent, naval training presences in Saudi Arabia and elsewhere in the Gulf, including in Bahrain, the UAE, Qatar and Oman.[76] A large number of former Pakistani servicemen also serve in security forces throughout the GCC states, recruited via semi-official Pakistani government service organisations. According to some reports, Pakistan keeps two army divisions on standby for deployment to Saudi Arabia.[77] The large Pakistani military presence reflects not only Pakistan's large population and well-trained armed forces but also a calculation by Arab leaders that Pakistani troops may be particularly useful for both internal and external security tasks. Pakistan's willingness to deploy armed forces to assist the Gulf states is not unlimited. In April 2015, it declined requests to provide military forces to assist Saudi Arabia in its military intervention in Yemen, possibly to avoid involving itself in internecine Sunni-Shia disputes.[78] However, the appointment of former Pakistan army chief, General Raheel Sharif, to lead the Saudi-sponsored Islamic Military Alliance points to an active and even growing military role for Pakistan in the Gulf.[79]

The nuclear factor also sustains and may, in the future, enhance Pakistan's strategic role in the Gulf. Pakistan's position as the only Muslim state with nuclear weapons gives it immense status in the Arab world which may be enhanced by understandings between Pakistan and Saudi Arabia relating to nuclear weapons. Saudi Arabia is suspected of providing considerable financial assistance to Pakistan to fund its nuclear weapons program during the 1980s and 1990s.[80] It has been claimed that, as a *quid pro quo*, Pakistan now provides a *de facto* nuclear umbrella for Saudi Arabia.[81]

On the other hand, competition with Islamabad also acts as a driver for India's desire to build relations with GCC states. Strengthening its influence among GCC states is a way for India to weaken Pakistan's negotiating position on current areas of contention with India, including Kashmir and separatist/terrorist groups. GCC states could also be valuable partners in any potential efforts to neutralise tensions with Pakistan.

The US, as the predominant military power in the Persian Gulf, is pivotal to the development of India's security role in the region. Over the last decade or so, the US has encouraged the expansion of India's naval ambitions and capabilities throughout much of the Indian Ocean where it is seen as a *status quo* power that can play an important role in "burden sharing" of maritime security needs in the Indian Ocean region as a whole. But compared with other parts of the Indian Ocean, there is relatively little cooperation between the two countries in and around the Persian Gulf. It is not clear if the US has intentionally not encouraged a greater Indian naval presence in and around the Persian Gulf, or if India's strong preference for displaying autonomy has led it to decline to participate in various US-sponsored security initiatives such as the combined naval task forces that tackle maritime terrorism and piracy, particularly where the US cooperates with Pakistan. The Pakistan Navy is an active participant in regional security initiatives, including the US-sponsored international naval task forces which operate in the Persian Gulf and the Arabian Sea, which Pakistan has led on several occasions.[82] Nevertheless, Washington would likely see an enhanced Indian security role in the Gulf as consistent with US interests and potentially even as taking some strain off US defence resources.

More important is the diminishing interest and influence of the US, and the resulting space for other major powers. The growth of US domestic energy sources such as shale and renewables has reduced Washington's stakes in the Middle East. Political trends in the US increasingly reveal the public's increasing aversion to foreign policy adventurism. This coincides with the rise of powers like China and the reassertiveness of Russia to make for a more multipolar Middle East. Leaders in the Gulf are interested in diversifying their strategic partnerships with major powers. Beijing has already signed security and nuclear cooperation agreements with American allies such as Saudi Arabia, in addition to backing states feeling threatened by the US such as Iran.

China is becoming an important factor in India's calculations about the Gulf. China's economic and political influence in the Gulf is now increasing in line with its growing influence throughout the world. China is not yet a material military factor in the region despite maintaining a small anti-piracy presence in the Arabian Sea and the opening of China's first overseas military base in Djibouti in July 2017.[83] The gradually increasing Chinese military presence in the region threatens what India sees as its rightful sphere of strategic influence. Delhi's existing concerns regarding Beijing's intentions in bilateral relations will be compounded if China has leverage over India's energy security. In recent years, Pakistan has sought to make China a factor in the naval balance in the northwest Indian Ocean through encouraging China to develop a naval presence at the port of Gwadar in western Pakistan, around 600 kilometres east of the Strait of Hormuz. The development of a substantial Chinese naval presence at Gwadar, particularly in the context of a declining US military presence, could have considerable implications for India's role in the Gulf.[84]

What are India's options in face of these developments? Given the constraints India still faces in the region and its relatively limited power projection capabilities, India is likely to want to keep its options open for as long as possible. Its preference would be for the US to continue playing a stabilising role. In December 2013, amid speculation that Gulf states may be looking for new security partners, Indian Foreign Minister Salman Khurshid declared that India would not contemplate stepping into any vacuum left by the US. According to Khurshid:

> Because of the philosophical constraints that we impose on ourselves, we don't see ourselves as a replacement for any other power. We certainly don't believe that the presence of any other power, such as China or Japan, or what have you, would necessarily contribute to the security of the region. ... But will India be willing to step into a possible vacuum, if there might be the withdrawal of existing forces ... I think that is not the kind of thing that we – in terms of present strategic planning and understanding, that we would (contemplate).[85]

Although the current Modi government is far less bound than previous Congress governments by the "philosophical constraints" of Nehruvianism and non-alignment, there is little indication that Modi would rush to assume a military role in the Persian Gulf unless it saw China doing so. Indeed, a calculation that continued US military predominance in the Gulf, at least in the medium term, provides stability at a low cost to India may make considerable sense. It would also echo India's relatively benign attitude towards the Royal Navy's role in the Gulf during the declining years of the British Empire. Despite their anti-imperialist rhetoric, Nehru and his successors considered that the Royal Navy in the Persian Gulf was a stabilising force that should be allowed to fade away peacefully.[86]

The withdrawal of Britain in the early 1970s led to considerable strategic instability throughout the Indian Ocean, which India would not like to see repeated. Accordingly, it would be in India's interests to maintain the *status quo* for as long as possible.

Pull factors: the role of Gulf states in facilitating a greater Indian role in the Gulf

Like many countries around the world, the GCC states are diversifying their partnerships with major powers.[87] Until recent times, these countries have used the US as the sole guarantor of their security and for the maintenance of the established order. Given the advancement of India towards the status of a major power, there is an increasing desire in these countries to spread their security requirements through ties with India and also with China. A case in point is Saudi Arabia establishing stronger ties with China to complement and balance their existing ties with the US, even while Iran is strengthening its own ties with China.[88] The GCC states deepening strategic relations with India is not at odds with Washington, which indeed is encouraging India to play a greater regional role.

Another reason for diversifying strategic ties is the growing perception among the Arab nations that the US may gradually disengage from the Middle East. With the conclusion of the Iran nuclear deal in 2015, the Gulf countries believed that the US was aiming to balance between Israel, Iran and the GCC states to further Washington's own interests.[89] Iran, subject to reduced sanctions after the nuclear deal, is perceived by the Gulf states as a significant threat to their internal security. While ties between Saudi Arabia and the US have improved under Trump, it is unlikely to alter the diversification trend in the long term. The Arab Spring and the recent upheavals in the Middle East also brought into question the steadfastness of American loyalty. Leaders of GCC states could not have failed to see the hands-off position of the US when Egyptian President Hosni Mubarak was ousted, softening of relations with Libyan leader Muammar Gaddafi shortly before supporting rebels in his ouster, and the dispatch of Iraqi President Saddam Hussein who had been a recipient American military assistance during the Iraq-Iran War.

The moves by the GCC states to reach out to non-Western powers may also be driven by their perception that the US is losing its unchallenged supremacy in the region. This is coupled with the growing assertiveness of rising powers.[90] Even Russia's use of military force to defend the Syrian government and the seeming reluctance of the US to decisively support GCC states to overthrow the Syrian regime is seen as a defining contrast that the Gulf states have taken into their strategic calculations. To maintain regional security interests for the long term, the GCC states recognise that Western backing alone is insufficient.

Although the positions of India (and, as discussed in chapter 9, also of China) on issues such as Syria and Iran are markedly different to those of the GCC states, the Gulf states are nevertheless keen to strengthen their ties with them. For instance, India has maintained, albeit muted, support for the government of Syria President Bashar Assad throughout the conflict, reflecting its traditional non-interventionist stance and concerns about potentially worsening violent extremism in the region. This was even recognised by the Syrian government, which backed India's attendance at the Geneva II talks.[91] New Delhi hosted the Syrian foreign minister as the Assad government attempted to solicit international support before the peace talks, only a few months before Prime Minister Modi's visit to Saudi Arabia.[92] The Indian Ministry of External Affairs' website states that "Syria has deeply appreciated the support received from India … at the UNSC."[93]

In some ways maintaining relations with the GCC's rivals is advantageous for India as it can use this to gain extra leverage in dealings with Riyadh and other Gulf governments. India has had long-term relationships with both Iran and Syria, the two countries which are the main regional adversaries of the GCC states. This, combined with India's historic reputation of neutrality in foreign affairs, may also increase India's appeal to the GCC states both as a strategic partner and a channel for diplomatic persuasion. Using India as a diplomatic channel, however, is clearly more likely to appeal to states like Qatar and Oman, which have better relations with Iran than Saudi Arabia, particularly under the new Saudi Crown Prince Mohamed Bin Salman.

Conclusion

The size, proximity and historical links between India and the Persian Gulf seem to make India a natural leader in the Gulf. But for many years the relationship was constrained. India's inward-looking economic policies hampered its economic relationships in the region. This is now changing with burgeoning trade relationships (well beyond energy), bolstered by the presence of some 7 million Indian nationals in the Gulf region. While bilateral investment remains relatively thin, this is likely to change, especially with the liberalisation of the Indian economy under the Modi government. For many years, political relationships between India and the GCC states have generally been cordial, if somewhat restrained. During the Cold War in particular differing strategic alignments and the Pakistan factor placed limitations on relationships. However, over the last decade or so, there have been significant improvements in political and security ties between India and several GCC states. To some extent, this is driven by Indian concerns about the regional roles of China and Pakistan in the face of questions about the long-term role of the US as the main security provider in the region. It has also been driven by the desire of the GCC states to diversify relationships with other major powers. Over the long term, India is likely to play an ever greater role in the Persian Gulf. However, what type of role it will assume is not yet clear and may well be decided by developments elsewhere.

Notes

1 Andre Wink, *Al-Hind: The Making of the Indo-Islamic World* (Netherlands: E. J. Brill, 1990), p. 68.
2 Atul Sethi, 'Trade, Not Invasion brought Islam to India', *Times of India*, 24 June 2007.
3 P. N. Chopra, B. N. Puri, A. C. and Das, M. N., *A Social, Cultural and Economic History of India* (New Delhi: MacMillan India, 1974), pp. 28–9.

4 Kadira Pethiyagoda, 'The Influence of Cultural Values on India's Foreign Policy', (PhD diss., University of Melbourne, 2013), p. 97.
5 Pethiyagoda, 'The Influence of Cultural Values on India's Foreign Policy', p. 98.
6 Chopra et al., *A Social, Cultural and Economic History of India*, p. 29; Momin, A.R., 'Cultural Pluralism, National Identity and Development: The Indian Case', in Saraswati, B., (ed.), *Interface of Cultural Identity Development*, (New Delhi: IGNCA and D. K. Printworld Ltd, 1996), p. 290.
7 Sanjay Baru, 'Look West Policy', *Business Standard*, 8 March 2010.
8 Import Export Data Bank, Government of India, Department of Commerce. http://www.commerce.nic.in/eidb/default.asp
9 John Calabrse, '"Linking West" in "Unsettled Times"': India–G.C.C. Trade Relations', *Middle East Institute*, 11 April 2017. http://www.mei.edu/content/map/linking-west-unsettled-times-india-gcc-economic-and-trade-relations.
10 Import Export Data Bank, Government of India, Department of Commerce.http://www.commerce.nic.in/eidb/default.asp
11 'India–UAE Economic & Commercial Relations', Embassy of India, Abu Dhabi. http://indembassyuae.org/Com_bilateral.html.
12 'Investment flow between GCC, India "rising rapidly"', *TradeArabia*, 26 September 2017. http://www.tradearabia.com/news/IND_330665.html
13 Pradhan, 'India's Economic and Political Presence in the Gulf: A Gulf Perspective' in *India's Growing Role in the Gulf: Implications for the Region and the United States* (Dubai: Gulf Research Centre, 2009).
14 'India, UAE Expand Ties, But $75 Billion Investment Still in Limbo', *The Wire*, 25 January 2017. https://thewire.in/102968/india-uae-expand-ties-75-billion-investment-still-limbo/
15 U.S. Energy Information Administration (EIA), 'Country Analysis Brief: India', 1 June 2016. http://www.eia.gov/beta/international/analysis_includes/countries_long/India/india.pdf; K. Pethiyagoda, 'India–GCC Relations: Delhi's Strategic Opportunity', Brookings Doha Centre, p. 6.
16 Pethiyagoda, 'India–GCC Relations', p. 6.
17 Ibid.
18 'International', U.S. Energy Information Administration, 2015. http://www.eia.gov/countries/cab.cfm?fips=in
19 I. Bagchi, 'India Moving to the Centre of Global Energy Affairs', *Times of India*, 28 November 2015, http://timesofindia.indiatimes.com/india/India-moving-to-the-centre-of-global-energy-affairs/articleshow/49962339.cms
20 Ibid.
21 'Oiling the Wheels', *Business Today*, February 2015. http://www.businesstoday.in/stocks/falling-oil-prices-will-bring-a-windfall-for-india-inc/story/215108.html; Pethiyagoda, 'India–GCC Relations', p. 6.
22 U.S. Energy Information Administration (EIA), 'Country Analysis Brief: India'.
23 Bagchi, 'India Moving to the Centre of Global Energy Affairs'.
24 Pethiyagoda, 'India–GCC Relations'.
25 P. K. Pradhan, 'India and Gulf Cooperation Council: Time to Look BeyondBusiness', *Strategic Analysis*, Vol. 34, no. 3 (2014), pp. 409–19.
26 Bagchi, 'India Moving to the Centre of Global Energy Affairs'.
27 U.S. Energy Information Administration (EIA), 'Country Analysis Brief: India', June 2016.
28 Roche, E., 'UAE to store crude oil in Mangalore petroleum reserve', *LiveMint*, 11 February 2016.
29 D. Yergin, 'Ensuring Energy Security', *Foreign Affairs*, March/April 2006. https://www.foreignaffairs.org/articles/2006-03-01/ensuring-energy-security

30 World Bank, 'Remittances Growth to Slow Sharply in 2015, as Europe and Russia Stay Weak; Pick Up Expected Next Year', *Press Release*, 13 April 2015, http://www.worldbank.org/en/news/press-release/2015/04/13/remittances-growth-to-slow-sharply-in-2015-as-europe-and-russia-stay-weak-pick-up-expected-next-year
31 M. Azhar, 'Indian Migrant Workers in GCC Countries', *Diaspora Studies*, Vol 9., no. 2, (2016), p. 107.
32 A. Dinda, 'Indian Premier to Visit GCC Countries in 2015', *Gulf News*, 11 January 2015. http://gulfnews.com/business/economy/indian-premier-to-visit-gcc-countries-in-2015-1.1439706; A. Wadhwa, 'MEA Secretary (East) address at Second ORF-MEA West Asia Conference', New Delhi, 27 April 2015.
33 Pethiyagoda, K., 'Indian Workers in the Gulf: Too Little But Not Too Late', Policy Brief, Brookings Doha Centre, 2017.
34 MEA, 'Joint Statement Between the United Arab Emirates and the Republic of India', 17 August 2015. http://www.mea.gov.in/bilateral-documents.htm?dtl/25733/Joint_Statement_between_the_United_Arab_Emirates_and_the_Republic_of_India
35 Pethiyagoda, 'India–GCC Relations'.
36 David Brewster, 'India and the Persian Gulf: Locked Out or Staying Out?', *Comparative Strategy*, Vol. 35, no. 1 (2016), pp. 55–78.
37 Ibid.
38 'India well positioned to become a "net security provider" to our region and beyond: PM', *The Hindu*, 23 May 2013.
39 David Scott, 'India's "Grand Strategy" for the Indian Ocean: Mahanian Visions', *Asia-Pacific Review*, Vol. 13, no. 2 (2006), pp. 97–129; David Brewster, *India's Ocean: The Story of India's Bid for Regional Leadership* (London: Routledge, 2014).
40 Integrated Headquarters, Ministry of Defence (Navy), *Ensuring Secure Seas: Indian Maritime Security Strategy*, Naval Strategic Publication (NSP) 1.2, October 2015.
41 Chidanand Rajghatta, 'Singhing Bush's Praise', *Times of India*, 13 April 2001.
42 Manmohan Singh, 'PM's Address at the Combined Commander's Conference', 24 October 2004.
43 Manmohan Singh, 'PM Inaugurates Naval Academy at Ezhimala', 8 January 2009.
44 Anit Mukherjee, 'India as a Net Security Provider: Concepts and Impediments', RSIS Policy Brief, August 2014.
45 John Hawksworth 'The Long View: How Will the Global Economic Order Change by 2050?' PricewaterhouseCoopers, February 2017. https://www.pwc.com/gx/en/world-2050/assets/pwc-the-world-in-2050-full-report-feb-2017.pdf
46 George Tanham, 'Indian Strategic Thought: An Interpretive Essay', in George Tanham, Kanti P. Bajpai and Amitabh Mattoo (eds.), *Securing India: Strategic Thought and Practice in an Emerging Power* (New Delhi: Manhora, 1996), p. 73.
47 Stephen P. Cohen and Sunil Dasgupta, *Arming without Aiming: India's Military Modernisation* (Washington D.C.: Brookings Institution Press, 2010).
48 'India as a Great Power: Know your own strength', *Economist*, 30 March 2013; C.R. Mohan, 'Raja Mandala: A Movement in Coma', *Indian Express*, 20 September 2016.
49 C. Raja Mohan, *Crossing the Rubicon: The Shaping of India's New Foreign Policy* (New York: Palgrave Macmillan, 2004).
50 Pethiyagoda, 'India–GCC Relations', p. 22.
51 Ibid. p. 19.
52 'India, Qatar Ink Defence Pact', *The Financial Times*, 11 November 2008.
53 'India: PM Vows to Defend Tiny Qatar "If Needed"', *ADN Kronos International*, 12 November 2008; 'India, Qatar to Ramp Defence, Economic, Energy Ties', *Thaindian News*, 10 November 2008.
54 C. Raja Mohan, *Samudra Manthan: Sino–Indian Rivalry in the Indo-Pacific* (Washington, D.C.: Carnegie Endowment for International Peace, 2012), p. 163.

55 US Embassy Doha cable to US State Department, 'First-ever Indian PM Visit to Qatar Aims to Spark Better Ties', 18 November 2008. http://www.cablegatesearch.net/cable.php?id=08DOHA810
56 S. Priyadershini, 'Airlifted from Kuwait', *The Hindu*, 23 September 2016.
57 India, Ministry of Defence, *Indian Maritime Doctrine*, p. 64.
58 But India declined to respond to Omani calls for military assistance during the Dhofar War (1960–75) on the grounds that it did not wish to become involved in intra-mural Arab conflicts.
59 Saurav Jha, 'Naval Ties, Economic Interests Drive India's Outreach to Oman', *World Politics Review*, 7 January 2015. http://www.worldpoliticsreview.com/articles/14799/naval-ties-economic-interests-drive-india-s-outreach-to-oman
60 US Embassy Muscat cable to US State Department, 'Oman – Government's Number Two Gives His Views of The Region', 22 February 2010. http://www.cablegatesearch.net/cable.php?id=10MUSCAT99
61 Donald L. Berlin, 'India–Iran Relations: A Deepening Entente', Asia Pacific Center for Security Studies Honolulu, October, 2004; Pethiyagoda, K., 2018 'India–Iran Relations', *Analysis Paper*, Brookings Doha Centre [soon to be published].
62 Press Information Bureau – Government of India, 'Prime Minister's Visit to Iran: Text of Tehran Declaration', n. d. http://pib.nic.in/archieve/pmvisit/pm_visit_iran/pm_iran_rel4.html; Ministry of External Affairs – Government of India, 'The Republic of India and the Islamic Republic of Iran "The New Delhi Declaration"', 25 January 2003. http://mea.gov.in/bilateral-documents.htm?dtl/7544/The+Republic+of+India+and+the+Islamic+Republic+of+Iran+quotThe+New+Delhi+Declarationquot
63 'Modi in Iran: Chabahar Port Deal Can Enable India to Break Out of Strategic Encirclement', *Times of India*, 24 May 2016. http://blogs.timesofindia.indiatimes.com/toi-editorials/modi-in-iran-chabahar-port-deal-can-enable-india-to-break-out-of-strategic-encirclement/
64 Christine Fair, 'India-Iran Security Ties: Thicker than Oil', *Middle East Review of International Affairs*, Vol. 11, no. 1, (March 2007), pp. 260–81, p. 279.
65 Pethiyagoda, 'India–Iran Relations'.
66 Fair, 'India–Iran Security Ties'.
67 Pethiyagoda, 'India–Iran Relations'.
68 Fair, 'India–Iran Security Ties: Thicker than Oil', p. 262.
69 Pethiyagoda, 'India–Iran Relations'.
70 Ministry of External Affairs – Government of India 'India–Iran Joint Statement' Civilisational Connect, Contemporary Context during the visit of Prime Minister to Iran', 23 May 2016. http://www.mea.gov.in/bilateral-documents.htm?dtl/26843/India__Iran_Joint_Statement_quot_Civilisational_Connect_Contemporary_Contextquot_during_the_visit_of_Prime_Minister_to_Iran
71 Ibid.
72 Pethiyagoda, 'India–Iran Relations'.
73 Fair, 'India–Iran Security Ties: Thicker than Oil', p. 279.
74 Pethiyagoda, 'India–Iran Relations'.
75 Brewster, 'India and the Persian Gulf: Locked Out or Staying Out?'.
76 See Sehar Kamran, 'Pak-Gulf Defense and Security Cooperation', Centre for Pakistan and Gulf Studies, January 2013.
77 Bruce Riedel, 'Saudi Arabia: Nervously Watching Pakistan', Brookings Institute, 28 January 2008; Syed Saleem Shahzad, 'Pakistan Ready for Middle East Role', *Asia Times*, 2 April 2011.
78 Ankit Panda, 'Pakistan's Neutrality in the Yemen Crisis: Brought to You by China', *The Diplomat*, 28 April 2015.
79 Salman Masood and Ben Hubbard, 'Pakistan Approves Military Hero to Head Tricky Saudi-Led Alliance', *The New York Times*, 2 April 2017.

80 Feroz Khan, *Eating Grass: The Making of the Pakistani Bomb* (Palo Alto: Stanford University Press, 2012), p. 383.
81 Arnaud de Borchgrave, 'Pakistan, Saudi Arabia in Secret Nuke Pact: Islamabad Trades Weapons Technology for Oil', *The Washington Times,* 22 October 2003; Riedel, 'Saudi Arabia'; *Hugh Tomlinson*, 'Saudi Arabia to Acquire Nuclear Weapons to Counter Iran', *The Times*, 11 February 2012.
82 Brewster, *India's Ocean*, ch.6.
83 David Brewster, 'China's Announcement of Its First Overseas Military Base Is the Taste of Things to Come', *Lowy Interpreter*, 2 December 2015. http://www.lowyinterpreter.org/post/2015/12/02/Chinas-first-overseas-military-base-in-Djibouti-likely-to-be-a-taste-of-things-to-come.aspx
84 Brewster, 'India and the Persian Gulf: Locked Out or Staying Out?'
85 William Maclean, 'Rising Power India Sees no US-Style Gulf Security Role', *Reuters Online*, 7 December 2013. http://uk.reuters.com/article/2013/12/07/uk-gulf-security-india-idUKBRE9B60DV20131207
86 David Brewster, 'Indian Strategic Thinking About the Indian Ocean: Striving for Strategic Leadership', *India Review*, Vol. 14, no. 2 (2015), pp. 1–16.
87 Pethiyagoda, 'India–GCC relations', p. 13.
88 Ibid.
89 Washington's accommodation of Israel amidst past and present tensions with Palestinians (particularly under the Netanyahu Government) continue to make the optics of allying with the US problematic for Gulf leaders (Turki Al Faisal, 'Failed Favoritism toward Israel', *Washington Post*, 10 June 2011).
90 Pethiyagoda, 'India–GCC relations', p. 13.
91 Pethiyagoda, K., 'India on Syria –The Rising Power's Position on a Global Conflict', *Huffington Post*, January 2016.
92 Pethiyagoda, 'India on Syria'.
93 'India–Syria Relations', Ministry of External Affairs, December 2014. http://www.mea.gov.in/Portal/ForeignRelation/Syria_Dec2014.pdf

9 Striking a balance between economics and security
China's relations with the Gulf monarchies

Jonathan Fulton

Introduction

Leaders in the People's Republic of China (PRC) have always considered the Gulf monarchies strategically, but that is not to say that they were always considered important. Far beyond China's traditional sphere of interests and with more pressing foreign policy concerns in its immediate neighborhood, events in the Gulf rarely had a direct impact on the PRC. Similarly, rulers on the Arabian side of the Gulf oriented westward toward the United Kingdom (UK) and United States (US), had long perceived China as a marginal actor at best, or a hostile one at worst. These perceptions have changed significantly in the post-Cold War era, and China's role in the Gulf has become an important determinant of national interests in China and the Gulf Cooperation Council (GCC) member states.

The Gulf features heavily in China's foreign policy, both in terms of political economy and strategic thought. Gulf leaders have similarly adopted a "look east" orientation in recent years. The result is a thickening of political and economic interactions, which leads to an important question: will its deeper regional footprint lead to a security or military role for China in the Gulf? To address this, the chapter begins with a brief historical overview of China's relations with the GCC member states in order to emphasize the increasing depth of engagement. This includes a discussion of China's strategic hedging approach to the Gulf region, which has allowed China to pursue denser ties to regional actors without a corresponding security commitment. An analysis of China's economic and strategic interests in the Gulf follows, demonstrating that, while there are significant areas of concern on China's side, its commitment to its Gulf position should increase, especially as China's Belt and Road Initiative (BRI) takes shape, extending Chinese interests across Eurasia. The last section of this chapter discusses two competing approaches to Gulf security emphasized in Chinese discourse: security through development and security through power projection. These competing visions are important in attempting to understand what type of regional security role China could reasonably be expected to play.

China and the Gulf monarchies: a historical overview

China's relations with the Gulf monarchies has changed significantly over the years, and these changes can be categorized into four general periods: indifference

(1949–66), hostility (1966–71), transition (1971–90), and interdependence (1990–present).[1] While there is some variation in China's relations with individual states, especially in the transition period, as a whole the time frames are representative of changes in policy or approach, and these changes are indicative of either a re-evaluation of Chinese leaders' perceptions of the international system or their domestic political situation, which in turn influenced their views on the relative importance of the Gulf in their strategic thought.

The first period reflects mutual indifference, motivated largely by systemic features of the Cold War alliances of the bipolar system. The PRC was aligned with the Soviet Union and the Gulf monarchies were aligned with the West. There had been few interactions prior to the establishment of the PRC in 1949, and there were few issues where their interests converged or diverged. The PRC's Foreign Ministry did not even have a department dedicated to the Middle East North Africa (MENA) region, let alone the Gulf.[2] After the Bandung Conference in 1955, China made efforts to enhance its nearly non-existent presence in MENA, but any nascent gains were soon lost during the domestic upheaval of the Great Leap Forward. When Chinese leaders thought of the Gulf monarchies, it was through an ideological lens, and the sheikdoms were perceived as "reactionary monarchies" or "puppets," reliant upon foreign powers for their continued rule.[3] For their part, Gulf rulers also had negative perceptions of the PRC, shaped by an aversion to communism as well as the accounts of Chinese Muslims who had immigrated to MENA after the Chinese Communist Party (CCP) took power. Some from Xinjiang had resettled in Cairo and met Saudi Arabia's king Ibn Saud in 1950, and complained that "the Communist seizure of Xinjiang had been accompanied by chaos and a large-scale offensive against the Muslims."[4] With few common interest areas and negative perceptions of each other, "it was not evident what, if anything, China and the Middle East could offer each other."[5]

The period of hostility was a result of the Cultural Revolution when China pursued a revolutionary foreign policy in an attempt to challenge Soviet leadership of the communist bloc. At this time, the Middle East was transformed from a theater of collaboration between China and the Soviet Union into a theater of open rivalry. Oman was directly affected as the focus of the PRC's revolutionary ambition. The Omani sultan, Said bin Taimur, was facing a domestic challenge from Dhofar province. Chinese leaders, with scant resources in the region and a poor understanding of events on the ground, understood the Dhofari rebellion as an anti-colonial struggle rather than a regional power play against an unpopular leader. The PRC saw Oman as a venue to export their revolution throughout the Gulf monarchies:

> the excellent situation of the victorious developing armed struggle of the Dhofar people is bound to promote and inspire the development of the national liberation struggle of the people of the entire Arabian Gulf region.[6]

With this goal, China provided military training and aid, including anti-aircraft missiles, explosives, and machine guns.[7] This brief period of ideological and material hostility drove a wedge deeply between China and the Gulf monarchies, especially Saudi Arabia, which would not recognize China diplomatically until 1990.

The transition period was marked by a reinterpretation of the international system and the Gulf's place in it. By 1971, Mao had come to consider the Soviet Union, rather than the US, as China's greatest threat. The US, bogged down in Vietnam, seemed a declining threat, while the Sino–Russian border had hundreds of thousands of troops facing each other from either side. Given this reinterpretation of the international environment facing China, the time was right for Sino–US rapprochement. In the Gulf, the UK's departure from the region in 1971 led to the perception of a power vacuum that would benefit the Soviet Union; China's destabilizing efforts in Oman could have the unintended consequences of benefitting the Soviets. Furthermore, the Omani rebellion was losing steam by 1971 after the UK and Iran provided material support and Sultan Qaboos replaced his unpopular father. The Dhofari rebellion was increasingly seen as a lost cause in Beijing. This was compounded by the diplomatic efforts of Iran and Kuwait, both of which recognized the PRC diplomatically in 1970. Chinese leaders had come to place more value on a stable Gulf as a means of checking Soviet expansion, and as such, maintaining the status quo was perceived as meeting Chinese interests. With this reevaluation of the Gulf, China began a charm offensive, expressing support for the Gulf monarchies and pursuing diplomatic relations with the other sheikhdoms. Oman was the first to establish such relations, recognizing China in 1978, a development described as "probably the most striking example of the transformation in China's position in the Middle East."[8] Others slowly followed suit: the UAE in 1984, Qatar in 1988, Bahrain in 1989, and finally, Saudi Arabia in 1990.

China–GCC interdependence

The interdependence period begins with the establishment of diplomatic relations between China and Saudi Arabia. Recognized by all states in the region, the PRC began to adopt a multifaceted approach that built ties in trade, diplomatic initiatives, people-to-people exchanges, and infrastructure projects.[9] This period too is largely a result of systemic pressures, in this case the end of the bipolar Cold War order and the beginning of the US-led liberal order. The US had long been the decisive power in the Gulf, and without the constraining factor of Soviet interests, America could pursue its vision of a Gulf order. This took shape shortly after Operation Desert Storm, as the US established a security umbrella that protected its GCC allies, using its regional preponderance not to transform the Gulf but rather to maintain the status quo.[10] The US established Defense Cooperation Agreements with Kuwait (1991), Bahrain (1991), Qatar (1992), and the UAE (1994), and has a Facilities Access Agreement (FAA) with Oman that was signed in 1980 and renewed in 1985, 1990, 2000, and 2010. There are approximately 35,000 US troops in the Gulf, with approximately 13,500 in Kuwait, 10,000 in Qatar, 8,000 in Bahrain, 5,000 in the UAE, and a few hundred in Oman.

In addition to the troops, there are substantial military installations throughout the five states. Kuwait hosts US personnel at Camp Arifjan, Camp Buehring, Ali Al-Salem Air Base, Shaykh Ahmed al-Jabir Air Base, and Camp Patriot. After Desert Storm, up to 60% of Kuwait's territory was occupied by US military.[11] Bahrain has had a US naval command presence since 1948, although it was not an especially large one until after the Reagan administration established Central Command and the Bahraini base housed the naval component, NAVCENT. Post Desert Storm, the onshore command presence was established and the Fifth Fleet was reconstituted in 1995. All of this is housed at the Naval Support Activity (NSA) Bahrain. This facility has undergone a $590 million expansion that started in 2010, bringing the total US cost of the facility to approximately $2 billion.[12] Bahrain's Khalifa bin Salman Port accommodates US aircraft carriers and amphibious ships, and its Shaykh Issa Air Base has undergone a $45 million upgrade, funded by the US, and hosts US military aircraft. The US has also put $19 million into a facility for US Special Operations Forces, and has authorized $90 million in further military construction in Bahrain.[13] Qatar hosts US Air Force personnel at the Al Udeid Air Base, which was built at a cost of $1 billion in the 1990s and has since undergone expansion and enhancement with some US funding.[14] The UAE hosts US military personnel at the Jebel Ali Port, which is the US Navy's busiest port of call, as well as the Al Dhofra Air Base and naval facilities in Fujairah.[15] Oman, under its FAA with the US, gives the US access to military airfields in Muscat, Thurait, Masirah Island, and Musanah. As part of the FAA, the US paid to upgrade Omani facilities initially spending $260 million between 1981 and 1987, and then further upgrades totaling $120 million while negotiating the renewal in 2000.[16]

This US security umbrella has created an environment where China has been able to pursue denser, multifaceted ties to the GCC states without having to take on a larger regional security role, which has been the source of some friction between China and the US. American leaders have long called on China to adopt a larger role as a "responsible stakeholder" within the US-led international system.[17] This is not an entirely unreasonable expectation from Washington, as this system has provided a relatively stable environment under which the PRC has been able to focus on domestic development while establishing itself as a power with global interests. From the American perspective, China has been freeriding in the Gulf, taking advantage of the US military commitment to maintaining the regional status quo and providing public goods, such as patrolling the international waterways through which Gulf energy passes to get to China in order to continue with its impressive development.[18] This view is loudly rejected in China. One Chinese Middle East analyst articulates the response to this critique, claiming that China is actually "a victim of regional instability as a result of the U.S.' reckless military actions and presence."[19] He then describes the PRC's contribution to regional order and security as a complementary one, stating: "Political mediation and economic engagement, which can help mitigate tensions within and among regional countries, should definitely be regarded as security public goods as well."[20]

Whereas the US has taken an active role in the Gulf based on alliances, China has taken a strategic hedging approach.[21] It maximizes the benefits of engagement with the GCC at relatively little cost, using strategic partnerships rather than formal alliances. Strategic hedging is an approach common to second-tier powers that want to avoid antagonizing the dominant power, while at the same time expanding their economic and military regional capabilities.[22] Goh defines strategic hedging as "a set of strategies aimed at avoiding (or planning for contingencies in) a situation in which states cannot decide upon more straightforward alternatives such as balancing, bandwagoning, or neutrality."[23] In the case of China's role in the Gulf, neither balancing against nor bandwagoning with regional powers meets its goals, as both strategies would disrupt an order that, for the time being, meets Beijing's interests. Neutrality does not advance its ambitions as a growing regional actor with interests on both the Arabian and Iranian sides of the Gulf. Strategic hedging has therefore allowed the PRC to build relations with all regional actors under the US-dominated system.

In contrast, the active role played by the US in the post-Cold War era has put significant strain on US–GCC relations. Despite the significant US commitment to maintaining the regional status quo, several major events – 9/11, the US-led invasion and occupation of Iraq, the US response to the Arab Spring, and the Joint Comprehensive Program of Action (JCPOA) – have all contributed to a perception of a divergence of interests between the US and the GCC. Snyder's work on alliance security dilemmas tells us that asymmetrical alliances tend to be difficult to manage, as the weaker ally will fear abandonment if the alliance commitment seems vague or uncertain.[24] Al Shayji sees current US–GCC relations as a "textbook example" of the alliance security dilemma, describing tensions between the two sides as a structural consequence of the relationship, resulting in a more assertive regional foreign policy from the GCC as its leaders doubt the US's continued commitment to their security.[25] Confusion with the Trump administration's response to the dispute between Qatar and the Saudi–Emirati–Bahraini bloc further clouds the role the US can be expected to play in the Gulf.

The Chinese approach, on the other hand, does not use alliances but diplomatic partnerships. The non-alliance policy is believed to date to 1983, when Deng Xiaoping, paramount leader of China from 1978 to 1989, articulated this strategy, and successive Chinese leaders have reiterated the position.[26] The PRC's aversion to alliances is consistent with Snyder's analysis; Liu and Liu state that the Chinese foreign policy establishment perceives alliances as "an archaic and entangling system that only increases the chances of costly military conflict."[27] A partnership is defined as a "diplomatic instrument that allows for hedging against all eventualities while allowing for the common pursuit of mutual interests."[28] Struver developed a framework for understanding strategic partnerships, stating that they are:

- based on a structured collaborative framework at a level beyond normal diplomacy, with frequent exchanges between ministries, departments, or agencies;
- characterized by a high level of flexibility, with low entry and exit costs;

- based on pursuit of shared interests and goals, and tend to work around conflict issues;
- process-oriented, as a means of "cooperation for the sake of cooperation."[29]

Goldstein notes that among strategic partners, the expectation is not purely cooperative relations, but rather a shared commitment to "managing unavoidable conflicts so that they could continue to work together on vital areas of common interest."[30] In terms of China's relations with the GCC, this partnership system allows China to continue its hedging strategy, developing interest-based relations while avoiding taking a costly stand on issues of potential conflict, such as the Sino–Iranian relationship.

Not all strategic partnerships are created equal, and the PRC has devised a hierarchy of relationships. In defining its diplomatic partnerships, there is some variation in the names of different levels, but they are generally described as follows, in descending order:

- Comprehensive strategic cooperative partnership: involves full pursuit of cooperation and development
- Comprehensive strategic partnership: involves close coordination on regional and international affairs
- Comprehensive cooperative partnership: involves maintaining sound momentum of high-level exchanges, enhanced contacts at various levels, and increased mutual understanding on issues of common interest
- Cooperative partnership: involves developing cooperation on bilateral issues, based on mutual respect and mutual benefit
- Friendly cooperative partnership: involves strengthening cooperation on bilateral issues such as trade[31]

The variables that differentiate between levels are not explicit. However, when former premier Wen Jiabao described the Chinese–European Union (EU) comprehensive strategic partnership in 2004, he provided a description that gives a sense of how the PRC perceives these partnerships:

> By 'comprehensive', it means that the cooperation should be all-dimensional, wide-ranging and multi-layered. It covers economic, scientific, technological, political and cultural fields, contains both bilateral and multilateral levels, and is conducted by both governments and non-governmental groups. By 'strategic', it means that the cooperation should be long-term and stable, bearing on the larger picture of China-EU relations. It transcends the differences in ideology and social system and is not subjected to the impacts of individual events that occur from time to time. By 'partnership', it means that the cooperation should be equal-footed, mutually beneficial and win-win. The two sides should base themselves on mutual respect and mutual trust, endeavor to expand converging interests and seek common ground on the major issues while shelving differences on the minor ones.[32]

Strategic partnerships are usually announced by the president or premier, and partnerships are often upgraded during state visits.[33] This was the case when President Xi visited both Saudi Arabia and Iran in January 2016 and announced in both countries that the bilateral relationships were being elevated to the highest level of comprehensive strategic cooperative partnership. Qatar and the UAE have both been designated as strategic partners, and China and the GCC have agreed to establish a multilateral strategic partnership as well.[34]

That Iran and Saudi Arabia were elevated to this level during the same week demonstrates both the benefits of partnership diplomacy as opposed to alliances and the difficulty China confronts in navigating its relationships in the Gulf. Chinese leaders emphasize the pursuit of common interest in their partnerships, and the preference to avoid issues of potential conflict. Having the highest level of diplomatic recognition for competing regional powers, both of which are major energy and trading partners for China, can put China in a difficult position. Chinese leaders present it as an opportunity, however; it can maneuver on both sides because it is not aligned against any regional actor. In March 2017, Foreign Minister Wang Yi emphasized this point, offering China's services to mediate between Iran and Saudi Arabia, saying: "China is friends with both Saudi Arabia and Iran. If there is a need, China is willing to play our necessary role."[35] No other external power can credibly make the same offer, lacking the depth of diplomatic relations and mutual interests with both states.

This hedging strategy in the Gulf has allowed China to develop a significant regional presence with deep economic and strategic interests, upon which the next sections will elaborate.

China's economic interests in the Gulf

Economic relations have been the driving force of China–GCC relations, with trade playing a central role, but finance and investment becoming increasingly important as well. This is consistent with what Sun and Zoubir describe as a geo-economic approach to the Middle East, in which China avoids military and security issues while promoting development strategies as an alternative means of creating stability.[36] Political cooperation has largely been a method by which China strengthens its economic relationships in the Middle East. Three Sino–Saudi official visits illustrate this. In August 2016, then Deputy Crown Prince (and current Crown Prince) Mohamed Bin Salman led the Saudi delegation at the G-20 summit in Hangzhou, and used the occasion for an official visit before the summit began. Meeting with Vice Premier Zhang Gaoli, the two initiated a joint Sino–Saudi council with the goal of deepening bilateral cooperation. To this end, they signed fifteen Memorandums of Understanding (MoUs) on a range of energy, infrastructure, and cultural issues.[37] This was followed by a state visit from Mohamed Bin Salman's father, King Salman, in March 2017, during which the MoUs began to take shape, as deals worth up to $65 billion were signed.[38] Notably, talks involved China Investment Corp, the $814-billion state-owned enterprise, investing in the state-owned oil behemoth

Economics and security 147

Saudi Aramco, a deal that is still under negotiation at the time of writing.[39] In August 2017, Vice Premier Zhang Gaoli visited Riyadh, where a series of bilateral deals worth an estimated $70 billion were signed.[40] These three political exchanges demonstrate the economic focus in developing closer ties, and are consistent, albeit on smaller scale, with China's relations with the other five GCC member states.

Trade is the strongest pillar in the China–GCC economic relationship, and bilateral trade has grown significantly in recent years. In 2000, China–GCC trade was valued at just under $10 billion; by 2016 it had reached nearly $115 billion[41] (Table 9.1). Collectively, the GCC is China's eighth-largest export destination and eighth-largest source of imports. Energy is at the heart of this trade. China became the world's largest net importer of oil in 2013 and is projected to remain so for the foreseeable future, and despite Chinese efforts to diversify its energy sources, it is projected to surpass the US in terms of oil consumption by 2034.[42] At the same time, domestic production, while projected to increase modestly, will not be able to meet its growing energy needs. As such, the GCC states play an important role in China's energy security strategy. 52% of China's crude oil imports come from the Middle East, and of that, 33% is supplied by the GCC. At 34%, natural gas imports from Qatar are China's largest source of liquefied natural gas (LNG).[43] Given the strategic nature of this energy trade, the economic relationship is complementary; the Gulf states require reliable long-term export markets, and Chinese demand is forecast to increase steadily between now and 2040 (Table 9.2).

Because of the substantial Gulf energy exports to China, trade is balanced in favor of Saudi Arabia, Oman, Kuwait, and Qatar; only with the UAE and Bahrain does China export more than it imports. In Bahrain's case, this is a result of relatively insignificant hydrocarbon exports and a relatively small volume of trade with China; in 2016 bilateral trade was valued at $862 billion, and of that $818 million was Chinese exports.[44] In the UAE's case, the trade imbalance is in spite of substantial crude oil exports to China. In 2016, Emirati imports from China outweighed exports by a ratio of nearly three to one, a result of the UAE's position as a re-export hub through which products from around the world are traded throughout the Middle East.

This trade could receive a substantial boost should the long-planned China–GCC free trade agreement (FTA) be concluded. Under negotiation since 2004, the FTA seemed permanently stalled, but the implementation of the China–GCC Strategic Dialogue in 2010 revived talks. China views the FTA as part of a larger overall relationship, with Foreign Minister Wang Yi describing it as "a driving force to boost pragmatic cooperation in all fields."[45] During President Xi's visit to Riyadh in 2016, he stressed China's desire to complete the negotiations by the end of the year,[46] although at the time of writing the talks have not yet resulted in a completed FTA.

Finance has become an emerging pillar in China–GCC economic relations. The UAE is at the forefront. To support a business community of 4,200 Chinese companies in the UAE,[47] China's four largest banks – Industrial and Commercial Bank

Table 9.1 China–GCC trade value (all figures in US dollars)

Year	China–GCC	China–Bahrain	China–Kuwait	China–Oman	China–Qatar	China–Saudi Arabia	China–UAE
2005	34,827.08	255.89	1,648.97	4,465.92	676.25	16,111.28	11,465.71
2006	45,970.81	349.44	2,785.69	6,043.44	998.31	20,140.91	15,094.14
2007	59,623.69	486.9	3,626.98	7,020.10	1,209.08	25,360.16	21,472.91
2008	94,285.24	784.75	6,794.84	12,179.34	3,384.88	41,853.27	30,126.73
2009	69,106.88	686.57	5,064.38	5,689.24	2,245.08	32,568.26	22,853.35
2010	93,669.47	1047.71	8,536.37	10,220.61	3,306.22	43,230.42	27,328.14
2011	135,057.7	1204.73	11,298.53	15,287.29	5,888.35	64,369.64	37,009.16
2012	156,913.24	1550.83	12,543.25	18,590.93	8,464.38	73,396.39	42,367.46
2013	165,166.81	1541.59	12,240.14	22,893.87	10,136.2	72,233.48	46,121.53
2014	175,172.93	1416.71	13,432.23	25,883.39	10,565.38	69,270.83	54,604.39
2015	136,606.11	1126.05	11,254.51	17,170.32	6,873.76	51,834.87	48,346.6
2016	114,077.72	882.2	9,475.39	14,088.83	5,554.37	43,278.28	40,798.65

Source: International Monetary Fund, Direction of Trade by Country.

Table 9.2 China's oil production and consumption

Year	China's oil production (millions of barrels per day)	China's oil consumption (millions of barrels per day)
2014	4.6	10.7
2016	4.6	11.3
2020	5.1 *(projected)*	13.1 *(projected)*
2030	5.5 *(projected)*	16.9 *(projected)*
2040	5.7 *(projected)*	20.8 *(projected)*

Source: U.S. Energy Information Agency, China International Energy Data and Analysis, May 14, 2015.

of China, Agricultural Bank of China, Bank of China, and China Construction Bank – have established branches in Dubai. Another important element of the financial relationship is currency swap agreements that China has signed with the UAE and Qatar. With increased regional trade and investment, the renminbi (RMB) is coming into wider use. In 2012, China and the UAE signed a three-year $5.5 billion currency swap agreement, which they renewed in 2015. While the swap has yet to be activated, it is seen as an important first step should the UAE aim to become a regional trading hub for RMB-dominated investment.[48] Qatar followed suit in 2014 with a slightly larger agreement, valued at $5.7 billion, although this was made in conjunction with $8 billion worth of construction and infrastructure deals[49] and therefore seems a mechanism to finance projects rather than a strategy to establish Doha as a regional investment hub. Saudi Arabia has also announced that it is increasing its RMB holdings.[50] This also has coincided with the announcement of several contracts for Chinese firms operating in Saudi, and as such appears related to funding projects. Speculation in late 2017 that China would finance oil purchases from Saudi Arabia in RMB indicates further development of financial integration between China and the GCC.

As the third pillar of China–GCC economic relations, investment has also seen significant increases in recent years. Gulf sovereign wealth funds have teamed up with Chinese financial organizations to create joint investment funds. The UAE's Mubadala and China's China Development Bank Capital and China's State Administration of Foreign Exchange formed the UAE–China Joint Investment Fund in 2015, with $10 billion in capital, funded equally by both governments.[51] The Qatar Investment Authority and CITIC Group Corp announced the creation of a $10 billion investment fund in 2014.[52] In 2017, Saudi Arabia and China signed an MoU to create a $20 billion joint investment fund as well, to fund projects related to the BRI and Saudi Vision 2030, the economic diversification program championed by Crown Prince Mohamed bin Salman.[53]

Taken together, trade, finance, and investment demonstrate a deepening of economic ties between China and the GCC that indicates a set of relationships far more intricate than the "oil for trade" narrative supposes. These ties will continue to thicken, as unimpeded trade and financial integration are highlighted as key cooperation priorities of the BRI.

The strategic element: the Belt and Road Initiative

Denser economic relations in turn complement the strategic significance of the Gulf for China as a crucial hub in the BRI, which has been described as "the most significant and far-reaching initiative that China has ever put forward."[54] Announced in a set of 2013 speeches by President Xi, the BRI consists of the Silk Road Economic Belt, the overland component, and the 21st Century Maritime Silk Road. Together, these two initiatives are designed to promote connectivity through infrastructure investment across Eurasia, ultimately connecting China to markets as far away as Africa and Europe. Participation in the BRI is guided by a set of five cooperation priorities: policy coordination, facilities connectivity, unimpeded trade, financial integration, and people-to-people bonds.[55] In the case of the GCC, these priorities are consistent with pre-BRI relations, meaning the initiative does not represent a fundamental change in existing relationships.

The BRI is often referred to as the signature foreign policy initiative of the Xi administration, and he has certainly committed substantial financial and political capital to the initiative. At the same time, it has become clear that Beijing sees this as a project that will outlast Xi's leadership, evident when it was enshrined in China's constitution during the 19th National Congress of the Chinese Communist Party in October 2017. The constitution was amended, with the inclusion "following the principle of achieving shared growth through discussion and collaboration, and pursuing the Belt and Road Initiative."[56] By including the BRI in its constitution, the CCP has committed to linking its long-term strategic vision with the BRI's success.

The architecture of the BRI has been established as a set of economic corridors that begin in China and cross through several states and regions. Initially, six of these corridors were announced: China–Mongolia–Russia; the New Eurasian Land Bridge; China–Central and West Asia; China–Indochina Peninsula; China–Pakistan; and China–Myanmar–Bangladesh–India. The Arabian Peninsula does not feature in any of these corridors, although both the China–Pakistan Economic Corridor (CPEC) and China-Central and West Asia Economic Corridor (CCWAEC) are oriented toward the Gulf. CPEC ends in Gwadar Port, 600 nautical kilometers from the Hormuz Straits, and Iran is prominent in CCWAEC. This absence of a formal economic corridor has not hampered the GCC states' ability to participate in the BRI; as a Chinese diplomat in the Gulf recently said, "any type of bilateral cooperation can be considered part of the Belt and Road."[57] Each of the GCC states has articulated an interest in participating in BRI, and several China–GCC initiatives are consistent with the BRI cooperation priorities.

The GCC is well-positioned to partner with China in the BRI. Each of the Gulf monarchies has embarked upon ambitious national development programs, such as the Saudi Vision 2030 and New Kuwait 2035. These programs involve significant infrastructure construction and present foreign direct investment opportunities, both of which are BRI cooperation priorities. Chinese firms and state-owned enterprises can build upon well-established presences on the Arabian Peninsula to further coordinate Gulf development programs with the BRI.

The future shape of China–GCC Belt and Road cooperation was articulated at the China–Arab States Cooperation Forum (CASCF) in Beijing in 2014, when President Xi announced the 1+2+3 cooperation model.[58] This was eventually inserted into the 2016 China Arab Policy Paper, which outlined China's vision for Sino–Arab cooperation, as countries would:

> upgrade pragmatic cooperation by taking energy cooperation as the core, infrastructure construction and trade and investment facilitation as the two wings, and high and new technologies in the fields of nuclear energy, space satellite and new energy as the three breakthroughs.[59]

This model of cooperation has been evident in China's relations with the GCC states, with energy technology, infrastructure construction, and nuclear energy all contributing as especially important components.

Given the centrality of the BRI in its foreign policy, China's interests in participating states and regions will intensify. The Arabian Peninsula, geostrategically in the middle of much of the Belt and Road, will therefore be an important feature in the initiative's development.

Chinese role in Gulf stability: two approaches

Given this increased strategic significance of the Gulf and the importance of the China–GCC economic relationship, it stands to reason that China's military and security presence in the region will also intensify to protect its assets, interests, and citizens on the Arabian Peninsula. American preponderance has largely negated the need for China to take on such a role, but the US's diminishing regional role and China's emergence as a power with global interests indicates that the Chinese government will be more proactive in securing its interests in the Gulf.

In articulating its views on a Middle East security role, the PRC has been somewhat vague. In January 2016 it released "China's Arab Policy Paper" in which cooperative endeavors predominate. Section Five, "Cooperation in the Field of Peace and Security," begins by stating:

> China calls for a concept of common, comprehensive, cooperative and sustainable security in the Middle East, and supports Arab and regional countries in their efforts to build an inclusive and shared regional collective cooperation security mechanism, so as to realize long-term peace, prosperity and development in the Middle East.[60]

How this will be achieved is unclear, however. The document states that China will deepen cooperation and exchanges in anti-terrorism, military, and non-traditional security measures, but does not provide details. In a speech delivered in China that coincided with the release of the Arab Policy Paper, President Xi stated that China did not plan to fill the void left should the US's pivot to Asia reduce its Middle East role, but rather that China would promote peace talks and cooperative endeavors.[61]

In the absence of an articulated regional security policy, there are two distinct approaches to security that may explain what type of security role China could play in the Persian Gulf. The first approach is that which Chinese officials and several Chinese academics describe: security through development. This approach is articulated in official statements and speeches, and is used as a counterpoint to what Chinese officials describe as a "cold war mentality" of Western powers in geostrategic approaches to international politics. Sun Degang makes this point explicit, describing China's military presence in the Middle East as a reflection of geo-economics, whereby China is pursuing development goals, while Western countries' presences reflect geopolitical ambitions that focus on military goals.[62] Rather than seeking military solutions to security problems, this approach expresses the belief that economic development would eliminate many existing security problems. Foreign Minister Wang Yi articulated this approach when he said:

> we believe that development holds the key and serves as the foundation for solving all problems. Any solution to hotspot and political issues hinges on economic growth and better lives for the people. As far as Arab countries are concerned, the most crucial task facing them is national development and economic revitalization.[63]

Ambassador Li Chengwen, who is China's representative to the China–Arab States Cooperation Forum (CASCF), said: "The root problems in the Middle East lie in development and the only solution is also development."[64] This approach believes that China does more for security in the Middle East through trade and investment than it could through military means, and this is described as a public good provided by the PRC.[65]

The second approach anticipates a more traditional military-security role, in which Chinese power projection would be used to protect assets and Chinese citizens in the Gulf. This would represent a dramatic shift from the PRC's approach to international politics, which has long operated under Deng Xiaoping's famous 24-character dictum: "Observe calmly; secure our position; cope with affairs calmly; hide our capacities and bide our time; be good at maintaining a low profile; and never claim leadership." As described above, China has not pursued formal alliances, and with that, had not developed overseas military installations. The recently opened Chinese base in Djibouti – its first overseas military installation – indicates a reevaluation of this approach. The port in Gwadar could also serve to project Chinese power in the Arabian Sea, as it will deploy naval ships to safeguard the port.[66] There have long been calls within China to take a more assertive international role, including the adoption of both overseas bases and alliances. In 2010, Shen Dengli wrote an influential article in favor of establishing bases, stating: "With the continuous expansion of China's overseas business, the governments are more accountable for protecting the overseas interests."[67]

He then outlined four specific responsibilities the government has which overseas bases would address: the protection of Chinese citizens and wealth overseas, the guarantee of trade, the prevention of external intervention in key trading partners, and defense against foreign invasion. Yan Xuetong, perhaps China's most prominent international relations scholar, wrote that "non-alignment suited our country during the cold war when it was weak. However, in the coming decade, China will no longer be the weak country it was. To stick to the non-aligned strategy would not only be unhelpful but also potentially harmful."[68]

This approach signals a more assertive Chinese foreign policy, in which the strategic hedging approach to the Gulf would no longer serve China's ambitions for the region.

Of the two approaches, the first, representing the PRC's official policy, is a better description of China's current role in the Gulf and in its relations with the Gulf monarchies. In the 2014 CASCF ministerial conference, President Xi indicated the approach the PRC envisions for its future involvement in the region when he announced the 1+2+3 cooperation pattern, discussed above. The Gulf monarchies already have well-established cooperative relations with China in (1) energy cooperation and (2) infrastructure construction and economic cooperation, and are working toward each of the fields discussed in (3) nuclear energy, aerospace, new energy. This reinforces the geo-economic approach to China's role in the Gulf, and the concept of security through development.

Beyond pursuing cooperative development projects, this approach to the region includes what Sun has described as a soft military presence.[69] He notes three forms of security involvement that China has already engaged in within the Middle East: the ongoing naval escort in the Gulf of Aden; naval visits, primarily on the Arabian Peninsula; and peacekeeping forces in Lebanon, Sudan, and South Sudan. The 'soft' designation is in contrast with Western states' 'hard' presence; Sun describes Western states' engagement in the Middle East as driven by issues of national security, whereas China's engagement can thus far be explained as a response to domestic concerns of overpopulation and resource scarcity. Thus for Sun, China's soft military presence is a means of expanding investment opportunities and fostering energy and trade cooperation in order to achieve domestic stability: "by increasing the well-being of the Chinese people and developing the domestic economy, China seeks to maintain stability."[70] Li Guofu, another Chinese researcher on Middle Eastern affairs, also equates a stable Gulf with China's domestic stability, stating: "China has a growing stake in energy, security, and trade in the region, so it hopes for a stable and peaceful Middle East, otherwise our domestic development will be affected."[71]

At the same time, there is evidence that China's security relationship with the Gulf monarchies is edging beyond this soft presence toward a harder, geostrategic one. As described above, the commercial elements of the China–GCC relationship are strong, and the energy component of that is important to China's own economic development. The strategic element of the BRI attaches further significance to stability on the Arabian Peninsula, given its geostrategic centrality to many of the end-points of economic corridors and connecting regions.

Nascent security and military cooperative endeavors could well signal an emerging security role for China in the region. In a recent study, Parello-Plesner and Duchatel demonstrate that in states and regions where China has significant interests, including commercial assets and expatriate citizens, the PRC has proven willing to pursue more assertive foreign policies when those interests were threatened or perceived to be so.[72] Chinese nationals working in Saudi Arabia, for example, have expressed concern about their safety. An engineer with a Chinese National Petroleum Corporation subsidiary firm employing 5,500 Chinese in Saudi Arabia's northwest region, bordering Iraq, worried: "Although we received anti-terrorism training before coming here, we are really afraid of unexpected conflicts. What if someone rushes into our building and takes us hostage?"[73] This is an especially important consideration for the CCP; with an estimated 5 million Chinese nationals living and working overseas, it needs to demonstrate that it is able to secure their safety. In cases where Chinese expatriate workers have been killed, such as in Pakistan in the summer of 2017[74], there is tremendous public scrutiny expressed on social media and online articles, and ministries and officials are usually the targets of this anger.[75] The responsibility to protect its overseas nationals is therefore an important test of legitimacy for the CCP.

There is evidence that security is an emerging focus in bilateral meetings between China and the GCC states. Joint communiques from official visits between China and the Gulf monarchies rarely offer specific details discussed during meetings, but in 2016 and 2017 security cooperation has been highlighted, and shortly after there have been developments that demonstrate more military cooperation. Saudi Arabia's Crown Prince and Minister of Defense Mohamed bin Salman visited Beijing in August 2016, and met with his Chinese counterpart, Defense Minister Chang Wanquan, who said that China was "willing to push military relations with Saudi Arabia to a new level."[76] Two months later, Saudi Special Forces went to Chengdu for a 15-day joint military exercise, where they trained in anti-terrorism drills, hostage situations, and extreme weather conditions.[77] This marked the first time that Chinese forces had cooperated in military exercises with an Arab state. This was followed by the aforementioned state visit from King Salman in March 2017, during which China and Saudi Arabia signed a MoU to build a factory in Saudi Arabia to assemble Chinese hunter-killer aerial drones in a joint project with the China Aerospace Science and Technology Corporation (CASTC). This is the only such factory in the Middle East, and only the third that CASTC has set up outside of China, the others being in Pakistan and Myanmar. Because the factory will also assemble associated equipment on-site, it allows CASTC to service other regional client states, which include Egypt, Iraq, and Jordan.[78] A recent official visit to Beijing from UAE Minister of State for Defense Mohammad Ahmed al Bowardi can be expected to yield similar outcomes. He also met with Defense Minister Chang, who said, "China is willing to join hands with the UAE in deepening cooperation in various fields and pushing for higher-level development of military ties."[79] Qatar, the other GCC state that has been designated a strategic partner by China, has also expressed an interest in a deeper military–security relationship with China. In November

2015 Fang Fenghui, who is a member of China's Central Military Commission and chief of staff of the People's Liberation Army (PLA), received Ghanem bin Shaheen Al-Ghanem, chief of staff of the Qatar Armed Forces, who stated that Qatar would like to develop deeper bilateral military relations in military training, military academic education, personnel training, anti-terrorism, and military trade.[80] Taken together, it is clear that security cooperation is becoming a larger factor in the China–GCC relationship.

Conclusion

The PRC's hedging strategy in the Gulf continues to serve a purpose, and it is unlikely that it would alienate any regional actors by adopting a balancing position. Its non-alliance policy further indicates that China will continue to approach the Gulf by developing its ties to all regional actors, and the 'development as security' approach will continue to dominate in Chinese discussion of its Gulf policy.

At the same time, its deepening economic and strategic interests imply that hedging is not a viable long-term strategy. The call within China for a more traditional power projection, as discussed above by Yan Xuetong and Shen Dengli, is consistent with the expansion of Chinese power projection to Gwadar Port and its naval facility in Djibouti. As the Gulf region becomes increasingly multipolar, it is likely that China will adopt a more assertive position. Its regional interests are such that China cannot be expected to rely on a US-maintained order. This is especially so as the BRI gains momentum, and China transitions from a power with global interests into a global power.

Notes

1 This borrows from and expands upon Christopher Davidson's analysis in *The Persian Gulf and Pacific Asia: From Indifference to Interdependence*. (London: Hurst and Company, 2010).
2 Lilian Harris. *China Considers the Middle East*. (London: I.B. Tauris & Co. Ltd, 1993), 82.
3 Mohamed Huwaidin. *China's Relations with Arabia and the Gulf, 1949–1999*. (London: Routledge, 2003), 96, 102–3.
4 Yitzhak Shichor. *East Wind Over Arabia: Origins and Implications of the Sino–Saudi Missile Deal*. (Berkley: Berkley Center for Chinese Studies, 1989), 1.
5 Harris. *China Considers the Middle East*. 82.
6 Ibid.
7 Hashim Behbehani. *China's Foreign Policy in the Arab World: 1955–1975: Three Case Studies*. (London: KPI, 1981), 178.
8 Yitzhak Shichor. *The Middle East in China's Foreign Policy: 1949–1977*. (Cambridge: Cambridge University Press, 1979), 177.
9 Jonathan Fulton. "China's Relations with the Arab Gulf Monarchies: The Case Studies," PhD diss., University of Leicester, 2017.
10 F. Gregory Gause, III. "American Policy in the Persian Gulf: From Balance of Power to Failed Hegemony." In *Gulf Politics and Economics in a Changing World*, ed. Michael Hudson and Mimi Kirk. (Singapore: World Scientific, 2014), 181–2.
11 David Roberts, "Kuwait." In *Power and Politics in the Persian Gulf Monarchies,* ed. Christopher Davidson. (New York: Columbia University Press, 2011), 92.

156 Jonathan Fulton

12. Kenneth Katzman. "Bahrain: Reform, Security, and U.S. Policy." Congressional Research Service Report for Congress, 2017, 18.
13. Ibid.
14. Kenneth Katzman. "Qatar: Governance, Security, and U.S. Policy." Congressional Research Service Report for Congress, 2017, 13.
15. Kenneth Katzman. "The United Arab Emirates (UAE): Issues for U.S. Policy." Congressional Research Service Report for Congress, 2017, 18.
16. Kenneth Katzman. "Oman: Reform, Security, and U.S. Policy." Congressional Research Service Report for Congress, 2016, 9.
17. Robert Zoellick. "Whither China: From Membership to Responsibility? Remarks to National Committee on U.S.–China Relations," U.S. Department of State Archive, September 21, 2005. https://2001-2009.state.gov/s/d/former/zoellick/rem/53682.htm
18. "The Obama Interviews: China as a Free Rider." *New York Times*, August 9, 2014. https://www.nytimes.com/video/opinion/100000003047788/china-as-a-free-rider.html
19. Jin Liangxiang. "China's Role in the Middle East: Current Debates and Future Trends." *China Quarterly of International Strategic Studies* 3, no. 1 (2017), 42.
20. Jin. "China's Role." 44.
21. See Mohammad Salman, Moritz Pieper and Gustaaf Geeraerts. "Hedging in the Middle East and China–U.S. Competition." *Asian Politics & Policy* 7, no. 4 (2015), 575–96; Mordechai Chaziza. "Strategic Hedging Partnership: A New Framework for Analyzing Sino-Saudi Relations." *Israel Journal of Foreign Affairs* 9, no. 3 (2015), 441–52.
22. Brock Tessman. "System Structure and State Strategy: Adding Hedging to the Menu." *Security Studies* 21, no. 2 (2012), 192–231.
23. Evelyn Goh. *Meeting the China Challenge: The United States in Southeast Asian Regional Security Strategies*. (Washington: East–West Center, 2005), 2.
24. Glenn Snyder. "The Security Dilemma in Alliance Politics." *World Politics* 36, no. 4 (1984), 475.
25. Abdullah Al Shayji. "The GCC–U.S. Relationship: A GCC Perspective." *Middle East Policy* 21, no. 3 (2014), 62.
26. Liu Ruonan and Liu Feng. "Contending Ideas on China's Non-Alliance Strategy." *The Chinese Journal of International Politics* 10, no. 2 (2017), 153.
27. Liu and Liu. "Contending Ideas." 153.
28. Vidya Nadkarni, *Strategic Partnerships in Asia: Balancing Without Alliances*. (London: Routledge, 2010), 46.
29. Georg Struver, "China's Partnership Diplomacy: International Alignment Based on Interests of Ideology." *The Chinese Journal of International Politics* 10, no. 1 (2017), 36–7.
30. Avery Goldstein. *Rising to the Challenge: China's Grand Strategy and International Security*. (Stanford: Stanford University Press, 2005), 135.
31. "Quick Guide to China's Diplomatic Levels," *South China Morning Post*, January 20, 2016. http://www.scmp.com/news/china/diplomacy-defence/article/1903455/quick-guide-chinas-diplomatic-levels
32. In Feng Zhongping and Huang Jing, "China's Strategic Partnership Diplomacy: Engaging with a Changing World." *European Strategic Partnerships Observatory Working Paper 8* (2014), 8–9.
33. Feng and Huang, "China's Strategic Partnership." 8.
34. Ministry of Foreign Affairs of the People's Republic of China, *Third Round of China-Gulf Cooperation Council Strategic Dialogue Held in Beijing*, January 17, 2014. http://www.fmprc.gov.cn/ce/cenp/eng/zgwj/t1121625.htm
35. "Ahead of King's Visit, China Says Hopes Saudi, Iran Can Resolve Problems." *Reuters*, March 8, 2017, http://uk.reuters.com/article/china-parliament-mideast/ahead-of-kings-visit-china-says-hopes-saudi-iran-can-resolve-problems-idUKL3N1GL2E5
36. Sun Degang and Yahya Zoubir. "China's Economic Diplomacy Towards the Arab Countries: Challenges Ahead?" *Journal of Contemporary China* 24, no. 95 (2015), 907.

37 "Saudi Arabia, China Sign Multiple Deals, MoUs," *Al Arabia*, August 30, 2016. https://english.alarabiya.net/en/business/economy/2016/08/30/Saudi-Arabia-and-China-sign-multiple-deals-MoUs-.html
38 Ben Blanchard. "China, Saudi Arabia Eye $65 Billion in Deals as King Visits," *Reuters*, March 16, 2017. https://english.alarabiya.net/en/business/economy/2016/08/30/Saudi-Arabia-and-China-sign-multiple-deals-MoUs-.html
39 "China, Saudis to Discuss CIC, CNCP Investment in Aramco IPO," Bloomberg, March 16, 2017. https://www.bloomberg.com/news/articles/2017-03-16/china-saudis-said-to-discuss-cic-cnpc-investment-in-aramco-ipo-j0bynknm
40 Charlotte Gao. "Closer Ties: China and Saudi Arabia Sign $70 Billion in New Deals," *The Diplomat*, August 27, 2017. https://thediplomat.com/2017/08/closer-ties-china-and-saudi-arabia-sign-70-billion-in-new-deals/
41 International Monetary Fund, Direction of Trade by Country.
42 U.S. Energy Information Agency, "China Country Report," May 15, 2015.
43 U.S. Energy Information Agency, "China Country Report," May 15, 2015.
44 International Monetary Fund, Direction of Trade by Country.
45 "China, Gulf States Outline 2014–2017 Cooperation," *Xinhua*, January 17, 2014. http://www.china.org.cn/china/Off_the_Wire/2014-01/17/content_31229860.htm
46 "GCC and China Decide to Speed Up Free Trade Talks," *Saudi Gazette*, January 18, 2017. http://saudigazette.com.sa/article/147021/?page=1
47 Dania Saadi, "China Considers UAE to be More Than an End Market," *The National*, December 5, 2016. https://www.thenational.ae/business/china-considers-uae-to-be-more-than-an-end-market-1.223813
48 Adam Bouyamourn, "UAE Renews Renminbi Swap Deal with China," *The National*, December 14, 2015. https://www.thenational.ae/business/uae-renews-renminbi-swap-deal-with-china-1.104179
49 Peter Alagos. "Qatar and China Sign $8bn Infrastructure Deals in '14," *Gulf Times*, April 8, 2014.
50 Reem Shamseddine and Katie Paul. "Saudis May Seek Funding in Chinese Yuan," *Reuters*, August 24, 2017. https://www.reuters.com/article/us-saudi-china/saudis-may-seek-funding-in-chinese-yuan-idUSKCN1B413R
51 Mubadala. *UAE–China Joint Investment Fund*. https://www.mubadala.com/en/what-we-do/capital-investments/uae-china-joint-investment-fund
52 Kristian Coates Ulrichsen. *The Gulf States in International Political Economy*. (Basingstoke: Palgrave MacMillan, 2016), 125.
53 "Saudi Arabia Eyes Joint Investment Fund with China, with a Focus on Energy," *Al Bawaba*, August 23, 2017. https://www.albawaba.com/business/saudi-arabia-joint-investment-fund-with-china-1013606
54 Michael Swain. "Chinese Views and Commentary on the 'One Belt, One Road' Initiative," *China Leadership Monitor* 47, no. 2 (2015), 3.
55 National Development and Reform Commission, Ministry of Foreign Affairs, and Ministry of Commerce of the People's Republic of China, with State Council Authorization, *Vision and Actions on Jointly Building Silk Road Economic Belt and 21st-Century Maritime Silk Road*, March 28, 2015. http://en.ndrc.gov.cn/newsrelease/201503/t20150330_669367.html
56 An Baijie. "Xi Jinping Thought Approved for Party Constitution," *China Daily*, October 24, 2017. http://www.chinadaily.com.cn/china/19thcpcnationalcongress/2017-10/24/content_33644524.htm
57 Author interview, Spring 2017.
58 "Backgrounder: China–Arab States Cooperation Forum," *Xinhua*, May 12, 2016. http://news.xinhuanet.com/english/2016-05/12/c_135354230.htm
59 "Full Text of China's Arab Policy Paper," *Xinhua*, January 13, 2016. http://news.xinhuanet.com/english/china/2016-01/13/c_135006619.htm
60 *Xinhua*, "Full Text."

61 *Xinhua*, "China Lends More Economic, Security Support to Middle East," January 22, 2016.
62 Sun Degang. "China's Soft Military Presence in the Middle East." *Middle East Institute*, March 11, 2015. http://www.mei.edu/content/map/china's-soft-military-presence-middle-east
63 Ministry of Foreign Affairs of the People's Republic of China, *Wang Yi Gave an Interview to Al Jazeera*, January 9, 2014. http://ae.china-embassy.org/eng/gdxw/t1116924.htm
64 "Development Key to Solving Middle East Problems: Chinese Diplomat," *Xinhua*, August 25, 2016. http://news.xinhuanet.com/english/2016-08/25/c_135630804.htm
65 Jin. "China's Role in the Middle East," 44.
66 "Chinese Navy Ships to be Deployed at Gwadar in Arabian Sea," *The Tribune*, November 25, 2016. http://www.tribuneindia.com/news/nation/chinese-navy-ships-to-be-deployed-at-gwadar-in-arabian-sea/328306.html
67 Shen Dengli. "Don't Shun the Idea of Setting Up Overseas Military Bases," *China.org*, January 28, 2010.
68 In Charles Clover and Luna Lin. "China's Foreign Policy: Throwing Out the Rule Book," *Financial Times*, August 31, 2016. https://www.ft.com/content/810b4510-6ea4-11e6-9ac1-1055824ca907
69 Sun. "China's Soft Military Presence."
70 Sun. "China's Soft Military Presence."
71 *Xinhua*, "China Ready to Coordinate."
72 Jonas Parello-Plesner and Mathieu Duchatel. *China's Strong Arm: Protecting Citizens and Assets Abroad*. (London: The International Institute for Strategic Studies, 2015)
73 Kristin Huang. "Need for China to Take Greater Military Role in Middle East, Analysts Say," *South China Morning Post*, September 18, 2016. http://www.scmp.com/news/china/diplomacy-defence/article/2020329/need-growing-china-take-greater-military-role-middle
74 Drazen Jorgic. "Pakistan Says Chinese Killed by Islamic State Were Preachers," *Reuters*, June 14, 2017. https://www.reuters.com/article/pakistan-china/pakistan-says-chinese-killed-by-islamic-state-were-preachers-idUSKBN1931DE
75 Parello-Plesner and Duchatel. *China's Strong Arm*. 39–41.
76 "China Willing to Advance Military Relations with Saudi Arabia: Defense Minister," *Xinhua*, August 31, 2016. http://news.xinhuanet.com/english/2016-08/31/c_135648206.htm
77 "Saudi, Chinese Special Forces Conclude Their Joint Exercises," *Asharq Al-Awsaf*, October 23, 2016. https://eng-archive.aawsat.com/theaawsat/world-news/saudi-chinese-special-forces-conclude-joint-exercise
78 Minnie Chan. "Chinese Drone Factory in Saudi Arabia First in Middle East," *South China Morning Post*, March 26, 2017. http://www.scmp.com/news/china/diplomacy-defence/article/2081869/chinese-drone-factory-saudi-arabia-first-middle-east
79 Ministry of National Defense of People's Republic of China. *China and UAE Defense Ministers Hold Talks in Beijing,* May 18, 2017. http://eng.mod.gov.cn/news/2017-05/18/content_4780862.htm
80 "China, Qatar Vow to Strengthen Military Ties," *China Military Online*, November 27, 2015. http://english.chinamil.com.cn/news-channels/china-military-news/2015-11/27/content_6789781.htm

10 South Korea–Gulf relations and the Iran factor

Jeongmin Seo

Introduction

South Korea and the Gulf states have always enjoyed a cooperative economic relationship. During the twentieth century, there was no obvious security dimension to the increasingly interdependent relationship between South Korea and the Gulf. However, the Gulf countries have recently started to find an alternative or at least supplementary security partners. This is because the twenty-first century has witnessed the straining of relations between the Arab world and the West, due especially to the events of 11 September 2001, the invasion of Afghanistan, and the 2003 invasion of Iraq.[1] This has meant that the dependence of the Gulf countries on a Western security umbrella has become somewhat problematic. Some GCC countries have, therefore, begun seeking positive alternatives to dependence on the West. This has opened the doors for Asian countries to seek a more active role in the security and defense arena with their primary energy suppliers.[2] Furthermore, this new international and regional atmosphere fitted with the South Korean foreign policy vision and strategy of "middle power diplomacy," which has been a prominent aspect of its diplomatic narrative for more than a decade. In seeking to present itself as a newly advanced Asian country in the post-Cold War era, South Korea has initiated a more proactive diplomatic role especially when it comes to promoting the so-called MITKA (Mexico, Indonesia, South Korea, Turkey, and Australia), a middle power network.[3] This new identity and initiative has also contributed to its more active involvement in not only economic but also strategic and military cooperation in the Gulf region.

The turning point was the year 2009 when South Korea and the United Arab Emirates (UAE) signed a number of cooperation agreements related to the construction of nuclear power plants. Especially important was the $20-billion contract between the Emirates Nuclear Energy Corporation and a consortium of South Korean companies, led by the Korea Electric Power Corporation (KEPCO), to design, build, operate, and maintain four civil nuclear power plants as part of the UAE's peaceful nuclear energy program.

The nuclear deal was packaged with the dispatch of South Korean military personnel, the Akh unit to the UAE. This was a military training unit which started deploying in January 2011 on a two-year mission to train special Emirati warfare troops. This constituted a dramatic development in South Korea's cooperation with the Gulf countries. Never before had it dispatched troops abroad, except under the umbrella of a multinational force or in peacekeeping operations. This military cooperation, moreover, has facilitated other forms of strategic cooperation between South Korea and the Gulf. In recent years, South Korea and some of the Gulf countries have been in active discussion over ways to foster bilateral military exchanges and strategic cooperation in the defense industry. For instance, Saudi Arabia recently established a military attaché office at the Saudi Embassy in Seoul, which is the country's first in the Far East.

Participation in security initiatives in the Middle East and other areas has also elevated South Korea's status and reputation in the international community as a rising middle power with increasing economic and political clout. South Korea's rising power and stature have compelled Seoul to contribute to international efforts to address global conflicts and threats. Moreover, engagement in military deployments and operations has provided valuable operational experience for its military forces to either go it alone or to act in concert with international partners. The practical experience of such military operations has allowed South Korea to accumulate precious field experience and skills for possible future defense challenges in the Korean Peninsula. These joint operations may also strengthen security diplomacy with the Gulf states in censuring provocative actions by North Korea. The latter, for example, has not abated its attacks against the South as underlined by the Cheonan ship sinking and the Yeonpyeong island skirmish. The Cheonan sinking occurred on 26 March 2010, when the Cheonan, a Republic of Korea Navy ship carrying 104 personnel, sank off the country's west coast after it was hit by a North Korean torpedo fired by a midget submarine; 46 seamen were killed. The bombardment of Yeonpyeong island was an artillery engagement between the North Korean military and South Korean forces stationed on Yeonpyeong island on 23 November 2010. Following a South Korean artillery exercise in waters close to the maritime line of military control between the two countries, North Korean forces fired around 170 artillery shells and rockets at Yeonpyeong island, hitting both military and civilian targets. The shelling caused widespread damage on the island, killing four South Koreans and injuring 19. In this regard, the military circle in South Korea believed that the active participation in international peace as a middle power would also be able to improve considerable actual warfare experience and skills to counteract possible military threats from North Korea. Finally, South Korea is of the opinion that strategic diplomacy with the Gulf may deter North Korea from cooperating with more countries in the Middle East on issues such as labor contracts, missile sales, and nuclear proliferation.

This chapter begins with a brief survey of the largely economic relations between the Gulf and South Korea, including an overview of economic and military cooperation between the two sides. It then analyzes the expansion of South Korea–Gulf relations into military cooperation and strategic partnership. Finally, it will address how Iran's recent reintegration into the international community may affect South Korea's burgeoning relations with the Gulf states.

Fluctuations in South Korea–Gulf cooperation

During the first years after its establishment in 1948, South Korea was preoccupied with nation building, economic development, and reconstruction efforts following the Korean War (1950–53). This left relations with the Gulf outside of South Korea's interest.

The surge during the era of President Park Chung-Hee

Under President Park Chung-Hee (1963–79), the Gulf remained relatively unimportant to the South Korean economy and people. The Cold War division affected South Korea's diplomatic and political relations with the Arab countries. Seoul selected its trading partners among the countries with which it could establish diplomatic relations and there was competition between Seoul and Pyongyang in establishing diplomatic relations with countries around the world.[4] It was relatively easy for South Korea to establish diplomatic relations with the pro-Western Gulf monarchies (see Table 10.1) in comparison to socialist republics as Syria, Egypt, and Algeria.

The 1970s witnessed a dramatic change in South Korea's foreign economic policy towards the Gulf region. This was largely a result of the emergence and influence of South Korean business conglomerates keen to export their products and services. Cognizant of the need to reduce the country's dependence on the United States (US), President Park focused on promoting industry and trade. The Gulf Cooperation Council (GCC) countries were seen as potential targets for the expansion of South Korean construction companies in particular. This was because the oil boom in the 1970s led many oil-producing Gulf countries to launch ambitious modernization programs in building infrastructure, roads, and power stations, all of which opened up opportunities for South Korean companies to expand their activities into the Gulf.

Moreover, the rapidly growing South Korean economy and the huge cost of energy imports into an energy-poor country necessitated a more assertive approach by the South Korean government and companies in the Gulf. To support its domestic companies, the South Korean government provided direct and indirect assistance through low-interest loans, tax reductions, and other incentives.[5]

Table 10.1 The establishment of formal relations between the two Koreas and the GCC

	South Korea	North Korea
Bahrain	April 17, 1976	May 23, 2001
Kuwait	June 11, 1979	April 4, 2001
Oman	March 28, 1974	May 20, 1992
Qatar	April 18, 1974	January 11, 1993
Saudi Arabia	October 16, 1962	None
UAE	June 18, 1980	September 17, 2007

For example, the South Korean government facilitated the activities of construction companies by recruiting most of the workers for these training facilities and even offering soldiers an early discharge if they signed up for the Middle East.[6] Thanks to their experience with reconstruction efforts at home and their low labor costs, this first wave of South Korean business in the Gulf countries succeeded in completing substantial infrastructure projects more quickly than other international companies.[7] The South Korean government and companies were also very attractive because they did not profess any overt political, military, and strategic agenda or ideological aspirations in the Gulf and focused only on mutually beneficial trade relations.[8] It is particularly notable that this period was bereft of any military or security cooperation.

The slump period in the 1980s and 1990s

Political instability in the Middle East negatively affected the South Korea–Gulf relationship in the 1980s and the 1990s. The Iran–Iraq War and the Gulf War underlined perceptions about the volatility of the Gulf and the risks of doing business in the region. Furthermore, the drop in the price of oil and the consequent decline of the oil boom in the mid-1980s resulted in drastic cuts to state budgets in the Gulf, which consequently reduced the number of construction projects. In this situation, South Korean companies were obliged to participate in riskier projects or to diversify into alternative markets such as Iraq and Libya.[9] For example, Dong Ah Construction, a South Korean company, won a $9 billion project to develop a river project to distribute water to Libya's coastal strip. Following the end of the Iran–Iraq War in 1988, many South Korean companies participated in reconstruction projects in Iraq. However, the Iraqi invasion of Kuwait two years later halted almost all of the projects. Many companies lost money: Samsung was left holding a $100 million debt owed by the Iraqi government and Hyundai's projects for the Housing Ministry estimated at $860 million were jeopardized.

Despite the depressed economic conditions, the 1990s were the starting point of Seoul's political and military engagement in the Middle East. For the first time, South Korea offered financial assistance to the Palestinian National Authority (PNA) after the Oslo Accords in 1993. According to the South Korean Ministry of Foreign Affairs and Trade, Seoul invested more than $10 million in the PNA between 1994 and 2005 and continues to grant funds for PNA projects.[10] More importantly, Seoul participated in the first Gulf War in 1991; 314 troops with medical and logistics expertise were stationed in Saudi Arabia. It was the first direct military presence of South Korea in the Gulf region and proved highly controversial. Seoul was disinclined to send forces to Iraq but understood that the alliance with the United States included a price that Seoul needed to pay, even if it did not want to send forces into war zones. In any case, the deployment of the troops onto Arab soil provided a physiological catalyst for South Korea to take the first step towards contributing to the maintenance of regional and international order.[11]

Increased interdependence in the new millennium

The new millennium brought with it an upgrade in South Korea's relations with the Gulf[12] and was a response to the deteriorating regional security situation in the Middle East. The 9/11 attacks of 2001, the US "war on terror," the Afghanistan War in 2001, the Iraq War in 2003, and the Israel–Hezbollah War in 2006 implicated South Korea in related military operations since Seoul offered tacit support to the US "war on terror" and dispatched troops to Afghanistan, Iraq, and Lebanon. South Korea largely acquiesced with the US in these conflicts partly due to the Mutual Defense Treaty between the two countries that had been signed on 1 October 1953, two months after the armistice agreement with North Korea. The agreement commits the two nations to provide mutual aid if either was faced with an external armed attack.[13] The South Korean military involvement in the region was not opposed by the pro-Western Gulf governments and, in fact, facilitated a strengthening of South Korea's strategic ties with the monarchies. The more active security and military involvement ushered in the so-called "second wave" of a construction boom in the Gulf countries, which once again attracted South Korean construction companies to the region, where they have secured a large number of projects. The GCC, for instance, accounted for over 50% of all South Korean global construction contracts in 2013, which amounted to some $17.3 billion.[14] Many of the projects won by South Korean companies were accompanied by undertakings to transfer technology and skills to local companies.

The most important achievement with far-reaching implications was Seoul's success in winning the $20-billion contract to build the UAE's nuclear power stations. This was the largest contract ever won by a South Korean company abroad. The UAE nuclear project also helped the South Korean economy to diversify the products and services it exports to the Gulf. Furthermore, the nuclear deal ushered in a new era of security and defense cooperation. South Korea signed an agreement with the UAE to transfer unmanned aerial vehicles (UAVs) and other technologies and has also been negotiating with some of the Gulf and Arab countries regarding the sale of its T-50 Golden Eagle trainer jets[15]. Seoul also concluded a security agreement with the UAE government, in what became a turning point of South Korea's overseas military operation. In January 2011, Seoul dispatched the 130 members of the Akh unit to the UAE to train Emirati special warfare troops for a two-year period. Prior to this, South Korea had never dispatched troops abroad without the umbrella of a multinational force or a peacekeeping operation. The new type of military cooperation has, moreover, resulted in some further forms of cooperation between the two countries. In 2011, South Korea's chairman of its Joint Chiefs of Staff (JCS) visited the UAE and met top military commanders of the country in order to discuss ways to foster bilateral military exchanges and cooperation in the defense industry. It was the first official visit of South Korea's JCS chairman to the country. The new military dimension in Seoul's policy has coincided with incremental change in South Korea's broader foreign policy in the new millennium, as it has moved from being a passive global player to a more active player, not just on the Korean peninsula but also in international organizations and other regions as well.

The era of military cooperation

The tensions and conflicts in the region at the dawn of the twenty-first century have, to a degree, shaken the security reliance of the Gulf monarchies on the West. Some Gulf governments and political elites have begun to envisage a possible supplementary or alternative to dependence on Western countries. In this context, South Korea has sought to pursue a more positive role in regional security.

These changing attitudes can be found in the remarks of government officials. For example, in a meeting in February 2012 with Sheikh Salman bin Abdul Aziz Al Saud, the then Saudi minister of defense and current king, President Lee discussed ways to strengthen military cooperation. In a summit meeting with King Abdullah on the same day, the President also emphasized this field of cooperation and discussed the early conclusion of a defense cooperation pact, establishing a military attaché in Seoul, and exporting ammunition and howitzers. This initiative of the president encouraged government institutions and business circles in South Korea to accelerate their activities in the defense sector. The head of the Defense Acquisition Program Administration (DAPA), which oversees the defense industry and defense exports, visited Saudi Arabia, Jordan, and Israel in May 2012. With the encouragement of the DAPA, South Korean defense industry companies participated in defense-related exhibitions in the Middle East such as the Doha International Maritime Defense Exhibition and Conference (DIMDEX) and the International Defense Exhibition and Conference (IDEX) in Abu Dhabi. Eighteen South Korean companies took part in the First International Defense, Security and Aviation Exhibition in Baghdad in April 2012, and seven companies in the Special Operations Forces Exhibition and Conference (SOFEX) in Jordan in May 2012. This active participation contributed to doubling the amount of defense exports to the Middle East from $109 million in 2011 to $220 million in 2012.[16]

South Korea's military and defense-related commercial activities in the twenty-first century have been informed by three factors with roots in South Korea's domestic politics: involuntary military involvement and later voluntary cooperation, anti-piracy military operations, and concern about the Iran–North Korea nuclear connection. These issues have changed Seoul's overall perception of the Gulf and contributed to a reformulation of its strategic and economic policies as explained below.

Historically, South Korea had not taken a meaningful part in a war outside its borders, except in the Vietnam War, participation of which was colored by the Cold War. President Park Chung-Hee viewed the participation of the South Korean forces as part of the war against communism and as a means to sustain the alliance with Washington. He was also interested to avail of the foreign income from the US in return for the supply of 300,000 South Korean soldiers.[17] In contrast, the 1991 Gulf War occurred after the Cold War ended, so Seoul did not perceive the benefits of participating in the Gulf War as it had in Vietnam, and the financial need for economic assistance did not exist, all of which explains why South Korea's contribution was limited to a support rather than a combat role. Nevertheless, strategic considerations regarding the durability of the South Korea–US alliance led the South Korean government to join the multi-national coalition force. It also helped that the Saudi government had a positive attitude towards the deployment of South Korean troops.[18] In October 1991, the commander of South Korea's military medical unit, Colonel Choi Myong-ky, was awarded the King Abdul Aziz Medal by Saudi Arabia.

South Korea participated in its second military operation in the region under heavy pressure from Washington to send forces to Iraq in 2003. A senior official of the Blue House (South Korea's presidential office) offered the following explanation: "Korea does not want to be abandoned by the United States and hopes to maintain and strengthen its deterrence against North Korea. It shows how much South Korea feels obliged to the United States to prove itself a trustworthy ally."[19] Again, this was a controversial issue especially since the US was requesting the dispatch of several thousand combat troops. Civil societies in South Korea organized anti-US and anti-government demonstrations arguing that the Iraq War was not a "just" war and that South Korea could not dispatch "combat forces" abroad as Korea was technically still at war since no peace treaty has been signed between South Korea and North Korea. Besides, Seoul also wanted to be perceived positively by the Arab world and wished to prevent potentially damaging effects on its trade in the region. However, Washington was no longer willing to accept South Korea's limited involvement in Iraq as it had in the previous war. This was partly because the US needed a stronger military presence in Iraq to stabilize the turbulent situation there after violence had erupted in the second half of 2013. Then US Secretary of Defense Donald Rumsfeld even threatened to relocate the headquarters of the allies' combined military command out of Seoul.[20] After a lengthy debate, Seoul finally decided to dispatch 3,500 South Korean soldiers to Iraq in 2004. Although they were not in a battle zone, they were, nonetheless, present in Iraq while the low-intensity conflict continued. The South Korean forces participated in civilian projects despite Washington's preference for assigning them military tasks. This deployment signified a change in South Korea's level of involvement in the region; military forces as well as commercial and construction companies were now present in the region.

South Korea's decision to send forces to southern Lebanon as part of the UN peacekeeping forces after the 2006 Israel–Lebanon conflict stands as another example of Seoul's new policy towards the Middle East. Unlike the previous dispatches to Saudi Arabia, Afghanistan, and Iraq, the Dongmyeong unit was dispatched not as a result of US pressure but was a voluntary contribution in support of the United Nations Security Council (UNSC) resolutions 425 and 426 to activate the United Nations Interim Force in Lebanon (UNIFIL).[21] Since none of the sides in the conflict suspected Seoul of having a hidden political or ideological agenda, it was therefore a perfect candidate for participating in a peacekeeping force. The Dongmyeong unit consisted of 300 people, including one battalion of South Korean Special Forces and specialist troops filling various roles, including engineering, communications, transport, maintenance, and medical support roles.

The largest military contribution of South Korea to the region relates to anti-piracy operations in the Gulf of Aden. In March 2009, the South Korean National Assembly approved the first foreign deployment of South Korea's naval forces to join the US-led Combined Task Force (CTF-151). The purpose of CTF-151 is to conduct anti-piracy operations in the Gulf of Aden and off Somalia's east coast. South Korea joined the navies of 24 other countries that participated in the Combined Maritime Forces (CMF) through one of three combined task forces, CTF-150, CTF-151, and CTF-152. South Korea has been a regular participant in CTF-151, contributing a destroyer, a helicopter, and special operations personnel (the Cheonghae unit) to support counter-piracy efforts. This participation was premised on the security of South Korea's commercial and energy fleet and its citizens who work on shipping and fishing vessels since South Korea had seen an increasing number of its ships seized with demands for ever-higher ransoms. A case in point was the hijacking (and subsequent rescue) of the Samho Jewelry chemical tanker. It is difficult to calculate in monetary terms the benefit of the Cheonghae unit's presence, but given South Korea's dependence on ocean-borne shipping, the approximately $33 million spent annually to fund the deployment is money well spent.[22] The deployment also put an end to the wave of hijackings of South Korean ships. According to one report, the high ransoms paid by South Korean shipping companies, particularly the $9.5 million paid for the Samho Dream tanker, may have marked South Korean ships as easy targets.[23] In the end, successful rescue operations, such as in the case of Samho Jewelry, demonstrated that South Korea was willing and able to use force when necessary to protect its interests.

The dilemma of Iran's nuclear issue

One would have expected a country like South Korea, which has to live with North Korea's nuclear intimidation, to be watchful with respect to the Iranian nuclear issue, but Seoul has prioritized economic interests and above all its insistence on being a nonpolitical economic partner, especially with Iran; it has tried to keep its more assertive military involvement in other Middle East affairs separate from the Iranian issue. This is because Iran has traditionally been one of its most important markets and trade partners. Ever since the issue of Iran's nuclear program was raised in 2003 at a meeting of the International Atomic Energy Agency in Vienna, Seoul has sent conciliatory messages to Tehran reaffirming its balanced position. At least until September 2010 South Korea's policy had been to follow the obligatory sanctions imposed on Iran by the UNSC while refraining from the voluntary harsh measures towards Iran, which other US allies, including Japan, have taken. These voluntary sanctions would have required a political decision to pay an economic price for coordinated international counter-proliferation efforts – a price that Seoul was not ready and not required to pay.

Prior to 2010, the tension between Iran and the United States did not prevent South Korean companies such as LG, Samsung Electronics, Hanjin Heavy Industries, Hyundai, Daewoo Shipbuilding, and others from signing billion-dollar contracts with Iran.[24] Trade between the two states, comprising mainly South Korean energy imports, had not suffered greatly either. Iran was South Korea's biggest trade partner and export market in the greater Middle East region, but the volume of bilateral exchanges reached an all-time high of more than $20 billion, including formal and informal transactions.[25] A bigger number of South Korean businesses, even top tycoons, were willing to invest in Iran and market South Korean goods and services throughout the country. Additionally, a sudden hike in oil prices after 2008 and a more vigorous East-looking foreign policy pursued by Tehran promoted a positive view of Korea. In an interview with a South Korean newspaper, Hassan Taherian, Iranian ambassador to South Korea said, "Korean companies have been involved in a wide range of construction and development projects in Iran, and Korean goods and products are popular in Iran, having their own many fans in the country."[26]

The Lee administration (2008–13) tried to balance South Korea's global relationships with its significant vested interests in Iran. Like previous South Korean administrations over the past three decades, President Lee was prudent enough not to raise the North Korean issue in Seoul's relationship with Tehran. The nature and raison d'être of Iranian and North Korean nuclear programs were kept separate for fear of antagonizing Iranian officials and consequently harming Seoul's crucial commercial ties with Tehran. On top of that, a majority of South Koreans had yet to be fully convinced that Iran's relationship with North Korea was detrimental to the peace and security of the Korean Peninsula. This is despite the fact that since the 1980s, North Korea has become a reliable supplier of arms to other countries, including Iran. Weapons sales between North Korea and Iran increased significantly during the Iran–Iraq War and has been expanded to include the development and exchange of nuclear technology. North Korea and Iran also have an active exchange of military expertise particularly in relation to special operations and underground facilities. North Korea has earned a considerable amount of hard currency from such arms sales and technological cooperation with Iran.[27]

However, 2010 witnessed a change in South Korea–Iran relations. In September, after an internal struggle that pitted financial interests against diplomatic interests and strained the US–Korean alliance, South Korea reluctantly joined the US-led drive to enact sanctions against Iran. The names of 102 Iranian firms and 24 people were added to the blacklist of those with whom South Korea was banned from doing business; it also promised to inspect cargo from Iran more diligently and to hold back on investing in Iranian oil and gas enterprises. Furthermore, when the EU and the United States in January 2012 agreed to a much harsher sanctions regime – an oil embargo on Iran effective from July and a freeze on the assets of Iran's central bank – South Korea was obliged to participate as well since global shipping insurers based in Europe were unable to underwrite shipments of Iranian oil.

The sanctions on Iran presented Seoul with at least three inconvenient dilemmas. First, Western sanctions linked Iran's nuclear issue to the North Korean nuclear program: Seoul was therefore in no position to seek an exemption from the requirements dictated by sanctions bills since its own security was on the line. Second, sanctions targeting Tehran's petroleum exports left Seoul with no option but to decrease the import of Iranian oil. Since the beginning of the sanctions regime in 2012, twenty of the countries importing Iranian oil, including South Korea, had qualified for periodic waivers. For instance, the US State Department extended a six-month sanctions waiver in November 2013 to China, India, South Korea, and other countries in exchange for their compliance in reducing imports of Iranian crude oil. As South Korea had been dependent on Iran for some 8–10% of its crude imports before 2012, a temporary ban on oil supply from the country had serious consequences for the health of South Korea's domestic economy. At the same time, however, the United States reserved the right to sanction any oil-consuming country, including South Korea, should it suddenly increase its demand. Third, constraints on banking and financial transactions between Seoul and Tehran or any beneficiary third party were very detrimental to the interests of some 3,000 small- to medium-sized South Korean companies doing businesses with Iran.[28]

The Lee administration first attempted to compensate for the petroleum it could no longer import by traveling to Saudi Arabia, Qatar, and the UAE. Saudi Arabia, in particular, promised to provide Seoul with as much oil as it required. This sense of relief was, however, short-lived since Tehran threatened, through its embassy in South Korea, that it was considering a total ban on imports of South Korean goods if Seoul complied with the sanctions regime. This pushed the Lee administration to use back channels to ultimately remove South Korea from the list of countries that were not allowed to do oil business with Iran.

The Lee administration also addressed the sanctions on banking and financial transactions. It initially tried to settle the problem through bilateral banking cooperation, such as opening a special account with the Korean Woori Bank and letting the Iranian Bank Mellat operate a branch in Seoul. A further step was a barter arrangement through which South Korea could ship manufactured products and luxury goods to Iran in return for energy imports from the country. A third measure, taken by both parties, was to implement a sudden yet temporary increase in the import of oil and export of manufactured products in the run-up to the implementation of sanctions. A final tactic was to pour South Korean products into Iran's neighbors, especially the UAE so that Iranian importers had easy access to made-in-Korea goods. Iran has, in fact, conducted the lion's share of its informal trade in recent years with the UAE.

South Korea has no doubt that Iran and North Korea have cooperated on missile technology and nuclear ambitions. This belief was reaffirmed when 38 North, a website devoted to analysis about North Korea in the US, reported in September 2016 on North Korea's ground test of a liquid-fueled engine ballistic missiles and the launch of three modified-Scud missiles.[29] As tensions between the US and Iran rose, Seoul increasingly found itself caught in the middle as its economic and national security interests came into conflict: should it take part in sanctions that could harm South Korea's own economic interests or should it back its closest ally in an effort to bring Iran back to the negotiation table over its suspected nuclear weapons program? Like Iran, North Korea presented the world with pressing nuclear proliferation concerns. While South Korea expressed half-hearted support for US efforts to check Iran's nuclear ambitions, it simultaneously attempted to reduce the economic consequences[30] and also tried to ensure that US efforts to bring other Asian nations on board the sanctions regime were not undermined by South Korea's actions.[31]

South Korea–Gulf relations in the post-sanctions era

Turmoil in the Middle East has raised concerns about South Korea's military and civilian personnel working in the region. The recent instability in Syria and Iraq, caused by the Syrian civil war and the emergence of the Islamic State, is regarded as a possible threat to South Korean soldiers in southern Lebanon. Any deterioration in the conflict in Lebanon that will endanger the South Korean forces might lead Seoul to consider withdrawing its forces from the country. Nevertheless, economic interests are still a major priority. According to the Korean Trade-Investment Promotion Agency, South Korean construction companies are completing projects in other countries in the Middle East, where turmoil threatens the safety of the South Korean workers. The government has prepared a contingency plan if the crises in those countries escalate, and it has maintained a ban on traveling to five Arab countries, namely Iraq, Syria, Yemen, Libya, and Somalia. The biggest concern for South Korea is the stability of the wider Gulf region since seven regional states – Saudi Arabia, UAE, Qatar, Oman, Kuwait, Iraq, and Iran – are the main oil and gas exporters to South Korea (see Table 10.2). Political instability there would imperil the activities of South Korean companies and energy imports into South Korea.

The significance of the wider Gulf region to South Korea does not, however, end with oil. The new millennium began with improved trade volumes between South Korea and these states. Their importance to South Korea's economy, especially to its construction companies, is clear from the numerous overseas

Table 10.2 Amount of crude oil imports from the GCC states, Iraq, and Iran

	2015	2016
Saudi Arabia	305 million barrels	324 million barrels
Kuwait	141 million barrels	159 million barrels
UAE	99 million barrels	87 million barrels
Qatar	123 million barrels	88 million barrels
Oman	2 million barrels	16 million barrels
Iran	42 million barrels	119 million barrels
Iraq	126 million barrels	138 million barrels

Source: Petronet, Korea National Oil Corporation, http://www.petronet.co.kr/main2.jsp

construction projects; regional instability therefore has significant political and economic costs for South Korea. Consequently, a gradual resolution of tensions over Iran – including the lifting of international sanctions at the beginning of 2016 and the return of Iran to regional and international markets – appears to offer a chance for South Korea to revive bilateral economic relations with Iran, which had been its largest trade partner in the Middle East before the UN-led sanctions. The rivalry and conflicts between the Saudi-led Sunni monarchies and Iran-led Shia belt countries in recent years have also changed South Korea's strategic cooperation in the region from "middle power" assertiveness to "fence-sitting," low-profile or even "by-stander" attitudes mainly focused on economic opportunities from the re-opening of Iran. In this regard, the next section will briefly compare the recent visits of South Korea to the Gulf states in 2015 and to Iran in 2016, and discuss the extent to which the South Korean government is eager to improve and strengthen its economic ties with Iran.

The presidential visit to Gulf's countries in March 2015

The 2015 visit of South Korean President Park Geun-hye to four of the Gulf states – Kuwait, Saudi Arabia, the UAE, and Qatar – reflected increased mutual interests and expanding cooperation between the two sides. A total of 44 MoUs were signed on deals worth up to $906 million, thereby underlining the potential of the partnership between South Korea and the Gulf countries. The agreed fields of cooperation indicate that the latter intend to benefit from the technological expertise and the knowledge-based skills of South Korea while strengthening economic ties through investment. In turn, South Korea seeks to support the expansion of its SMEs into overseas markets.

Some of the details agreed upon during this visit are as follows. Seoul–Kuwait cooperation included technology-intensive high-value-added industries such as smart grids and research and development (R&D) on building energy efficiency. In terms of investment, the agreement on establishing a joint venture for a biaxially oriented polypropylene film production plant in Kuwait appears to be a good example of cooperation between South Korea technology and Kuwaiti capital. Seoul–Riyadh cooperation is also set to improve. For example, South Korea's SK Telecom and Saudi Telecom Company signed an MoU to collaborate on the development of the innovation capabilities in Saudi Arabia by benchmarking South Korea's Creative Economy Concept. This is the first private-level cooperation between South Korea and Saudi Arabia that has been developed out of the previous agreement between the South Korean Ministry of Science, ICT, and Future Planning and Saudi Arabia's Ministry of Science and Technology.

South Korea's cooperation with Qatar is also expanding into new growth areas. These include the signing of a Letter of Intent between the Korea Institute for the Advancement of Technology and the Qatar Science and Technology Park for cooperation in R&D on IT, renewable energy, and green technology. Qatar's Education Above All and the Korea International Cooperation Agency signed an agreement to enroll thousands of children, particularly refugee children, into quality basic education in developing countries. Based on the agreement, the two partners will allocate $20 million over three years for their joint project.[32] In the case of the UAE, the emphasis has been on cooperation in advanced agricultural technology and cultural exchange. South Korea's nuclear cooperation with the UAE also serves as a model for other GCC countries, particularly Saudi Arabia, can follow.

Thus, the 2015 visit to the four Gulf states clearly demonstrates South Korea's comparative advantage in economic relations with the Gulf states, namely its willingness to custom-tailor and transfer its expertise and know-how to serve the development needs of the GCC countries. The main fields of cooperation include renewable energy, higher education, environment, ICT, defense industry, and power plants. The newly introduced South Korea–GCC joint business model of making commercial inroads into a third country shows that the partnership between South Korea and the GCC states is evolving into innovative cooperation between emerging market economies. The South Korea–Saudi joint business partnership targeting the small- and medium-size nuclear power plants market exemplifies such a trend in South Korea–GCC relations. Overall, the South Korea–GCC partnership has opened up possibilities for comprehensive and multilateral relationship-building, including economic, educational, environmental, military, and cultural cooperation.

The presidential visit to Iran in May 2016

President Park's government inherited the stance taken by the Lee administration, whereby South Korea would halfheartedly support US efforts to check Iran's nuclear ambitions while attempting to reduce the impact on its economy as a consequence of the sanctions imposed on Iran. Fortunately, a cautious change in the Iranian nuclear issue occurred by the end of 2013. On 24 November 2013, the Geneva interim agreement, officially titled the Joint Plan of Action was signed between Iran and the UNSC's permanent members and Germany (P5+1) in Geneva, Switzerland. And the final deal on Iranian nuclear issue, officially known as the Joint Comprehensive Plan of Action (JCPOA) was reached in Vienna on 14 July 2015. As a result, UN sanctions were lifted on 16 January 2016. On that day, it was announced by the International Atomic Energy Agency that Iran had adequately dismantled its nuclear weapons program, allowing for the UN to lift some sanctions immediately.

Considering the economic and security importance of Iran, South Korea moved quickly to respond to the new political and economic environment in the Middle East. Foreign Minister Yun Byung-se visited officially on 7 November 2015, just three weeks after the international community, led by the P5+1, and Iran had agreed on the JCPOA. During the visit, the foreign ministers of the two countries agreed to strengthen and diversify their partnership into various fields such as trade and economy, culture, tourism, development cooperation, and academic exchange.[33] In his meeting with Minister Yun, the Iranian president,

Hassan Rouhani, said that Iran, as a country with significant regional status, and South Korea, as an important country in East Asia, have remarkable capacities for expansion of economic, cultural, and political ties.

President Park's visit to Iran in May 2016 with a delegation of 236 businessmen and women aimed at recovering, improving, and strengthening bilateral relations with the latter; bilateral trade had plummeted to $6.1 billion in 2015, compared with $17.4 billion in 2011.[34] Park was the third president to visit Iran after sanctions were lifted, following Chinese President Xi Jinping and South African President Jacob Zuma. To facilitate Seoul–Tehran cooperation, President Park held talks with the Iranian president and the Supreme Leader Ayatollah Ali Khamenei on building a strategic partnership and on reviving and expanding industrial and energy cooperation. President Park emphasized that South Korea and Iran could produce a win-win situation if they worked together on infrastructure projects in the Islamic Republic. Sixty-six MoUs worth up to $45.6 billion were signed, although only six are legally binding. Seoul hopes the MoUs will pave the way for South Korean companies to eventually win massive infrastructure projects underway in Iran and "secure momentum for the development of bilateral relations and to strengthen substantial cooperation."[35]

The sanctions relief in January 2016 and the visit of President Park to Iran in May have undermined the blossoming relationship between South Korea and the Gulf in view of the escalating tensions between the Gulf rivals. In this regard, a South Korean newspaper pointed out that the most serious challenge to improving South Korean–Iranian economic cooperation was the uneasy bilateral relations between Saudi Arabia and Iran.[36]

An editorial in another newspaper, the *Hankyoreh*, warned that over-playing the Seoul–Tehran economic relations may mar South Korea's friendship with Saudi Arabia, although they positively support Iranian efforts toward denuclearization of the Korean Peninsula.[37] In any case, the shift towards Iran had to do with domestic politics. Just before the visit to Iran, President Park suffered a serious setback in the 2016 general elections as her ruling Saenuri Party lost both its majority and its status as first party in the National Assembly. Park had also been criticized for her involvement in the elections and the party's nomination process, and other Saenuri members blamed the pro-Park faction in the party for the defeat.[38] The foreign policy success in Iran was, therefore, a way to shore up her domestic political credibility and legitimacy as a leader.

For its part, Iran, which is seeking to rebuild its post-sanctions economy, has likewise been eager to boost its economic ties with South Korea. In March 2017, oil imports from Iran into South Korea were around 18 million barrels, up 126% from the same period last year, making Iran South Korea's second-largest oil supplier after Saudi Arabia.[39] However, since the impeachment of Park by the National Assembly on charges related to influence peddling by her top aide, Choi Soon-sil, in December 2016, the South Korean government and companies have adopted a more careful and low-profile approach towards economic cooperation with Iran. This would minimize being ensnared in an Iran–Saudi Arabia conflict.[40]

Conclusion

The relationship between South Korea and the Gulf states has grown in scope and depth over the past several decades. This relationship has also evolved in the new millennium,[41] with South Korea gradually shifting and diversifying its interests from economic and cultural cooperation to more strategic areas such as the nuclear energy sector and military cooperation, ultimately leading to a more comprehensive strategic partnership. These diverse linkages between South Korea and the Gulf countries are expected to accompany a fresh wave of opportunities for South Korean and Gulf governments and companies to work together.

The more assertive diplomacy in the first decade of the new millennium was based on the initiative of the South Korean government to establish its 'middle power' status not just in Asia but also in the Gulf and wider Middle East. By dispatching peacekeeping forces to Lebanon, participating in anti-piracy operations, increasing support for humanitarian and peace-building projects in Syria and Palestine, South Korea hoped to develop its new regional status while remaining politically neutral in the region.[42] At the same time, South Korea was happy for the United States to continue in its role as the protector of the Gulf States.[43] South Korea's ultimate goal has been to delegitimize North Korea's military provocations and persuade more countries to oppose North Korea's nuclear weapons ambitions.

However, the instability in the Middle East after the Arab Spring, the increasing terror threats to businesses and citizens, and the escalating rivalry between Iran and the Saudi-led Sunni bloc have raised doubts and concerns in Seoul. The geopolitical risks have kept the government nervous and pushed it to pursue more careful and balanced diplomacy in the region and to avoid backing one side over the other. Seoul's current "fence-sitting" position prioritizes geoeconomics over geopolitics. South Korea today has moved away from its middle-power assertiveness to more traditional economy oriented interests and behavior in the Gulf states, which will continue to be key energy suppliers and markets for infrastructure projects.

Notes

1 Ben Simpfendorfer, *The New Silk Road: How a Rising Arab World Is Turning away from the West and Rediscovering China*, (New York: Palgrave Macmillan, 2011).
2 Balbina Y. Hwang, "The US Pivot to Asia and South Korea's Rise." *Asian Perspective* 41, no. 1 (2017): 72–4.
3 Sung-Mi Kim, "South Korea's Middle-Power Diplomacy: Changes and Challenges," *Research Paper Chatham House* (June 2016). https://www.chathamhouse.org/sites/files/chathamhouse/publications/research/2016-06-22-south-korea-middle-power-kim.pdf
4 B. K. Gills, *Korea versus Korea: A Case of Contested Legitimacy*, (London: Routledge, 1996), 64.
5 Jung-en Woo, *Race to the Swift* (New York: Columbia University Press, 1991), 180.
6 Nigel Disney, "South Korean Workers in the Middle East," *MERIP Reports*, no. 61 (1977): 23.

7 John Lie, *Han Unbound: The Political Economy of South Korea* (Stanford: Stanford University Press, 1998), 92.
8 Disney, "South Korean Workers in the Middle East," 22.
9 Alon Levkowitz, "The Republic of Korea and the Middle East: Economics, Diplomacy, and Security," *Academic Paper Series of Korea Economic Institute* 5, no. 6 (August 2010): 5.
10 "Palestinian National Authority," Ministry of Foreign Affairs and Trade, Republic of Korea. www.mofat.go.kr/english/regions/meafrica/20070824/1_1363.jsp?
11 Brian Bridges, "South Korea and the Gulf Crisis," *The Pacific Review* 5, no. 2 (1992): 141.
12 Christopher Davidson, "Persian Gulf–Pacific Asia Linkages in the 21st Century: A Marriage of Convenience?" *Research Paper of Kuwait Programme on Development, Governance and Globalisation in the Gulf States* 7 (January 2010): 18.
13 "Mutual Defense Treaty Between the United States and the Republic of Korea; October 1, 1953," The Avalon Project. Lillian Goldman Law Library. http://avalon.law.yale.edu/20th_century/kor001.asp
14 Myeongkwang Kwon, "Dreaming a New Middle East Take-off," *Construction and Economy* (Seoul), January 23, 2014. http://www.cnews.co.kr/uhtml/read.jsp?idxno=201401221115288770419
15 Sung-ki Jung, "South Korea to Transfer UAV, Missile Technologies to UAE," *Korea Times* (Seoul), January 7, 2010.
16 "2013 Statistics of Defense Acquisition Program Administration", DAPA (Seoul). http://www.dapa.go.kr/internet/information/statistics/list_statistics.jsp. The Korean government and DAPA do not publicize details of military contracts due to political sensitivity.
17 Pyong-guk Kim, *The Park Chung Hee Era* (Cambridge: Harvard University Press, 2011), 427–28.
18 "Seoul, Riyadh to Sign Accord on Korean Medical Team Members," *Korea Herald* (Seoul), January 9, 1991.
19 Yoichi Funabashi, "Japan, South Korea Agonize over Troop Dispatch to Iraq," *The Asia-Pacific Journal* 1, no. 12 (December 10, 2012). http://apjjf.org/-Yoichi-Funabashi/1593/article.html
20 Jong-Heon Lee, "Analysis: Rumsfeld Tests Seoul's Friendship," *UPI*, November 17, 2003. https://www.upi.com/AnalysisRumsfeld-tests-Seouls-friendship/61881069079567/
21 Brian Lee, "South Korea to Field Troops for UN in Lebanon," *Joongang Daily* (Seoul), January 15, 2007.
22 Terence Roehrig, "South Korea's Counterpiracy Operations in the Gulf of Aden." *Global Korea: South Korea's Contributions to International Security* (2012): 28–30.
23 Stephen Kurczy, "Top 5 High-Profile Captures by Somali Pirates," *The Christian Monitor*, November 15, 2010. https://www.csmonitor.com/World/Global-Issues/2010/1115/Top-5-high-profile-captures-by-Somali-pirates/Samho-Dream-biggest-ransom.
24 Aejung Kim and Mohammad Arjmand, "The Foreign Relations of Iran and South Korea: Separation of Economy and Politics," *Iranian Review of Foreign Affairs* 7, no.1 (Winter–Spring 2016), 36.
25 Ibid., 37–8.
26 Jack Park, "South Korea, Iran to Deepen Relationship Based on Common Shared Values," *Business Korea* (Seoul), June 30, 2016. http://www.businesskorea.co.kr/english/embassy-row/interviews/15094-interview-iranian-ambassador-s-korea-iran-deepen-relationship-based.
27 Samuel Ramani, "The Iran–North Korea Connection," *The Diplomat* (Seoul), April 20, 2016. https://thediplomat.com/2016/04/the-iran-north-korea-connection/
28 Shiraz Azad, "Déjà vu diplomacy: South Korea's Middle East Policy Under Lee Myung-bak," *Contemporary Arab Affairs* 6, no. 4 (2016): 562–3.

29 Michael Elleman, "North Korea-Iran Missile Cooperation," *38 North*, September 22, 2016. http://www.38north.org/2016/09/melleman092216/
30 Il Hyun Cho, *Global Rogues and Regional Orders: The Multidimensional Challenge of North Korea and Iran* (New York: Oxford University Press, 2016), 16–17.
31 Jeffrey W. Knopf, "Security Assurances and Proliferations Risks in the Trump Administration," *Contemporary Security Policy* 38, no.1 (2017): 28.
32 "EAA, KOICA to Support Out-of-school Children," *Qatar Tribune*, May 20, 2015. http://archive.qatar-tribune.com/viewnews.aspx?n=A25A8578-CF29-4C67-8E6C-AF227E4F003E&d=20150520
33 Minju Lee. "South Korea's Diversifying Economic Cooperation in the Gulf," *Middle East-Asia Project Series*, Middle East Institute (29 Feb. 2016). http://www.mei.edu/content/map/south-korea%E2%80%99s-diversifying-economic-cooperation-gulf
34 "Park to Meet with Rouhani, Supreme Leader," *The Korea Herald* (Seoul), May 2, 2016. http://khview.heraldm.com/view.php?ud=20160502000641
35 "Park: S. Korea, Iran can Create Win-Win Biz Situation," *Yonhap News Agency* (Seoul), May 3, 2016. http://english.yonhapnews.co.kr/news/2016/05/03/0200000000AEN20160503009753315.html
36 Kyuwon Kim, "Obstacles in Korea–Iran Economic Cooperation," *Hankyoreh* (Seoul), May 25, 2016. http://www.hani.co.kr/arti/economy/economy_general/745411.html
37 "South Korea's Leading Role in Solving the North Korean Nuclear Issue," *the Hankyoreh* (Seoul), June 22, 2017. http://english.hani.co.kr/arti/english_edition/e_editorial/799820.html.
38 Hyo-jin Kim, "Saenuri's Defeat Brews Political Upheaval," *The Korea Times* (Seoul), April 14, 2016. http://www.koreatimes.co.kr/www/news/nation/2016/04/116_202637.html.
39 Gijun Kang, "Korea Imports the Largest-ever Amount of Oil from Iran," *Money Today* (Seoul), May 1, 2017. http://news.mt.co.kr/mtview.php?no=2017043013001663480&outlink=1&ref=http%3A%2F%2Fsearch.naver.com
40 Yongchang Song, "A Task to Appease Iran's Archrival Saudi Arabia," *Korea Times* (Seoul), January 3, 2017. http://www.hankookilbo.com/v/506d114d18944391b714d4ae1d28d34f
41 Daniel Moran and James A. Russell, (eds.) *Energy Security and Global Politics: The Militarisation of Resource Management.* (London: Routledge, 2008), 4–7.
42 Alon Levkowitz, "South Korea's Middle East Policy." *Mideast Security and Policy Studies*, no. 106 (December 2013): 25.
43 Junyoung Yang, "Dilemma of US in the Post-ISIS Middle East," *Korea Economy* (Seoul), November 16, 2017. http://news.hankyung.com/article/2017111667181

11 Technology for oil

Japan's multifaceted relations with Saudi Arabia

Koji Muto

Introduction

In 2015, Saudi Arabia and Japan celebrated the 60th anniversary of the establishment of diplomatic relations, which had been relatively stable throughout several historical phases related to the energy-based political economy, including the establishment of joint venture (JV) companies, cooperation on social development and, more significantly, Saudi royal-Japanese imperial relations. The value-laden bilateral relations increasingly became salient in terms of not only energy security but also industrial diversification in the period of inexpensive oil. In general, it might be argued that the beginning of the two countries' relations originated in dealings with oil supply and demand in a transitional period of energy shift from coal to oil in Japan after the Second World War (WWII). There were several reasons why the two countries primarily anchored in economic relations rather than in political or defense and security relations. First, as an energy-scarce country, Japan decisively prioritized a policy of secured oil supply for post-war industrial development. Secondly, concerning its foreign policy, Japan was constitutionally constrained from deploying international military activities. The alliance with the US in defense and security also influenced Japanese policymakers' diplomatic decision.

This research analyzes how the Saudi–Japanese bilateral "multi-layered" relationship has developed since the establishment of diplomatic relations in 1955. Four distinctive phases of relations are Japan's first oil development and the 1973 oil crisis (1955–75), agreement on economic and technical cooperation (1975–90), enhancement of multi-layered reciprocal relations (1990–2010), and techno-economic diplomacy on energy and security (2010–17). Throughout the historical phases above, Saudi–Japanese relations were described as "oil for (Japanese) technology, cooperation for (Saudi) oil."

Similar to recent Saudi–Japanese relations, Gulf Cooperation Council (GCC)–Asia relations have been shifting from economic relations to widely ranged collaborations in energy-saving technologies, infrastructure projects, and defense/security fields.[1] To supplement these vital economic trends, GCC officials' recent diplomatic visits have been increasingly focused toward Asian countries.[2] In particular, Saudi Arabia's foreign policy, based on its omni-balancing diplomacy,[3] has increasingly been oriented toward East Asian, and Japan has featured prominently.[4]

How were Japan and Saudi Arabia able to establish wide-ranging reciprocal relations? The fact is that in recent years Saudi Arabia has chosen Japan as a partner to diversify its petrochemical-anchored industry, while Japan selected Saudi Arabia to revitalize its "Abenomics" strategy for economic growth. These relations were not based on a simple trading arrangement, but on multi-layered reciprocal relations. The bilateral initiative of the "Saudi–Japan Vision 2030," which was advocated in October 2016, is a symbol of these reciprocal relations. This initiative is a response to a paradigm shift of the existing macro-economic development models for both states. The Saudi economic development process was moving from a government-centric model to a market-driven model,[5] while Japanese policymakers were trying to reverse the inward trend of economic protectionism to an international business expansion model. Secondly, both governments held broad and complementary ambitions to capitalize on economic or trade disparities with neighboring regions. Geographically, the Saudi government was keen to leverage its comparatively principal position in the region and capture unexplored business opportunities in Africa, while the Japanese business approach was limited to markets in South East Asia. Thirdly, as modern societies, both countries valued economic sustainability inspired by socio-cultural factors. Japanese decision-makers, for example, prioritized invigorating service-based industries, such as tourism, healthcare, and entertainment, which were familiar to the modernized younger generation in Saudi Arabia.

In this context, the two economic initiatives – Abenomics and Vision 2030 – are moving in a complementary direction. Abenomics aims to achieve long-term growth through developing its own economy and expanding to the international market, while Vision 2030 ambitiously attempts to place Saudi Arabia at the center of the Arab and Islamic world as an investment powerhouse and the hub for trade and business connections in the region. The envisioned joint investments are aimed to increase globally, for example through participation in each other's backyard markets by offering complementary strategic directions in the markets in the Middle East, Africa, and South Asia. Leaders in both states chose to pursue this initiative because it meets development and economic objectives. For Saudi Arabia, the Japanese package of cooperation for investment, technology transfer, and human resource development is a political tool to revitalize its economy and local industries, while the Japanese government identified synergy effects on their economic growth initiative of Abenomics. Such reciprocal relations make up the core of the 60-year bilateral history and have resulted in socio-economic interdependent relations.

The first communication: Japanese Muslims in the Hajj pilgrimage and mosque in Tokyo

Saudi–Japanese relations predate the foundation of the Saudi kingdom and started with the Hajj pilgrimage by Japanese Muslims performed in the early 1900s.

In December 1909, an Islamic–Jewish studies scholar, Kotaro Omar Yamaoka, successfully performed his Hajj pilgrimage as the first Japanese Muslim guided by a Russian-born Tatar Muslim, Abdulrashid Ibrahim.[6] A Russian-speaker, Yamaoka was probably working in intelligence services, as he collected information on Islam[7] and published travelogue books in 1912[8] and in 1921, detailing the austere Hajj pilgrimage.[9] Another Japanese, Ippei Tanaka, an expert on Chinese philosophy, became a Muslim when he was in China and carried out his Hajj pilgrimage in July 1924 (after which he penned a pilgrimage travelogue) and March 1933, respectively. Tanaka wrote another pilgrimage travelogue book in 1925.[10]

Islamic knowledge was brought into Japan in the Nara era (710–94) through Japanese envoys to the Tang Dynasty in China. In the Kamakura era (1185–1333), Japanese Buddhist priests who were staying in China had contacts with Tajik Muslims there.[11] In addition, knowledge of Islam was introduced through Chinese literature in the middle of the Edo era (1603–1868). Early in the Meiji era (1868–1912), Kowashi Inoue, a viscount as well as a bureaucrat, referred to Islam in his research book on China, and Tadasu Hayashi, an earl as well as ambassador to the UK, published the *Book of Prophet Muhammad* (1876) based on English-language sources. Detailed research on political, social, and legislative systems in Islamic Middle Eastern countries under European colonialism was introduced into Japan. However, the purpose of the research was not purely a study of Islamic law or philosophy, but an investigation of practical procedures of treaty revisions, consular jurisdiction systems, and treaties on commerce. Japan was keen to understand how European countries governed the Islamic Middle Eastern countries.[12]

The Meiji Restoration began in 1867 and prioritized the establishment of diplomatic relations with Western governments, in order to obtain knowledge of modern Western technologies as well as social systems and philosophy.[13] The government encouraged the gathering of foreign intelligence by dispatching foreign missions and exchange students in the 1870s. In international politics, Japanese policymakers began to expand their presence by concluding the Anglo–Japanese Alliance in 1902 and engaging in the Sino-Japanese War in 1894 and the Russo–Japanese War in 1905.

Afterwards, several Japanese Muslims successfully conducted Hajj pilgrimages between 1935 and 1939. Much Islamic research related to East–West Asian diplomatic relations, history and languages was encouraged by a governmental initiative during this period. The first mosque in Japan was built in the commercial city of Kobe in 1935, followed by the Tokyo mosque in 1938 by Islamic scholars and Muslim merchants, mainly from Turkey and other Asian regions. Many diplomats from Islamic countries attended the inauguration ceremony of the Tokyo mosque.[14] From Saudi Arabia, HE Mr. Hafiz Wahhabi, a *chargé d'affaires* at the Royal Embassy of Saudi Arabia to the UK, attended the ceremony. This was the first official trip to Japan by a Saudi government representative.

The Japanese government dispatched Mr. Masayuki Yokoyama, a *chargé d'affaires* at the Embassy of Japan in Egypt, to Saudi Arabia in March 1939, when he took a five-day trip to Riyadh via Suez and Jeddah. His delegation was honored to be granted an audience with King Abdulaziz Al-Saud, discussing issues such as a friendship treaty, diplomatic relations, and the economy. However, the negotiations for establishing diplomatic relations were interrupted by the outbreak of the WWII.

In any case, Tomoyoshi Mitsuchi, a geologist and member of Yokoyama's delegation, had a secret mission to look into the possibility of new oil-field development in Saudi Arabia. The kingdom was trying to bring a competitive mechanism into the domestic oil-development market by suggesting that Japan could participate in the possible development of three new oil fields: the eastern inland al-Dahna desert area, the south-eastern desert area Wadi Sirhan, and the Saudi–Kuwaiti neutral zone.[15] However, Japan was forced to abandon negotiations due to potential risks associated with such a large-scale investment, lack of proper technology and experience, the doubtful safety of the transportation sea lane, and direct and indirect interferences from the existing major oil development companies. The Japanese government resumed negotiations regarding the establishment of diplomatic relations with Saudi Arabia in 1953 and relations were formally established in June 1955.

The first phase: Japan's first oil development and the 1973 oil crisis: 1955–75

Oil supply and demand relations remain vital for both countries in terms of oil security. It is not an exaggeration that the securing of energy is a principal lifeline of Japanese industry and economy since Japan has few indigenous oil resources.[16] The Arabian Oil Company (AOC), the Japanese company that obtained Japan's first oil concession in the Middle East, was, in a sense, an essential bridge between the two countries and the symbol of prominent reciprocal relations throughout the bilateral history.

For two decades from 1955, Saudi Arabia was in the process of unique economic development, described by Niblock as "laying the basis for development (1962–1970)" and "planning for transformation (1970–1985),"[17] during which Saudi Arabia tried to implement national reform focused on industrial diversification. Japan contributed to the process by offering JV business formation in relation to infrastructural, administrative, and industrial development as well as by concluding the governmental agreement on economic technical development cooperation for enhancing pivotal economic relations.

AOC: symbol of Saudi–Japan relations

Japan's crude oil imports increased rapidly through the substantial and constant demands of post-war reconstruction projects,[18] and most of the oil came from the Middle East.[19] Without political influence, financial power, appropriate technology, and experience of original oil development, Japan was dependent on the major Middle Eastern oil suppliers.[20] In the 1950s the oil-producing countries came to appreciate Japan's large and growing demand and offered the country the opportunity to participate in developing new oil fields, driven largely by a need to diversify their export markets, and also because of dissatisfaction with the stranglehold of international oil companies over their domestic resources. Japan's rapid post-war redevelopment was also a factor, representing a substantial steady long-term customer.

A Japanese businessman, Taro Yamashita, became the first AOC president. He visited Saudi Arabia in February 1957 with a letter of introduction from then Prime Minister (PM) Taizan Ishibashi, Foreign Minister Nobusuke Kishi, and former PM Shigeru Yoshida. King Saud welcomed Yamashita's delegation and they reached an agreement "to start an official negotiations for right of interests in acquisition of an oil field within six months."[21] Yamashita returned home, established the AOC on July 9, and returned to Saudi Arabia on July 26, 1957.

The Saudi negotiating partner was Eng. Abdullah ibn Hamoud Tariki, director-general of petroleum and mineral affairs in the Ministry of Finance and National Economy who would later become the first minister of the Ministry of Petroleum and Mineral Resources. He suggested that the neutral zone between Saudi Arabia and Kuwait was the most promising field to explore.[22]

Following contentious negotiations, a concession agreement was finally signed in December 1957, with AOC remaining a Japanese-registered company, contrary to the preferences of the Saudis. The Saudi intention was to rebalance existing oil-granting rights which were completely devoted to the US and European companies.[23] The new company, AOC, was registered as a Japanese company in February 1958. AOC was also able to sign a concession agreement with Kuwait in July 1958 as a result of intense negotiations. After technical excavation and extraction works began on the site, later named the Khafji oil field, crude oil gushed out of the field from 1,670 meters below ground in January 1960. It was confirmed that the Khafji oil field was one of the world's most significant oil fields with enormous reserves. However, it had high sulfur content and contained heavy crude oil, which required AOC to install desulfurization facilities.

As for the political situation in the Middle East in the 1950s, the influence of former colonial powers and the bipolar Cold War system created a complex dynamic in the region.[24] Pan-Arab nationalism spread across the Middle East, leading several Arab states to review diplomatic relations with the US and Europe.[25] As such, Western oil majors were in a less advantageous position in negotiations for the acquisition of the Khafji oil field, creating an opportunity for AOC. The international political atmosphere throughout the Middle East therefore benefitted Japan, opening the door for the first instance of "Asianization," whereby Saudi Arabia and Kuwait diversified oil concessions away from the Western majors, signing with the Japanese AOC instead.

Oil consumption in Japan increased rapidly, and it became the primary source of energy. It increased to 55.9% in 1965 and peaked at 75.5% in 1973, with much of the imports originating from the Middle East,[26] demonstrating Japanese industry's shift from coal to oil, described in Japan as "a fluid revolution." Most Japanese electricity companies changed from coal to oil for power generation.

Petrochemical complexes became one of the core industrial developments in Japan. The Japanese government regarded the petrochemical industry as a new strategic industry, providing it with substantial financial support.

The 1973 oil crisis: the oil weapon and Japan's pro-Arab policy?

The oil crisis was a critical blow to the Japanese economy. For example, Japan recorded a so-called "frenzied inflation"[27] rate of more than 20% in 1974. For the first time in the post-war period, Japan's economy had a negative growth rate. Because of the oil crisis, rapid economic growth in Japan came to a complete halt. Consequently, Saudi Arabia was successful in encouraging Japan's oil-purchasing capacity and secured economic and technical cooperation by concluding a bilateral agreement which could secure financial resources to conduct domestic reform of the economic structure.

The oil crisis underlined the difficulty of oil diplomacy and exposed the fragility of Japan's economy. There was a considerable difference among the Arab countries regarding oil strategy. Japanese researcher Hosaka argued that some Arab countries, such as Kuwait and the UAE, were not in favor of suspending oil supply to Japan.[28] Japan was initially targeted by the oil-producing countries to withdraw its promises of economic development cooperation to Middle Eastern countries, including Iran, which was also of substantial benefit to them beyond just the selling of oil.

From a chronological viewpoint, there is a critical argument against the Japanese government's late response to the crisis. The oil weapon was unsheathed by the Arab countries on October 17, 1973, followed by the Japanese government's Chief Cabinet Secretary Nikaido's unequivocal statement clarifying Japan's so-called pro-Arab foreign policy on November 22[29] and a visit to the Middle East on December 10 by special envoy Takeo Miki.[30] Japan was subsequently recognized as a friendly nation on December 25. Despite the fact that the causes of the critical situation were clear and the necessary measures to solve the problem were also obvious, the Japanese government took an unexpected two months to prepare a short official statement and dispatch a special envoy to the Middle East.

The ministerial power balance in Japan was basically divided into two groups. The first group insisted on maintaining Middle East foreign policy along with the principal logic of Japan-US-anchored relations, while another group emphasized pro-Arab energy security policy based on downgrading relations with Israel to secure oil supply. Japan accepted the establishment of the Palestine Liberation Organization (PLO) office in Tokyo in February 1977. The Japanese government's late response was a result of concerned ministries' extensive efforts to approach the Saudi government, utilizing each ministry's domestic and international channels.

The fact that Japan is an energy-scarce nation, in terms of realistic energy acquisition and profitability, means that an energy security policy remains a constant priority for Japanese diplomacy. The oil crisis was not just a product of war in the Middle East, but a result of a rapid increase in global oil demand which outstripped the supplying capacity. After the oil crisis, oil-consuming countries in the industrialized world agreed to work on international economic issues. The Japanese government participated in the US-led initiative of the Energy Washington meeting while promoting dialogue with the Arab oil-producing countries. The Washington meeting resulted in the establishment of the International Energy Agency (IEA) as an extra-ministerial department of OECD in November 1974. Cooperation on energy issues led to unprecedented steady relations between US President Ronald Reagan and Japanese PM Nakasone in the 1980s. This represented active participation by the Japanese government in the US's new global economic strategy.[31]

The second phase: agreement on economic and technical cooperation: 1975–90

Through economic and business communications, the need for official economic technical cooperation was recognized between the two governments. Official negotiations were initiated by a visit to Tokyo by Prince Sultan bin Abdulaziz al-Saud, minister of transportation, in October 1960. In the discussions, Prince Sultan asked the Japanese government for cooperation on four business projects in the fields of telecommunications network, natural gas, steel, and fisheries. Subsequently, a large-scale business mission headed by Sohei Nakayama, chairman of Overseas Technical Cooperation Agency, was dispatched in January 1971 to extend relations with the Middle Eastern countries, mainly Saudi Arabia. King Faisal became the first Arab head of state to visit Japan in May 1971, and had an audience with His Majesty the Emperor of Japan, and met government leaders to request the early conclusion of the economic technical cooperation agreement. Finally, on March 1, 1975, the "Agreement on Economic and Technical Cooperation between the Government of Japan and the Government of the Kingdom of Saudi Arabia" was signed. The goal of the agreement was to promote cooperation in economic and technical fields, excluding security. In particular, it encouraged the establishment of JV companies and investment from Japan in petrochemical and other fundamental industries. The transfer of advanced technology from Japan was included.

During this period, Japan concluded a similar agreement with Iraq in August 1974 and exchanged notes of official credit with Egypt in July and with Jordan and Algeria in December 1974.[32] At the same time, Saudi Arabia was also aiming at economic development, trading, and technical cooperation with other foreign countries on the basis of reciprocal political economy interests.[33]

Ten Saudi–Japanese JV companies, mostly in manufacturing industries, were established based on the agreement on economic and technical cooperation between 1975 and 1990. These original JV companies continue to provide services and manufacturing products to this day. They include two petrochemical JV companies, Saudi Methanol (AR-RAZI) and Eastern Petrochemical (SHARQ).

The third phase: enhancement of multi-layered reciprocal relations: 1990–2010

The two decades following 1990 represent the most advanced period. During the 1990s, no large-scale JV projects were realized due to regional instability and low oil prices. However, an economic framework capable of shaping advanced economic relations was created by two different official agreements. The first was the Comprehensive Partnership towards the 21st Century (1997) and the other was the Japan–Saudi Arabia Joint Agenda (1998).

In the 2000s, the multi-layered economic relationship advanced. More than 20 JV companies were established, and three Japanese-style vocational and training institutes for car maintenance, plastic fabrication, and electronics and home appliances were set up in Jeddah and Riyadh. During another visit to Tokyo, this time in 2006, by the now Crown Prince Sultan the Joint Statement towards the Building of Strategic and Multi-layered Partnership between Japan and the Kingdom of Saudi Arabia was signed.

The Saudi economy developed despite fluctuating oil prices.[34] Thanks in part to Saudi initiatives to promote the introduction of foreign investment as well as human resource development, it created a socially balanced and diversified economy.[35] More specifically, the privatization and liberalization of state-owned companies were advocated in order to diversify the oil-anchored domestic industry, so that private companies could utilize their potential business efficiency and capabilities during this period.[36]

Many Japanese companies, mainly in the manufacturing industry, took advantage of the new legal environment to establish JV companies in Saudi Arabia despite its economic downturn and the fact that "the Kingdom could no longer count on a continuing upward drift in oil price."[37] Japanese companies introduced an 'All Japan' business initiative[38] in the Saudi Arabian market during that period, encouraged by the government's political commitment.[39] Similarly, the economic entities in Saudi Arabia also needed a governmental initiative as "the primary engine of growth" to enhance business relations with foreign countries.[40] In any case, trade continued to be significant throughout the 1980s and 1990s in terms of energy trade and security.[41]

It was in the early 2000s that Saudi domestic social problems became more apparent, including a financial gap among citizens, a huge inflow of foreign workers, overpopulation in urban areas, and differences in regional development levels.[42] Defense-related expenditures put pressure on the Saudi government's budget, as it sought to respond to regional turmoil as well as a financial downturn. The Iraqi invasion of Kuwait, the Gulf Crisis/War, 9/11 and subsequent military campaigns related to the global war on terror affected the international political economy, energy security, and diplomacy.[43] In particular, the historically strong relations between the US and Saudi Arabia also came under strain.[44] In the Gulf Crisis/War in the early 1990s, Japan made a controversial financial contribution to the US-led multinational force, and in the Iraq War in 2003, Japan conducted overseas deployment of the Self-Defense Forces under an Act on

Special Measures Concerning Humanitarian Relief and Reconstruction Work and Security Assistance in Iraq. It was a conceptual shift in international security for post-war Japan.[45]

Amid the changing political and economic situations in the region, the Saudi government was facing the impending need for comprehensive reform of its domestic politics, economy, and society, as a series of influential petitions signed by Saudi intellectuals and religious leaders were delivered directly to the government in the early 1990s.[46] The Saudi government needed cooperation from the global community, particularly developed countries' know-how and experiences of reform, in order to diversify its oil-dependent industry, stabilize the economic structure, create job opportunities for youth, and maintain social order and security in order to sustain the legitimacy of the al-Saud sovereignty and to survive as a member of the global community. Most analysts have linked reforms to Saudi authoritarian characteristics,[47] while Luciani generally explained the oil influence on domestic reform as well as regional balance and inter-Arab political relations.[48]

Such reform efforts provided avenues for energy-scarce Japan to begin to explore the potentially energy-rich Middle Eastern market for business expansion to compensate for its own shrinking domestic market. The Middle Eastern market was attractive for its business potential, and because Japanese companies could function as a business foothold to the promising African market in the future.[49] The timing of wide-ranging cooperation in the new economic development of Saudi Arabia also took place within the context of both countries' economic demand. The Japanese government implemented a business strategy of integrated public-private sectors to cope with this situation.

Inescapable human resource development: Japanese technical vocational institutes

Despite the Saudi government's launching of Saudization campaign in the 2000s which aimed at replacing foreign workers with Saudi nationals, the employment of foreign workers by Saudi companies continued substantially in many labor markets.[50] Many foreign workers took up employment, even in governmental jobs, in the Saudi labor market, which caused an increase in the unemployment rate among Saudi youth because of an aversion to private-sector employment.[51] As a result, the Saudi government came to rely on its international partners, including Japan, for support in developing its human resources capacity.

In Japan, knowledge of science and technology and a diligent work ethic was the engine of post-war reconstruction of its economy. In energy-scarce Japan, the government encouraged human resource development for an industrialized nation which required various technicians and engineers.[52] This experience was useful in supporting Saudi needs for human resources development, and as a result, the Japanese government established three vocational and training institutes between 2002 and 2009 in cooperation with the Saudi Technical Vocational Training Corporation (TVTC).

The first institute, the Saudi Japanese Automobile High Institute (SJAHI)[53] was established in 2002 and is a training institute specializing in vehicle repair and maintenance. This project was implemented as the last Official Development Aid (ODA) project of the Japan International Cooperation Agency (JICA).[54] Both governments collaboratively provided land, finances, and engineering support for facilities to build the institute, and it developed a favorable reputation because of its scale and quality. Secondly, the High Institute for Plastic and Fabrication (HIPF)[55] in Riyadh was established in 2007 in commemoration of the large-scale success of the petrochemical JV manufacturing company SHARQ (Mitsubishi group and Saudi Basic Industries Corporation (SABIC), a manufacturer of diversified chemicals) and specialized in training in processing and manufacturing plastic materials. This institute represented a successful JV business between Japan and Saudi Arabia and implied a social contribution for Saudi Arabia. The training machine and facilities installed in HIPF were distinctively practical for manufacturing plastic products, and the second-year training curriculum was designed for training operation and maintenance technicians in plastic-related industries. The third institute, the Saudi Electronics and Home Appliances Institute (SEHAI),[56] was established in Riyadh in 2009 to train Saudi youth to become technicians in electronics and home-appliance industries. Unlike the previous institutes, SEHAI's management was led by an executive committee comprised of Saudi distributing agent companies of Japanese electronics and home-appliance products, such as Sony, Toshiba, Hitachi, and Daikin, among others.

Despite these three institutes' small capacity, their continuous contributions to the bilateral multi-layered relations are significant. Human resource development, including training in work ethics, is indispensable for the manufacturing and commercial industries which will form the basis of sustainable economic development in a rapidly changing Saudi society.

The fourth phase: techno-economic diplomacy on energy and security: 2010–15

This section examines the fourth and most recent period of Saudi–Japanese relations –2010 to 2017. During the first half of this period, between 2010 and 2013, Japanese diplomatic activities stagnated. Significant political turmoil resulted in a drastic administrative change in Japan with the inauguration of the Hatoyama administration of the Democratic Party of Japan (DPJ) in August 2009 for the first time since its establishment in 1998. Japan's Middle East foreign policy during the DPJ administrations between 2009 and 2012 remained unclear due to its Asia-oriented foreign policy. The Great East Japan Earthquake in March 2011 completely changed the Japanese energy policy away from nuclear power in the wake of the disastrous accident at the nuclear power station in Fukushima. Despite the disaster, the Japanese government participated in Saudi Arabia's 26th National Festival for Heritage and Culture. The Japanese Pavilion was visited by more than 300,000 people, demonstrating Saudi popular interest in Japanese culture and products.[57]

Secondly, although this period was short, the reciprocal official visits continued and helped shape new bilateral relations, in particular in the field of energy-saving technology and defense and security cooperation. In the fields of foreign defense/security relations, the Japanese government legislated security-related bills to contribute to international peace in 2015, which enabled Japan's Self-Defense Forces to play a more active role in the international community. And thirdly, at the end of this period, King Salman succeeded to the Saudi throne and established his new administration, which has committed to significant economic and social reform through its Saudi Vision 2030.

The outlook for Japanese–Saudi JV businesses improved substantially, especially engineering work for the maintenance of technical services, for life-extension and effective utilization of the existing facilities and multi-industrial insurance services. As of 2015, more than 60 JV companies have been established since the governmental economic cooperation agreement in 1975 came into force, despite divergence of business interests.

Furthermore, cooperation on both energy-conservation technologies and security relations advanced in this period. Given that the Japanese government had carried out the development of full-scale energy conservation and storage technology and institutional system design worldwide, the Saudi government requested Japanese cooperation in bringing those technologies into the kingdom. The first reason was to export oil and gas to raise foreign currency revenues. The need to diversify energy resources, in particular renewable resources, to comply with domestic energy demand in the future was another reason. Finally, the Saudi government wanted to draw foreign investment in the energy sector to develop its energy industry.

As part of the Saudi "Look East" policy,[58] then Crown Prince (and now King) Salman visited five energy-scarce Asian countries in February and March 2014: Pakistan, Japan, Maldives, India, and China. British Petroleum (BP) statistics in 2015 showed that approximately 34% of the world's oil was consumed in the Asia Pacific region, with 12.4% in China alone.[59] Of the Middle Eastern countries' total oil production in 2014 (978.7 million tonnes), 171.7 million tonnes (m/t) were exported to China, 157.0 m/t to Japan, 121.1 m/t to India, and 237.0 m/t to other Asian countries.[60] Although economic and industrial cooperation was still significant,[61] the target of the 'Look East' policy[62] was to achieve not only economic success,[63] but also to enhance Saudi's diplomatic relations with these important trading partners.[64] This must be understood as a response to the US's pivot to Asia, which seemed to signal a downsizing of its commitments to the Middle East.

During Crown Prince Salman's visit to Japan, he and Prime Minister Abe expressed their commitment to the Comprehensive Partnership in all fields within the framework of the Joint Statement issued on April 30, 2013, and committed to continued discussion and cooperation at different levels. During the meeting, it was confirmed that bilateral cooperation would be strengthened in several fields. The governmental commitments during the meeting inferred a top-priority project which was agreed upon by both governments. Although a detailed description of defense cooperation could not be specified within that time frame, the description of defense exchanges and cooperation in the official document was significant in the process of the Japanese government's security-related legislation. The following, outlined in the Joint Statement in April 2013, symbolized the shape of bilateral relations in the fourth phase. This is a significant description because the two governments agreed on a package of cooperation on security, defense, and energy saving:

Cooperation in political and security affairs
Defense exchanges and cooperation
Cooperation in economic fields; 1) Energy Cooperation (joint oil storage, renewable energy, and energy efficiency), 2) Cooperation in private sectors, 3) Industrial cooperation (investment and technology transfer), 4) Infrastructure project cooperation (Metro projects and Water/Waste water), 5) Human resource development, 6) Health
Culture, Education, and People-to-People Exchanges[65]

Potential role for Japan in security in the Middle East?

In terms of defense and security, Japan experienced an unprecedented turning point in the defense industry in 2015, through the legislation of security-related bills. The Japanese Self-Defense Forces (SDF) are able to take on an active international role in the Middle East and other regions within the conditions of its legal framework. This does not mean that the Japanese government immediately dispatches the SDF to trouble spots worldwide, such as Iraq, Syria, or African countries. However, there is a possibility of future changing relations in politics and security between Japan and Middle Eastern countries, including Saudi Arabia.

In 2016 and 2017, Japan and Saudi Arabia proceeded to discuss future defense collaboration. Firstly, the agreement on the promotion of communications in the defense industry was confirmed between both ministries of defense in September 2016 when then Deputy Crown Prince Muhammad bin Salman made an official visit to Japan. According to media reports, the deputy crown prince asked Tomomi Inada, the Japanese defense minister, to promote a strengthening of relations in the field of defense equipment, while Inada replied that she wanted to discuss what kind of cooperation would be possible in the future. Muhammad bin Salman indicated expectations on the use of Japanese technologies in preparation for basic manufacturing systems of defense equipment in Saudi Arabia.[66] Prior to the meeting, the two governments signed a Memorandum of Understanding (MoU) on defense exchanges, including calls of SDF training naval vessels to Saudi ports, exchange programs of naval officers and other communications.

In May 2017, the Saudi government announced the establishment of a governmental organization, Saudi Arabian Military Industries (SAMI), under the budget of the Saudi Arabian Public Investment Fund (PIF), which would manufacture defense equipment for domestic use and create opportunities for Saudi nationals. According to news articles, SAMI would provide the Saudi government with four different military products and services, including aerospace and army systems, defense electronics as well as seek to establish a JV company with global original equipment manufacturers.[67] A Middle East analyst expressed his view on SAMI's establishment, noting that "expertise, supply chains, customer lines, finance, R&D infrastructure and more need to be developed," and that "they will need lots of outside help at first, but with the right training and education, investments and business development it is possible."[68]

Finally, from the political point of view of relations with the US, Japan is regarded as a pivotal ally in the Asia Pacific region, which is comparable to the political position of Saudi Arabia in the Gulf region. Both Japan and Saudi Arabia coordinate with the US to ensure security in the Gulf through sea lanes in East Asia, assuming this cooperation is reciprocal for all three states. The establishment of a strategic collaboration framework on the Gulf sea-lane security between the US, Saudi Arabia, and Japan represents an effective design of coordination. For the US, this combines partnerships with both Saudi Arabia in the Middle East and Japan in the Asia Pacific region – an attractive trilateral formation. However, the Japanese government's involvement in this security partnership will be deliberately implemented in response to the severely critical US public opinion against Japan's "free-riding" political attitude on the Gulf sea-lane security.[69]

In principle, the Saudi economy's next growing engine is expected to be based on diversified energy choices that include hydrocarbons, nuclear, and renewables[70]. This process of diversification is essential for its sustainable development. Japan will be able to play an important role in all but nuclear energy development. In addition, Saudi Arabia offers numerous investment opportunities for Japan, due to expansion in key areas such as the transportation sector, information technology and communication, and infrastructure.

Conclusion: evolving relations in energy and security

The economic realities resulting from the global economy shifting towards Asia facilitated diversification in diplomatic relations by the Saudi government.[71] Along with the Saudi government's global political–economic interests, it was understandable that Saudi Arabia pushed forward its diplomatic initiatives toward energy-thirsty and economically strong East Asian countries, particularly Japan.[72] The conventional special relationship with the US has diversified while remaining anchored in the fields of security and defense.

This chapter identified distinctive phases in the six-decade-long Saudi–Japanese relationship. Bilateral relations are mainly based on economic considerations that have evolved to encompass several issues, including cooperation on human resource development and cultural exchanges. The reciprocal relations are currently being re-consolidated by shaping contemporary Abe-Salman political relations through mutual visits.

On the other hand, to secure sustainable economic development, Japanese policymakers claim that they require a stable political situation in the Gulf oil-producing countries, particularly in the pivotal country of Saudi Arabia in order to provide an uninterrupted energy supply. The oil crisis of the 1970s represented an economic threat to Japan for decades, reinforcing the fact that political stability in the Gulf is indispensable for sustainable Japanese economic growth. As such, Saudi–Japanese relations are not one-sided but have always been reciprocal.

Notes

1 Naser M. al-Tamimi, *China–Saudi Arabia Relations, 1990–2012: Marriage of Convenience or Strategic Alliance?* (Oxon: Routledge, 2013), 59–77, (political), 126–144 (economy), and 181–93 (security).
2 Tim Niblock, *Saudi Arabia – Power, Legitimacy and Survival* (Oxon and New York: Routledge, 2006), 141; Anoushiravan Ehteshami, "Asian geostrategic realities and their impact on Middle East – Asian relations," in *The Middle East's Relations with Asia and Russia,* eds. Hannah Carter and Anoushiravan Ehteshami (London: RoutledgeCurzon, 2004), 1–18; Anoushiravan Ehteshami, "Regionalization, Pan-Asian Relations, and the Middle East." *East Asia* 32.3 (2015): 223–37.
3 Paul Aarts and Gerd Nonneman, *Saudi Arabia in the Balance – Political Economy, Society, Foreign Affairs* (London: C. Hurst & Co., 2005), 315.
4 Christopher M. Davidson, "The Gulf Monarchies and Pacific Asia: Towards Interdependency?" in *Covering Regions: Global Perspectives on Asia and the Middle East.* The International political economy of new regionalism series, Durham Research Online (2014), 143–60.
5 Steffen Hertog, "Chapter Nine. The New Corporatism in Saudi Arabia: Limits of Formal Politics" in *Constitutional Reform and Political Participation in the Gulf,* eds. Khalaf Abdulhadi and Giacomo Luciani (Dubai: Gulf Research Center, 2006), 270.
6 Abdul Karim Saitoh, "The historical journey of Islam eastward and the Muslim community in Japan today." *Journal Institute of Muslim Minority Affairs* 1.1 (1979), 117–26; Awang Hasmadi Awang Mois, "Some Issues Affecting Muslims in Japan." *Area Studies, University of Tsukuba* 20 (2002): 213–40, 220–4; Kingdom of Saudi Arabia and Japan, *The 50th Anniversary of diplomatic relations.* The beginning of exchanges and the establishment of the diplomatic relations, (1) Pilgrimage to Makkah by Japanese Muslims, The Royal Embassy of Saudi Arabia in Japan website (Tokyo, 2005), http://www.saudiembassy.or.jp/50years/3.htm
7 Renée Worringer, *Ottomans Imagining Japan: East, Middle East, and Non-Western Modernity at the Turn of the Twentieth Century* (New York: Palgrave Macmillan, 2014), 72–3.
8 Kotaro Yamaoka, *Sekai no Shimpi Kyo, Arabia Judan ki (Across the Arabia, the World's Mystery)* (Tokyo: Toado shobo, 1912).
9 Kotaro Yamaoka, *Kaikai-kyo no Shimpiteki iryoku (Mysterious Power of Islam)* (Tokyo: Shinko sha, 1921).
10 Ippei Tanaka, *Islamic Junrei – Haku-un yuu ki (Islamic pilgrimage – Journey on the White Cloud)* (Tokyo: Rekika shoin, 1925).
11 Yasuhiro Yokkaichi, "Chinese and Muslim Diasporas and the Indian Ocean Trade Network under Mongol Hegemony." *The East Asian Mediterranean: Maritime Crossroads of Culture, Commerce and Human Migration* 6 (2008): 73–4.
12 Ramon Hawley Myers and Mark R. Peattie, *The Japanese colonial empire, 1895–1945* (New Jersey: Princeton University Press, 1984), 80–6.
13 William Beasley, *The Meiji Restoration* (California: Stanford University Press, 1972), 405–11.
14 Tokyo mosque was closed due to architectural deterioration in 1983. The new mosque's construction project by the Turkish government began in 1998 and was completed in 2000. On the other hand, the Saudi government built the Arab Islamic Institute in Tokyo

(officially registered as 'Imam Muhammad ibn Saud Islamic University Branch') as an academic research institute of Islam in 1982. This research institute belongs to Saudi Arabian Embassy in Japan. Sequentially, the Saudi-financed Al-Tawheed Mosque Hachioji was newly built in the western part of Tokyo in 2002. This mosque also belongs to the Saudi Embassy.
15 Ikuo Nakajima, *Sekiyu to Nippon (Oil and Japan)* (Tokyo: Shincho-sha, 2015), 58–62.
16 Ministry of Economy, Trade and Industry (METI), Agency for Natural Resources and Energy, *Cabinet Decision on the New Strategic Energy Plan* (Tokyo, 2014), http://www.meti.go.jp/english/press/2014/0411_02.html
17 Tim Niblock and Monica Malik, *The Political Economy of Saudi Arabia* (London: Routledge, 2007), 52–4, 94–9.
18 Arabian Oil Company, *The 35-Year History of The Arabian Oil Company 1958–1993 – A Bridge Between the Arabian Gulf and Japan in War and Peace* (Tokyo: Arabian Oil Company Ltd., 1995), 34–42.
19 Ministry of Economy, Trade and Industry, Agency for Natural Resources and Energy, *Japan's Energy White Paper 2013, Part 2. Energy trends, Chapter 1. Domestic energy trends, Paragraph 3. Trends in primary energy, 1. Trends in fossil energy, (1) oil, ①Trends in supply*, (Tokyo, 2014), http://www.enecho.meti.go.jp/about/whitepaper/2013html/2-1-3.html
20 Paul Stevens, "National oil companies and international oil companies in the Middle East: Under the shadow of government and the resource nationalism cycle." *The Journal of World Energy Law & Business* 1.1 (2008): 9–16.
21 The Royal Embassy of Saudi Arabia Tokyo, *The 50th Anniversary*, (Tokyo, 2005), http://www.saudiembassy.or.jp/50years/En/11.htm
22 Arabian Oil Company, *The 35-Year History of The Arabian Oil Company*, 39–57.
23 Valerie Marcel, *Oil Titans: National Oil Companies in the Middle East*. (Maryland: Brookings Institution Press, 2006), 28–30.
24 Gregory Gause F., "Beyond Sectarianism: The New Middle East Cold War," *Brookings Doha Center Analysis Paper*, Number 11, July 2014 (2014): 8–15.
25 Robert R. Sullivan, "Saudi Arabia in International Politics," *The Review of Politics*, 32.4 (October, 1970): 436–60.
26 Ministry of Economy, Trade and Industry, Agency for Natural Resources and Energy, *Japan's Energy White Paper 2015, Part 2. Energy trends, Chapter 1. Domestic energy trends, Paragraph 1. Outline of energy demand and supply, 3. Trends in energy demand and supply*, 109, (Tokyo, 2015), http://www.enecho.meti.go.jp/about/whitepaper/2015pdf/whitepaper2015pdf_2_1.pdf
27 This term was originally used by the then prime minister, Takeo Fukuda. Yoshihiro Kobayashi, "Nihon shakai no kyoodootai teki tokushitsu to sono hyooka" (The feature of Japanese communal society and its evaluation)", *Hokkaido University Collection of Scholarly and Academic Papers, Economic Studies* 61.4 (2012): 75–95.
28 Shuji Hosaka, "Japan-Middle East-Oil: 40 years ago, 10 years ago, and 60 years ago," *Japan Cooperation Centre for the Middle East News* 2013.12–2014.1(2013): 70–1.
29 Akifumi Ikeda, "Sekiyu kiki to Chuto gaiko no 'tenkan' (Oil crisis and 'conversion' of the Middle East foreign policy)," *Kokusai Mondai (International Affairs), The Japan Institute of International Affairs*, No.638 (2015): 16–25. Ikeda argued Japanese diplomacy towards the Middle East in the 1970s was kept neutral. The so-called "economically high-profile, politically low-profile" stance preserved the US–Japan alliance despite Japan's pro-Arab policy.
30 Mana Ikeda, "Dai ichiji sekiyu kiki ni okeru nihon gaikoo – Arab shokoku to beikoku no hazama de (Japan's diplomacy in the 1st oil crisis – between Arab countries and the US)", *Kokusai seiji (International relations), The Japan Association of International Relations*, 2014.177 (2014): 142–55.
31 Kunio Katakura, "Japan and the Middle East: Towards a more positive role." *Energy Policy* 20.11 (1992): 1032–36.

32 Gaiko (Diplomatic) Bluebook 1974, Chapter 3. Diplomatic efforts made by Japan, Section 1. Promotion of relations with other countries, 6. Middle and Near East, Ministry of Foreign Affairs (MOFA), Japan website (Tokyo, 1974), http://www.mofa.go.jp/policy/other/bluebook/1974/1974-3-1.htm
33 William B. Quandt, *Saudi Arabia in the 1980s* (Washington, D.C.: The Brookings Institute, 1981), 3–4.
34 John Elder and Apostolos Serletis, "Oil price uncertainty." *Journal of Money, Credit and Banking* 42.6 (2010): 1137–59.
35 Niblock, *The Political Economy of Saudi Arabia*, 141.
36 Niblock, *The Political Economy of Saudi Arabia*, 83–93.Niblock referred to the Saudi economic situation in this period as 'after 1985, the (Saudi) government was no longer concentrating on mega-projects aimed at economic and social transformation'. (Niblock, *The Political Economy of Saudi Arabia*, 104.)
37 Niblock, *The Political Economy of Saudi Arabia*, 94.
38 Ministry of Economy, Trade and Industry (METI), Japan, A presentation material, "Economic situation of the Middle East and North Africa and METI's policy" at *Japan Cooperation Centre for the Middle East (JCCME)*, (Tokyo, 2013), http://www.jccme.or.jp/japanese/seminar_13/pdf_0825/01.pdf
39 The Japanese government usually initiates a comprehensive business framework by concluding a government-to-government (GtoG) agreement or, providing an official development aid (ODA) scheme followed by private companies' joint-venture manufacturing business, etc. and also supports business activities by providing them with governmental financial support and trade insurance schemes, etc. Kent Calder, *Strategic Capitalism: Private Business and Public Purpose in Japanese Industrial Finance* (New Jersey: Princeton University Press, 1995), 134–36; Min Chen, *Asian Management Systems: Chinese, Japanese and Korean Styles of Business* (Hampshire: Cengage Learning EMEA, 2004), 141–55. A survey by the governmental organization Japan External Trade Organization (JETRO) in 2016 found that many Japanese companies in MENA showed strong indications of business expansion, while still expecting substantial business support from the Japanese government. (Report on Japanese companies' activities in the market of the Middle East and Africa, Japan External Trading Organization (JETRO) website, (Tokyo, 2016), https://www.jetro.go.jp/news/releases/2016/258c29ac863240f1.html
40 Niblock, *The Political Economy of Saudi Arabia*, 97.
41 Shaykha Al-Shamsi and Magda Kandil, "On the Significance of Trade Relations Between GCC Countries and Japan," *Journal of Economic Integration* 16.3 (2001): 344–68.
42 Caryle Murphy, "Saudi Arabia's Youth and the Kingdom's Future," *Middle East Program*, Occasional Paper Series, Winter 2, 2011 (Woodrow Wilson International Centre for the Scholars, 2011): 1–9.
43 Waleed Hazbun and Abbas Amanat, "The Middle East through the lens of critical geopolitics: Globalization, terrorism, and the Iraq War," *Democracy* 53 (2001): 325–61. For the demographic problem, Dominique Tabutin, "The demography of the Arab World and the Middle East from the 1950s to the 2000s. A survey of changes and a statistical assessment," *Population* (English edition) (2005): 505–615.
44 Jean-Francois Seznec, "Business as Usual," *Harvard International Review* 26.4 (2005): 56–60.
45 In the Gulf Crisis/War in the early 1990s, Japan conducted a controversial financial contribution to the US-led multinational force with 13.5 billion US dollars in total which was unexpectedly criticized by some media. Japan's contribution was interpreted as a country which just paid the cost of international security (not military cooperation) and was uncooperative or limited to the recovery of regional security. On the other hand, in the Iraq War in 2003, Japan repeated an unprecedented discussion to affect constitutional interpretations about a possibility of the overseas deployment of

Japan's Self-Defense Forces for the first time after the WWII. As a result, the Japanese government decided to deploy Self-Defense Forces abroad, enacting the Act No. 137 of 2003, Special Measures concerning Humanitarian Relief and Reconstruction Work and Security Assistance in Samawah district, Muthannah governorate in Iraq.

46 Madawi Al-Rasheed, "God, the King and the Nation: Political Rhetoric in Saudi Arabia in the 1990s," *The Middle East Journal* (1996): 359–71.
47 Jean-Francois Seznec, "Stirrings in Saudi Arabia," *Journal of Democracy* 13.4 (2002): 33–40.
48 Giacomo Luciani, "Oil and Political Economy in the International," in *International Relations of the Middle East,* ed. Louise Fawcett (Oxford: Oxford University Press, 2013), 114–21.
49 Japan Cooperation Centre for the Middle East (JCCME), *Economic situation of the Middle East and North Africa and policy of Ministry of Economy, Trade and Industry (METI)*, (Tokyo, 2014).
50 Niblock, *The Political Economy of Saudi Arabia*, 99.
51 Martin Baldwin-Edwards, "Labour immigration and labour markets in the GCC countries: national patterns and trends," *LSE Global Governance paper* No.15, (2011): 14–21.
52 Hisashi Kawada and Solomon B. Levine, *Human Resources in Japanese Industrial Development*. (New Jersey: Princeton University Press, 2014), 3–22.
53 About SJAHI, Profile, SJAHI website (Jeddah, 2016), http://www.sjahi.org/Profile.aspx
54 Transitional era of Saudi – Japanese cooperation for development, JICA Newsletter website (Tokyo, 2009), http://www.jica.go.jp/egypt/english/office/saudi/pdf/newsletter_en_13.pdf
55 About us, Homepage, HIPF website (Riyadh, 2016), http://hipf.edu.sa/en/
56 About us, Homepage, SEHAI website (Riyadh, 2016), http://www.sehai.org/Home.aspx
57 "Displaying the Sumo, Kimono and Kendo, the Land of Bright Sun shines from Janadriyah," Saudi Press Agency, April 20, 2011.
58 U.S. Energy Information Administration, *Saudi Arabia Maintained Crude Oil Market Share in Asia in the First Half of 2015* (Washington, DC, 2015), http://www.eia.gov/todayinenergy/detail.cfm?id=22852
59 "Consumption," *BT Statistical Review of World Energy June 2015, 64th Edition*, (London, 2015).
60 "Inter-area movements 2014," *BT Statistical Review of World Energy June 2015, 64th Edition*.
61 "Saudi Arabia's Petrochemical Producers Look East," *Oxford Business Group*, (Oxford, 2015), http://www.oxfordbusinessgroup.com/news/saudi-arabia%E2%80%99s-petrochemical-producers-look-east
62 Anand Girdharadas, "Saudi Arabia Pursues a 'Look-East Policy,'" *The New York Times*, January 26, 2006.
63 Ibrahim Al-Ghamdi, "SABIC aims to expand its investment in China, Japan," *Arab News*, November 12, 2012.
64 Makio Yamada, "Saudi Arabia's Look-East Diplomacy: Ten Years On," *Middle East Policy Council*, Winter 2015, Volume XXII, Number 4 (2015).
65 Ministry of Foreign Affairs (Japan), *Countries and regions, the Middle East, 'Joint Statement on the occasion of the visit of Royal Highness Prince Salman bin Abdulaziz Al-Saud Crown Prince and Deputy Premier and Minister of Defence of Kingdom of Saudi Arabia to Japan'* (Tokyo, 2014), http://www.mofa.go.jp/files/000028395.pdf
66 "Saudi Deputy Crown Prince had a Meeting with Ms. Inada on Defence Equipment Cooperation," *Nikkei Shimbun*, September 2, 2016.
67 Shuja Al-Baqmi, "Saudi Arabia Launches 'SAMI' for Military Industries," *Sharq Al-Awsat*, May 18, 2017.

68 Glen Carey and Alla Shahine, "Saudi Wealth Fund Starts Defense Company to Meet Military Needs," *Bloomberg*, May 18, 2017.
69 A remark of Dr. Kent Calder, Director of Edwin O. Reischauer Centre for East Asian Studies, School of Advanced International Studies, Johns Hopkins University at the seminar titled, 'The United States, Japan and Gulf Region', organized by The Sasakawa Peace Foundation (Japan) on August 5, 2015 in Tokyo, Japan.
70 Andrew Roscoe, "Saudi Arabia's Nuclear Programme – The Kingdom Signalled its Nuclear Ambitions in 2007 and Aims to Generate 17.9GW by 2032," *MEED*, August 7, 2014; M. D. Rasooldeen, "KSA, China Sign Nuclear Energy Cooperation Deal," *Arab News*, August 10, 2014.
71 Gwynne Dyer, "Power Shift to Asia: No Need to Panic," *Arab News*, February 23, 2012.
72 "Kingdom Assures Asia of Uninterrupted Oil Supply," *Arab News,* April 10, 2011.

Index

Page numbers in **bold** denote tables.

2003 Iraq invasion 4
2008 financial crisis 3
2016 China Arab Policy Paper 151

Abdulaziz bin Abdulrahman Al Saud,
    King 17, 19
Abdullah, King 28, 30, 78, 115–16, 164
Abu Al Walid 40
Abu Dhabi 2030 2
Afghanistan 23, 26, 49, 129–30, 159
Africa 7
agricultural exports 8, 46, 90–2, 97–8, 100
al-Maliki, Nuri 28
Al-Nusra Front 40
al-Qaradawi, Youssef 85
Al Qaeda 24, 27–8, 39
al-Tarrah, Ali 25
Al-Udeid airbase 26, 31
al-Ulama, Hafsa 94
alternative energy 8, 11, *see also* nuclear
    power; renewable energy
anti-colonial rhetoric 59
anti-ISIS campaigns 30
anti-piracy efforts 12, 129, 132–3, 164–5
anti-war demonstrations 27
Arab diaspora 100
Arab–Israel conflict 22
Arab League 110
Arab–South America Summit (ASPA) 91
Arab Spring 5, 28–9, 38, 57, 63, 74, 79,
    90, 106, 115–16, 119, 134, 144
Arabian Oil Company (AOC) 179–80
Arabian Oil Company (Aramco) 20–1
arms deals 8–9, 23, 29, 36–7, 43, 45–6, 60,
    63, 69, 77–8, 81–3, 164
Asia 12, 32, 47, 176, 186, *see also*
    individual countries
Asian Infrastructure Investment Bank 32

Assad, Bashir Al 39, 44, 49, 79,
    118, 134–5
Assiri, Abdul-Reda 24
Association of Southeast Asian Nations 123
asymmetrical alliances 5, 144
Atatürk, Mustafa Kemal 107
Australia 11
Azevêdo, Maria Nazareth 93

Bahrain: criticism of 29, 63; defense
    cooperation agreements 24–5, 142–3;
    independence of 21; and India 123;
    military intervention in 40, 63, 80;
    Muslim Brotherhood 116; protests in
    93; and Turkey **108**, **110**, **111**, **113**, **117**;
    and the UK 64, 66; US military forces in
    23, 26, 142–3
Bahrain Petroleum Company
    (BAPCO) 19–20
bin Laden, Osama 18, 24–5
Bolivia 96
Brazil 6; economic ties with 12, 91;
    foreign policy 90–1, 97, 99–100, 100*n*2;
    investments in 94; and Kuwait 93; legal
    issues in 94–5; LNG imports 96; and
    Oman 90, 98–9; and Qatar 95–8; and
    Saudi Arabia 92; trade 8, 92, 97–8, 100;
    and the UAE 94–5
Brazilian Trade and Investment Promotion
    Agency (APEX-Brazil) 94
Brexit 57, 67–8
British Petroleum 65
Bush presidency (George W.) 12, 27–9

Californian Arabian Standard Oil
    Company (CASOC) 19
Cameron, David 63–5
Camp as-Saliyah 26

Canada 19
Carter doctrine 5, 22–3
Carter presidency 23
CENTO alliance 131
Central Planning Organization 21
Chechnya 40–1
Cheney, Richard 24
Chevron 19
Chile 8
China 6, 13, 132–4; Belt and Road Initiative 3, 7, 13, 140, 150–1, 153, 155; bilateral deals 146–7; early relationships 141–2; and the EU 145; expatriates 154; foreign policy 140; and the GCC 146; investment in energy companies 6; Navy 11; oil imports 10, 147; and Oman 141–2; perceptions of 140; proposed role 151–3; and Saudi Arabia 134, 146, 154; soft military presence 153; and the Soviet Union 142; and strategic hedging 144; strategic hedging/partnerships 140, 144–6, 155; trade 146–7, **148**; and the UAE 154; and the US 143
China–Arab States Cooperation Forum (CASCF) 151, 153
Chirac, Jacques 76
clean energy sources 8
Clinton, Hillary 29, 39
Cold War 22, 37, 79, 125–6, 129, 135, 161, 164
Colombia 92
Council of Foreign Relations 26
Crane, Charles 19
Crivella, Marcello 96
cultural heritage, defending 84
currency swap agreements 149

Daoud, Kamel 86
Davutoğlu, Ahmet 116
De Gaulle, Charles 75, 77, 86
Demirel, Süleyman 110
Dual Containment policy 25

economic diversification 7–9, 60, 67, 134, *see also* individual countries
economic interdependence 3
economic liberalization 7–9, 109, 135
Egypt 22, 64, 106, 115–17
Eisenhower doctrine 23
electric cars 15*n*40
electricity, energy sources for 10–11
emerging economies 6
Emirati Brotherhood (Al Islah) 65
energy consumption 10

energy security 10–11, 124
energy subsidies 10–11
energy trade 9–11
Erdoğan, Recep Tayyip 113–14, 119
European Economic Community 76
European Union 10, 45, 145
Evran, Kenan 109
extra-regional powers 6, 42–5
extremist Islamic groups 39, 41, 49
Exxon 20
ExxonMobil 96

Fabius, Laurent 80
Fahad al-Salim Al Sabah, Sheikh 21
Fair, Christine 130
Faisal bin Abdulaziz Al Saud 77, 182
France: Arab policy 76; arms deals 77–8, 82; defense agreements 78; early relationships 75–6; and the GCC 74; Gulf-bashing by 12, 85–6; internal criticism 84–5; investment in 83, 87; and Iraq 76; and Lebanon 81; military commitments 79; oil imports by 82; partnership with 12; and Qatar 78, 85; and Saudi Arabia 77–8; strategic priorities 87; strategic triangle 77; terrorism in 85–6; and the UAE 78–9
free trade agreements 29, 67, 147
Freedom and Justice Party 64, *see also* Muslim Brotherhood
'freeloaders' comment 18, 29, 143, 188

G7 countries, economies 6
Gadhafi, Muammar 76, 79, 134
Gaoli, Zhang 146
globalism 3
Goldberg, Jeffrey 29, 116
Goldstein, Avery 145
Great Britain. *see* United Kingdom
Gul, Abdullah 113, 115
Gulf Cooperation Council (GCC) 1, 18, 30–1, 90–1, 114–5, 118, 122, 131, 144, 146, **161**, 176
Gulf News 5
Gulf Oil Corporation 19
Gulf states, as 'penetrated region' 4
Gulf War (1991) 4, 17–18, 23–5, 60, 69, 76–7, 101*n*6, 110–11, 162, 164, 191–2*n*45

Haftar, Khalifa 43
Hagel, Chuck 5
Hamad bin Khalifa Al Thani 78, 95
hegemonic stability theory 2

Hezbollah 80, 81
Hollande, François 78, 80–1, 85
Hussein, Saddam 23–4, 27, 60, 76, 134
Hussein, Sharif 19

Ibn Al Khattab 40
India 6; culture 126–7; diaspora 13, 124–5, 129, 135; energy use 123–24; exports 123; foreign exchange remittances 124; foreign policy 125–7, 134–5; growth 126; and Iran 129–30, 135; Islam in 123; Look West policy 3, 124–5; Mughals 122; navy 126, 129; as 'net provider of security' 126; non-alignment 127, 130, 133; and Oman 123, 129; and Pakistan 125, 128, 131, 135; on the Persian Gulf 126; and Qatar 128; and the Soviet Union 126, 129; and Syria 134–5; under British rule 125; and the US 132
India-Africa Development Fund 7
Indonesia 8
İnönü, İsmet 107
International Center of Excellence for Countering Violent Extremism 48
International Monetary Fund (IMF) 21
Iran 115; 1953 coup 58; Chabahar 130; and China 134, 146; expansionism 22; increased influence of 28, 64; and India 129–30, 135; Islamic Revolution 22, 109; and North Korea 168; nuclear negotiations 18, 30, 65, 81, 115, 130, 134, 169; nuclear program 12, 44; oil exports **169**; and Russia 37, 41; sanctions against 44–5, 115, 131, 167–8; and South Korea 166–8, 170–2; support for Assad 80; Trump on 5; and Turkey 115; and the UAE 48–9, 168; and the UK 65–6; US rapprochement with 30; war with Iraq 22–3, 129, 134, 162
Iraq 22; 2003 invasion 4, 17, 27–8, 60, 69, 159, 165, 183–4, 191–2n45; and France 76; oil exports **169**; Sunni insurgency 28; war with Iran 22–3, 129, 134, 162, *see also* Gulf War (1991)
Iraq Petroleum Company 76
Iraq Study Group 28
Islamic Military Alliance 132
Islamic State in Iraq and Syria (ISIS) 26, 28, 39
Islamism 25, 116
Islamist extremist groups 26
Israel 37, 60, 75, 110–11, 165

Jaber al Ahmed Al Sabah 109
Japan 13; 2011 earthquake 185; Abenomics 177; early relationships 177–9; economics 176–7; foreign policy 176, 181, 183–4; investment in 7; JV companies 182–3, 188; and oil 176, 179–80; oil crisis 181–2, 188–9; and Saudi Arabia 176–9, 184–7; Self-Defense Forces (SDF) 186–7, 191–2n45; trade 8, 182; and the US 188
Jebel Ali free trade zone 99
jihad, calls for 49
Johnson, Lyndon B. 21
Joint Comprehensive Plan of Action (JCPOA) 5, 28–9, 46, 65, 69, 171
Justice Against Sponsors of Terrorism Act (JASTA) 18

Kadyrov, Ramzan 41
Khalifa bin Hamad al Thani 109
Khatami, Mohammad 25
Khomeini, Ruhollah 76
Khurshid, Salman 133
King-Crane Commission 19
Kirk, Alexander 20
Kirkuk–Incirlik pipeline 111
Kissinger, Henry 76
Kurdistan Workers Party (PKK) 110–12
Kuwait: and Brazil 93; defense cooperation agreements 24–5, 142–3; diversification by 8; and the Gulf War 23, 60, 69, 101n6; independence of 21, 59; and India 123; New Kuwait 2035 policy 2, 150; oil exports **169**; and Russia/Soviet Union 36; and South Korea 170; and Turkey **108, 110, 111, 113, 117**; US military forces in 26, 142–3

Latin America 90–2, 94
Le Pen, Marine 85–86
League of Arab States 76
Lebanon 81, 165, 173
Lee, Myung-bak 167–8
Lellouche, Pierre 86
Libya 43–4, 80, 115
liquid alliances 4
liquified natural gas industry (LNG) 11, 47, 69, 96–7, 128

Malacca Straits 11, 126
Malaysia 8
Masirah air force base 23
Mattis, James 31

Index

Memoranda of Understanding (MoU) 114, 146, 154, 170, 172, 187
Mexico 8
middle-power diplomacy 159, 173
MITKA network 159
Mobil 20
Modi, Narendra 125, 127, 129–30
Moffet, James 20
Mohamed Bin Rashid Solar Park 11
Mohammed bin Nawaf Al Saud 63
Mohammed bin Nayef 86
Mohammed bin Salman 31, 130, 135, 146, 154
Mohammed bin Zayed Al Nahyan 31, 65
Mohammed, Khalid Sheikh 26
Mohan, Raja 128
Moose, James 20
Morsi, Muhammed 106, 116
Moza bint Nassr 96
Mubarak, Hosni 5, 29, 134
Muhammad bin Salman 187
multilateralism, Russian 44, 50
multipolarity 3, 44
Muscat 18
museums 83–4, *see also* universities
Muslim Brotherhood 31, 64–5, 116

Nazer, Hisham 21
New Kuwait 2035 2, 150
New York Times 86, 116
Nixon Doctrine 22, 23
Nixon presidency 21
non-alignment 127, 130, 133
North Atlantic Treaty Organization (NATO) 37, 107
North Korea 160, **161**, 167–9
Norway 61
nuclear power 8, 11, 37, 45–6, 50, 84, 159, 163, 171

Obaid, Nawaf 29–30
Obama presidency 5, 12, 28–30, 66, 74, 81
Ocalan, Abdullah 111
Ocean LNG 96–7
offsets 8–9
oil, discovery of 19
oil concessions 17, 19, 58, 65, 180
oil prices 10–11, 67
oil reserves 8
Oman: agriculture 98–9; and Brazil 90, 98–99; and China 141–2; debt 8; defense cooperation agreements 25; and India 123, 129; Muslim Brotherhood 116; oil exports **169**; treaties with the US 18, 19; and Turkey **108**, **110**, **111**, **113**, **117**; US military forces in 23, 142–3
omnibalancing 4
OPEC (Organization of Petroleum Exporting Countries) 47
Organization of Islamic Conference 107–8, 110
Organization of Islamic Countries 37
Oslo Accords 162
Ottoman Empire 56, 58, 91, 107, 120n2
Özal, Turgut 109

Paes, Eduardo 96
Pakistan 125, 128, 131–2, 135
Palestine 37, 162
pan-Arab nationalism 107, 109
Park, Chung-Hee 161, 164, 170–2
Pedro, Antônio Carlos do Nascimento 93
personal networks 12, 18
Peru 92
petrochemicals industries 8, 46
Pompidou, George 75, 77
Popular Front for the Liberation of the Occupied Gulf 22
protests 39, 64, 80, 93, 115, *see also* Arab Spring
Putin, Vladimir 38–9, 41–2

Qaboos bin Said 19, 23, 142
Qatar: and Brazil 95–8; and China 146, 154–5; defense cooperation agreements 25, 142–3; and Egypt 116–17; and France 78, 85; gas reserves of 47; independence 21; and India 128; investment by 6, 61, 83; investment opportunities in 67–8; isolation of 31–2, 91, 97, 99, 117–19, 128–30; LNG development by 11, 69, 96–7; military agreements 118–19; Muslim Brotherhood 116; oil exports **169**; public opinion on the US 25; and Russia 37, 49; and Saudi Arabia 130; and South Korea 170–1; support for terrorists 26, 85; and Turkey 49, 106, **108**, **110**, **111**, **113**, **117**, 118–19; and the US military 18, 26, 142–3
Qatar Foundation 27, 96
Qatar Petroleum 96

radicalization 39
Red Line Agreement 19
regional stability 38–41, 68
renewable energy 10

Index

Roberts, Edmund 18
Roosevelt, Franklin 17, 20
Rouhani, Hassan 30, 130, 172
Rusk, Dean 21–2
Russia: arms deals with 36–7, 43, 45–6; economic interests of 45–8; as extra-regional power 42–45; growing presence of 3, 36, 43, 132; Gulf policy 12, 37–8, 50; and Iran 41; military presence 43–4; Muslims in 39; oil exports 47; and Palestine 37; and Qatar 37; sanctions against 47, 82; support for Assad 40, 119, 134; trade 8, 46, 48–9; and Turkey 113–14, *see also* Soviet Union
Russian Direct Investment Fund 37, 45, 50*n*5

Sabah al-Salim Al Sabah, Emir 21
Said bin Sultan 18
Sakwa, Richard 38
Salman bin Abdul Aziz Al Saud 164
Salman, King 78, 186
Sarkozy, Nicholas 78–9, 85
Saud al-Fasil, Prince 28
Saudi Arabia: and the Arab Spring 63–4, 116; and Asia 176–7; and Bahrain 80; and Brazil 92; British responsibilities for 20; and China 134, 146, 154; debt 8, 15*n*39; defense cooperation agreements 25; defense manufacturing 187–88; diversification by 8, 68, 176–7; and France 77–8; and the Gulf War 24; and India 123, 128; investment in the US 6; and Japan 176–9, 184–7; JV companies 182–3, 188; nuclear agreements with 37; oil exports 16*n*57, 47, 82, **169**; and Pakistan 131–2; and Qatar 130; and Russia 40–1, 48–9; Saudi Vision 2030 policy 2, 150, 177; social problems 183; and South Korea 170; support for Bin Laden 25; support for terrorists 26; and Turkey 107, **108**, **110**, **111**, **113**, **117**
"Saudi–Japan Vision 2030" 177
Sayyid Fahd bin Mahmoud Al Said 129
sectarian views 28, 82, 125, 128
September 11th, 2001 18, 26, 86, 115, 159
shale oil 10, 47
Sharif, Raheel 132
shipping, attacks on 23–4
Silva, Luiz Inácio Lula da 91, 95
Singh, Jaswant 126
Singh, Manmohan 123, 126
Singh, Sushmita 129
Sisi, Abd al-Fattah al 81

Socony-Vacuum 20
solar power 8, 11
South Korea 6; arms deals 164; bilateral military exchanges 160; construction projects 162–3; establishment 161; and the GCC **161**; and Iran 166–8, 170–2; and Kuwait 170; and middle power diplomacy 159–60, 173; military commitments of 3, 159–60, 163; and North Korea 160; nuclear power plants 159, 163; oil imports **169**, 172; and Qatar 170–1; and Saudi Arabia 170; trade 8, 161–2, 167, **169**; and the UAE 159–60, 163, 171; and the US 163–6; and the "war on terror" 163
South–North investments 6, 7
South–South investments 6
sovereign wealth funds 7, 57, 60–1, 83, 149
Soviet Union 23, 36, 38, 107, 120*n*3, 126, 129, 142, *see also* Russia
Standard Oil Company of California (SOCAL) 19
Standard Oil Company of New York 20
Stanford Research Institute (SRI) 21
steel industry 10
Straits of Malacca 126
strategic hedging approaches 2, 140, 144, 146, 155
Struver, Georg 144–5
Suez War 75
Sulayman, Abdullah 19–21
Sultan bin Abdulaziz 77, 182
Syria 28, 40, 110, 134–5, *see also* Assad, Bashir Al
Syrian civil war 12, 18, 30, 40, 80, 118, *see also* Assad, Bashir Al
Syrian National Coalition 80

Temer, Michael 98
terrorism 26, 28, 39–40, 65, 80, 84–6, 128, 132
Texaco 19
Texas Oil Company 19
Trans-Arabia Pipeline (Tapline) 21
Trucial States 20, 59, 86, *see also* United Arab Emirates (UAE)
Truman doctrine 23
Truman presidency 20–1
Trump presidency 5–6, 12, 18, 31, 134, 144
Tunisia 64, 79, 115
Turkey 6, 12–13; and the Arab Spring 106, 115, 119; diplomatic relations 108;

economic liberalization 109, 112; and Egypt 106, 116–17; financial crisis 112; and the GCC 114–15, 118; investment in 114, 118; and Israel 110–11; Istanbul Initiative 114; Justice and Development Party (JDP) 106, 112–13; military agreements 118–19; and Qatar 49, 106, 118–19; and Saudi Arabia 107; trade **108**, 109, **110**, **111**, **112**, **113**, 114, **117**, **118**
Turki bin Faisal Al Saud 30
Turkish Armed Forces 109, 111
Twin Pillars policy 22
Twitchell, Karl 19

Ukraine 38, 45
UN General Assembly 30
UN Human Rights Council 93
UN Security Council 30, 117
United Arab Emirates (UAE) 20; and the Arab Spring 64; and Brazil 94–5; and China 146, 154; defense cooperation agreements 25; diversification of 48, 68; and France 78–9; independence 21; and India 123; and Iran 48–9, 168; joint military actions 31; oil exports **169**; relations with Russia 37, 48; and South Korea 159–60, 163, 171; support for terrorists 26; trade 37, **108**, **110**, **111**, **113**, **117**; and the UK 64–5; US military forces in 26, 142–3, *see also* Trucial States
United Kingdom: and Arab dissidents 64; arms deals 60, 63, 69; defence agreements 63, 66; early relationships 57–9, 68–9; energy imports 61–2; "Gulf Initiative" 62; investment in 6, 61, 69; and Iran 65–6; military commitments of 66; military withdrawal of 18, 21–2, 59, 133–34; official visits to/from **62**; relationships with Gulf monarchies 12, 57, 59; trade 8, 61, 67

United States: and the Arab Spring 5, 28–9, 134, 144; arms deals 60; bilateral ties with 5; Central Command (CENTCOM) 17–18; and China 143; costs to 11; defense cooperation agreements 142–3; disengagement of 2, 29, 46, 66, 134; exports from 8; Fifth Fleet 17–18, 26; free trade agreements 29; and India 132; and Japan 188; joint military actions 31; Lend-Lease program 20; LNG industry 11; and the Malacca Straits 11; and oil 10, 17, 19, 124; 'pivot to Asia' policy 6–7, 29, 32, 46, 186; power of 3–4, 32, 126; public opinion on 25, 27; sanctions imposed by 45; Saudi investment in 6; security commitments 2, 18, 57; soft power 26–7; and South Korea 163–6; and the Soviet Union 5; trade with Oman 19; universities 27; "war on terror" 163
universities: satellite campuses 27, 79, 83, *see also* museums
US–GCC Security Committee 29

Valadares, Tadeu 90, 97
Vale 90, 98–9
Valls, Manuel 83, 86
van Buren, Martin 18–19

Waters, Richard 18
Wilson, Harold 21, 75
World War One 19, 58, 107
World War Two 20, 176

Yandarbiyev, Zelimkhan 37
Yemen 18, 22, 28–30, 118, 132
Yi, Wang 152

Zanzibar 18
Zayed bin Sultan Al Nahyan 109